IN SEARCH OF
SHAREHOLDER
VALUE

IN SEARCH OF

SHAREHOLDER

VALUE

Managing the drivers of performance

ANDREW BLACK ● PHILIP WRIGHT

with

JOHN DAVIES

FINANCIAL TIMES
Prentice Hall

An imprint of **Pearson Education**

London / New York / San Francisco / Toronto / Sydney / Tokyo / Singapore
Hong Kong / Cape Town / Madrid / Paris / Milan / Munich / Amsterdam

PEARSON EDUCATION LIMITED

Head Office
Edinburgh Gate
Harlow CM20 2JE
Tel: +44 (0)1279 623623
Fax: +44 (0)1279 431059

London Office:
128 Long Acre
London WC2E 9AN
Tel: +44 (0)20 7447 2000
Fax: +44 (0)20 7240 5771
Website: www.business-minds.com

———————————————

First edition published in Great Britain in 1998
This edition published in 2001

© PricewaterhouseCoopers 2001

The right of Andrew Black, Philip Wright and John Davies
to be identified as authors of this work has been asserted by them
in accordance with the Copyright, Designs and Patents Act 1988.

ISBN 0 273 65083 1

British Library Cataloguing in Publication Data
A CIP catalogue record for this book can be obtained from the British Library.

10 9 8 7 6 5 4 3 2 1

Typeset by Northern Phototypesetting Co. Ltd, Bolton
Printed and bound in Great Britain by Bell & Bain Ltd, Glasgow

The Publishers' policy is to use paper manufactured from sustainable forests.

ABOUT THE AUTHORS

Andrew Black is director of the Value-Based Management/Mergers and Acquisitions Team in PricewaterhouseCoopers Management Consultancy Services. He has worked extensively on shareholder value models and their application to corporate clients. Previously he was an analyst and strategist for various banks and fund managers, and is the author of a number of articles and papers on subjects such as corporate governance and government industrial policy.

Philip Wright is the European Leader in PricewaterhouseCoopers for Financial Advisory Services (comprising mainly corporate finance and business recovery). Based in London, he has more than 20 years' experience on major international assignments in privatization, corporate finance and shareholder value, including four years building the firm's German corporate finance business.

John Davies is a freelance journalist.

CONTENTS

PART 1 WHAT IS SHAREHOLDER VALUE?

PART 2 PUTTING IT INTO PRACTICE: THE VALUE MINDSET

PART 3 SHV IN ACTION

PART 4 BRINGING IT ALL TOGETHER

FOREWORD TO FIRST EDITION

Change is in the air. Within the last decade or so, most companies have seen the rapid transformation of their business and the climate in which they operate. Globalization, technological change and the increasing sophistication of the markets mean that as we approach the new millennium, successful companies are under pressure as never before: if they do not adapt to the new climate, they perish. They are finding that product excellence is no longer sufficient, nor is it enough to focus on profit alone. The key to success today is the simultaneous delivery of superior returns on capital, sustainable growth rates and the proactive management of risk.

We at Price Waterhouse [now PricewaterhouseCoopers] are not standing apart from this process. We have a long and successful history of financial analysis and assurance work that has adapted itself to, and transcended, a multitude of market and technology changes. The way we perform our services may have changed over the years – manual processes have become automated, for example – but the core business of giving credibility and clarity to the information and systems that we examine or implement has not changed. The provision of credible financial and management information is, and always has been, a necessary precondition for sound business decisions and access to financial markets.

But that's not all. We are fond of stating that we are more than just a financial services firm; rather we are in the business of "solving complex problems for top companies." This means, among other things, that we aim to focus on our clients' priorities and make the most of our capabilities to maximize value for them. In other words, we exist so that our clients can reach their full potential.

This is where shareholder value comes in. Our well-managed clients are on a relentless quest for value; in their businesses they want to create, preserve and realize value for owners, investors and employees. To progress in this quest, they need the latest and most effective techniques of business strategy and analysis – techniques that enable them to ensure that capital is not squandered but is used wisely. Shareholder value analysis provides just such an approach. That is why we have developed our ValueBuilder™ process which is proving its worth in helping top companies in a variety of fields to improve their performance. It is doing this by offering companies analysis and strategies that facilitate value creation and enhance communication and reporting – and by establishing appropriate ways of rewarding their employees when their targets are met.

Our research and client work in the area of shareholder value, then, is the basis for this book. In fields as diverse as banking and high technology, entertainment and energy, we are encountering enthusiastic responses when we explain shareholder value ideas and systems. We hope we can arouse similar enthusiasm among you, the readers of this book.

JERMYN BROOKS
Chairman, Price Waterhouse*

Since the time of writing Price Waterhouse has merged with Coopers & Lybrand, to create PricewaterhouseCoopers.

FOREWORD TO SECOND EDITION

In the three years since the first edition of this book, the culture of shareholder value has moved into the mainstream of corporate life across the globe. The first edition of *In Search of Shareholder Value* has been translated into nine languages, and understanding of the concepts behind shareholder value has become a requirement in every boardroom. In Europe, the first contested takeovers in Germany (Vodafone–Mannesmann) and in Italy (Olivetti–Telecom Italia) were fought around arguments on value, as was the bank merger in France of Paribas and BNP. In each case the spread of global institutional investors had a heavy influence on the outcome. All over the world, there has been a recognition that managers pursuing strategies divorced from shareholder value are not creating the same amount of wealth as those whose strategies are linked to shareholder value. Hence capital has been flowing at increasing speed to those stating clearly that they are out to create value.

If shareholder value has now reached a level of general acceptance, will not interest in it decline? We believe not.

Firstly, there are still very large issues to resolve with regard to how shareholders react with the other stakeholders in our society – employees, customers, governments and environmentalists for example. There is still much for corporates to do in demonstrating that optimizing returns to their shareholders is not irreconcilable with providing long-term satisfaction for other stakeholders; indeed, satisfied stakeholders are a precondition of creating sustainable value.

Secondly, the development of the information revolution and the integration of capital markets (and currencies in Europe) are gathering pace. Meanwhile the ability of investors, both institutional and retail, to compare and contrast corporate performance is increasing. The development of XML, a new-generation internet language, will act as a catalyst for the dissemination of financial information direct from company to investor, and new standards are being developed to cope with this.

Thirdly, the impact of e-business – the so-called "new economy" – has heightened interest in the value creation process. Creating value can be seen not simply as a matter of increasing returns, managing the cost of capital, or focussing on core businesses. The new economy is disrupting established value chains and allowing those who identify the value-creating options for doing business differently to create enormous value with their ideas. Indeed, as Rudolf G. Burkhard, winner of the first PricewaterhouseCoopers European Shareholder Value Award for innovative contributions to the debate has pointed out, the success of the "new economy" in creating value is based on identifying and removing constraints to growth and scale in business.

The success of this book's first edition has enabled us to update much of the text to reflect some of the changes alluded to above. In Chapter 10, we have taken into account the rise of e-business and expanded our treatment of the real options approach to the valuation process in the high-technology field. We have also expanded and extensively rewritten Chapter 11 to re-examine the development of shareholder value in a variety of countries across the world. Notable are more detailed sections on the UK, Germany and France; the inclusion this time of Canada, Singapore, South Korea and India; and a more general consideration of the impact of shareholder value on emerging economies. In Part 1, we have enlarged and, we hope, clarified our discussion of various shareholder value metrics, have additionally introduced the CVA model and developed further our discussion of cost of capital. The crucial concept of the competitive advantage period has also been explored in greater depth.

Indeed, every chapter contains new material – reflecting the way that more and more of the world is taking part in the search for shareholder value. We hope that you will join us in that search.

ACKNOWLEDGEMENTS

The collective knowledge and experience, over several years, of the Price Waterhouse Business Development Group and subsequent Pricewaterhouse-Coopers shareholder value groups has inspired and fed into the writing of this second edition of *In Search of Shareholder Value*.

In particular we would like to thank Likhit Wagle, Ian Coleman, Michael Melvill, Fredrik Weissenrieder, Eric Ottosen, Jeremy Booker, Timothy Luehrman and David Waller for encouragement while writing the book.

For some of the individual chapters we would like to thank the following: for Chapter 7, Mark Rowland and Mayvis Riveira; Chapter 8, Tom Wilson; Chapter 9, Alan Jamieson and John Soden; Chapter 10, Philippe Barsi, Ken Kasriel and Andrew Wardle. The revisions and updating of Chapter 11 was greatly assisted by Euan Friday, Greg Morris, Wesley Mark, Jan Japp Snell, Wim Holterman, Jochen Quaak, Michael Schwartz, Karl Spielberger, Patrick Frotiée, Chise Mori, Sherry Lee, Luis Menendez, Viren Malhotra, Ashwani Puri and Jihye Lee. For Chapter 12 we would like to thank Claire Fargeot, David Philips and Bob Eccles for their contributions and views.

Some of the material in Chapter 12 has already appeared in a different form in *Pursuing Value: The Emerging Art of Reporting on the Future* by Philip D. Wright and Daniel P. Keegan (PW papers 1997).

We are also grateful for the help provided by Kirsty Shaw in answering impossible questions and providing up-to-the-minute information; Michael Spracklin for furthering the development of ValueBuilder™; Reanne Fitz-George, Ramila Dhupelia and Anne Lima for keeping track of the manuscript and the authors; and finally to Gabi Black and Sigrid Wright for moral support and refreshment during the process of writing and revising the book.

Finally, all omissions and errors are the responsibility of the authors.

INTRODUCTION

You have probably heard about shareholder value. Perhaps your company has declared a commitment to shareholder value, or SHV as we will call it throughout this book, and you want an explanation. Perhaps you are an executive who wants to introduce an SHV approach in your company. You may have even thought of using some value-based management system to implement an SHV policy in your company. Or perhaps you are just curious about why *Fortune* magazine called shareholder value "the real key to creating wealth."

Certainly there is a veritable storm of acronyms out there for the interested lay person to weather. For a start, there is EVA™ (economic value added), SVA (shareholder value added) and CFROI (cash flow return on investment), to say nothing of value based management (VBM). We hope in this book to guide you around these and other sets of potentially important initials – for call them what you will, the ideas that cluster around these labels are ideas whose time has come. Corporations in Britain, the US and other parts of the world are increasingly putting SHV theories into practice – and benefitting from doing so.

This book aims to explain what shareholder value means, and how it can help companies and their managers make better, more informed and more proactive decisions. As we shall see in subsequent chapters, SHV takes the insights that market analysts, looking at a company from the outside, have developed, transfers them inside and transforms them into management tools – tools that can be used not just at the boardroom level but throughout a company to notch up genuine improvements in performance.

We at PricewaterhouseCoopers see ourselves as one of the leaders in the shareholder value trend. This book is not, however, a handbook for a particular system. Rather, it takes one step back to look at the philosophy of value creation and at the global financial environment in which value-based management can thrive. We do not promise easy solutions – and we hope we will succeed in dealing with some of the tricky questions raised by critics of the value-based approach.

What is unquestionable is that in the last decade or so there has been a global momentum in the economy. Capital markets – indeed, almost all financial institutions – are increasingly global in outlook. Investors are more sophisticated than ever and want to know more about a company; more than simply what dividends it has been paying in the past. Profit and loss statements drawn up in traditional ways are no longer enough; cash flow has become the most important measure.

As one of the oldest established and largest professional service providers in the world, PricewaterhouseCoopers is particularly well placed to observe such global trends. We are moving forward from the traditional audit that has been our bread and butter for so many years in order to keep pace with – and get ahead of – these trends. Indeed the core purpose of the firm can be described as to help clients build value: value for their shareholders, for their employees, and for their communities.

This book, then, is not only a result of our experience and thinking about financial value, but also an example of what PricewaterhouseCoopers does for its clients through financial and business analysis, implementation of systems and procedures that facilitate value creation, and enhanced communication and reporting to their shareholders and other stakeholders.

THE CONTENT OF THIS BOOK

The first part of *In Search of Shareholder Value* aims to introduce the basic concepts of shareholder value analysis, not only by describing the current economic and global conditions that make SHV so compelling, but also by arguing against a "stakeholder" view of business. We then look at the theory behind shareholder value, and the history behind that, before asking the all-important question: what does your capital cost?

It is not until you have established the true cost of your capital, then, that you will be able to calculate whether or not you are adding value in your day-to-day business. Working this out can, however, be a tricky business: we try to make it easier by dealing with matters such as risk-free rates of return, betas and market premia.

These calculations have to be made because, as we show in Chapter 4, the apparently straightforward figures of profit and loss cannot be relied on. Rather than look to such numbers and earnings per share, the market prefers increasingly to judge a company's performance on its cash flow. This is where SHV analysis come in, with its seven "value drivers" outlined in Chapter 5. Finally in this section, Chapter 6 outlines the various metric systems used for calculating shareholder value. Whatever refinements of calculation are used, the basic message is the same: cash is what counts.

Part 2 moves from theory to practice, and outlines the principles of value based management. First comes corporate analysis of a standard company – the application of the value drivers to its activities, and the tools by which value creation can be measured. We then turn to the "wartime" situation of mergers and acquisitions, and how SHV can help both acquirer and target company assess what their true worth, and hence their best course of action, might be. The other problem can be the "sickbed" situation – when a company is facing failure and it needs help to recover: here again SHV analysis can be a precious resource.

Part 3 stays in the practical sphere by reporting on our experience in a range of industrial sectors, noting that while the "value drivers" may vary, basic shareholder value analysis can apply to all of them. We also report on how shareholder value ideas are being received and applied in a selection of countries around the world, from the mature markets of the USA and the UK to the "stakeholder" economies of Europe and East Asia. We also look at how the shareholder value model can be adopted successfully in developing economies.

Finally, in Part 4, we bring everything together to look at the future of value reporting. We build on current trends to create a hypothetical company report of the future, where value creation is truly taken seriously – to the benefit of all concerned.

WHAT IS
SHAREHOLDER
VALUE?

SHAREHOLDER VALUE: FAD VERSUS FACT

Value. It's a five-letter word with a wealth of meanings – from "desirability" and "utility" as a noun to "appraise" or "have a high opinion of" when it is a verb. But more and more, when business people and investors talk about value, it's to do with shareholder value or similar "value-based" measurements of performance. In other words, techniques by which companies and corporations can be analyzed, re-oriented and then managed to conform with a value creation imperative.

Value for whom? What kind of value? In the business world it's certainly financial value that's the issue, and more specifically cash. By this we mean the cash that takes the form of the returns a company gives to its shareholders, and also cash flow – because that is the sign of a corporation's health in the eyes of the market.

But, you may ask, why should it matter what the market thinks? Isn't all this just another fad that management will have to adopt and then discard a few years later? Our answers to these two questions are: yes, the market does matter; and no, it is not a fad. Because shareholder value – the subject of this book – is founded on the facts of economic life as they confront us today. If you are to be part of a successful company, you cannot ignore these facts. The creation of value for its shareholders is fundamental to the success of any public company.

In this book, particularly in this opening chapter, we hope to convince you of the case for SHV. We will open our case by developing the argument under three headings: why it is not a fad; what it is; and why it is so controversial. Under the last heading we will be exploring some of the arguments against shareholder value that use "stakeholder" theories.

WHY SHV IS NOT A FAD

To put shareholder value into context, we must consider the changes that have taken place and are still taking place all over the world. In the past decade or so, companies have seen the rapid transformation of their businesses by a multitude of forces. Three forces in particular have contributed to a growing awareness of the importance of shareholder value and value-based management. They are the spread of private capital; the globalization of markets; and the information revolution including the internet. Let us look at them one by one.

Increasing amount and spread of private capital

The accumulation and spread of wealth has accelerated dramatically across the globe in the last 50 years, driven by technological advance, a long period of peace in the West and increased world trade. Inherited from the first half of the twentieth century, however, was a loss of faith in capital markets and an experience of war that led people to accept the expansion of the state into areas of commercial and financial life on a massive scale. In particular, many states entered into long-term obligations in the areas of pensions, health and social security. Combined with demographic developments – increased life expectancy, for example – this has meant that in the last 20 years these states have hit the limits of their taxing and borrowing powers and have begun to withdraw from at least some of their commitments and to shift provision back to the individual.

States and politicians have a multitude of differing and often complex claims and priorities to consider. But the individual is driven by a simpler and clearer set of objectives. At the practical level this means that more and more people are investing privately to secure their pensions, as well as taking out health and other insurances to protect themselves against a variety of risks. Depending on their circumstances, individual investors may make different choices: they may go for different combinations of growth, risk and return, and therefore different mixes of property, bonds and equity. But for longer-term commitments many take the higher-risk, higher-return option and invest in equities, often through unit trusts or mutual funds.

This in turn has led to an enormous expansion of the equity markets – in the first instance in the USA, the UK and Japan, but increasingly as a world-wide phenomenon. (The figures involved nowadays are truly enormous. In countries such as the UK, the USA, and Switzerland the total market capitalization of all the companies quoted on their stock exchanges is over 100 percent of their gross domestic product – see, in Part 3 of this book, Fig. 11.5.) Along with this expansion has come a rise in the proportion of equities held by institutions such as pension funds, as Fig. 1.1 shows. And, just as the individual investor expects funds to maximize their performance, so in their turn the funds increasingly demand value from the companies they invest in.

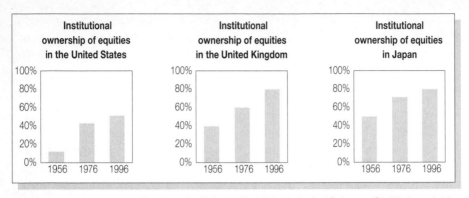

Source: International Federation of Stock Markets, London Stock Exchange, and Price Waterhouse calculations

FIG 1.1 ● **Growth in institutional ownership of equities**

Globalization of markets

Since 1970, true global markets have developed in an increasing range of goods and services, accompanied by various agreements under GATT (the General Agreement on Tariffs and Trade, now succeeded by WTO, the World Trade Organization). These agreements have successfully lowered trade barriers, leading, unsurprisingly, to an increase in international trade, so that companies have faced decisions about where to sell, and how to support those sales. (A strategy based on protecting or holding on to a domestic market has become doomed to failure in an increasing number of areas.)

The currency markets have grown in size and sophistication since the collapse, in the 1970s, of the Bretton Woods system of fixed exchange rates. This has enabled the management of currency and interest risks to keep pace, more or less, with the demands of global traders: investment in foreign markets requires the easy transfer of capital from one country to another, and arrangements for remitting profits back to the investor.

By the 1980s, along with widespread domestic financial de-regulation, most restrictions on capital flows had been removed by the OECD countries (essentially, the more developed markets of Western Europe, North America, and Japan). Following the establishment of global markets for financial assets, it has become possible to invest internationally in a much more proactive way than before. Companies are now competing internationally not only for customers, products and employees, but also for capital. Attracting capital depends on being best in class and the major criterion for this is the creation of shareholder value.

In "capital rich" countries, local companies can no longer expect to gain access to funds as cheaply as before. Many of the larger companies in countries such as Germany and Japan have come to realize that previous supplies of cheap long-term lending are drying up and that they must now concentrate on creating shareholder value in ways previously undreamed of. Equally, in capital-poor countries, companies have to offer investors not just what they would expect to get in their own countries, but an additional consideration to allow for their perceived riskiness as investment locations.

The move towards wider regional financial markets is something that is particularly apparent in Europe, facilitated by the euro as a common currency. Freed from the constraints of currency risk within the Euro-zone, the European investor is now starting to take a much closer interest in what is going on next door.

... but not everywhere is the same

In Part 3 of this book we will deal in greater detail with variations in practice between different countries, but it is worth noting at the outset that, broadly speaking, there have been two models for capitalism. The first, loosely called the "Anglo-Saxon" model, has been characterized by large and liquid capital markets, a growing concentration of power into the hands of institutional investors and a market for corporate control via takeover bids, many of them hostile. Institutional investors in the UK, for instance, have accounted for well over 70 percent of total equity, while over half of all European takeover bids have occurred in the UK.

By contrast, in Germany, much of the rest of Europe, and possibly Japan (countries where the "stakeholder" model has applied) equity markets have been – and to some extent still are – less liquid and often smaller. Shareholder power is concentrated among banks, governments and families. In Italy, for example, single majority shareholdings account for about 60 percent of the total market capitalization compared to just 5 percent in the UK and the USA. The largest five shareholders of Italian-listed companies typically hold nearly 90 percent of the shares between them, compared to only 21 percent in the UK. More significantly, mainland Europe has had a much less well developed market for corporate control. Hostile takeovers have in the past been rare in most European markets; changes in control have normally been negotiated by banks and governments, with the market typically informed after a transaction. This situation is now changing as the nascent European financial market makes it possible to raise what are, by local standards, huge sums of money for re-structuring and mergers and acquisitions. The successful takeover of the larger Telecom Italia by the smaller Olivetti was largely made possible by tapping into the Euro-bond market on a scale that was only previously possible in US dollars, and so had been closed to European investors.

Nevertheless, there are paradoxes. Portfolio investors now have the technical means to invest almost anywhere in the world, yet this freedom is limited. Restrictions are imposed on the liquidity and reputation of the markets where they can place their funds, and on the type of assets they can acquire. Like huge oil tankers unable to enter smaller ports, the large institutional funds are forced to stay in the deep-water channels of the financial markets. Asset and liability considerations also mean that such investors have to keep a weather eye open on their base currency: at the end of the day, liabilities in one currency have to be paid in that currency. Finally, valuable local tax concessions for entities such as pension schemes may prevent funds from investing outside their home markets.

Globalization, then, has not so far meant that every developed country's financial market is the same, nor that investment is flowing freely across national boundaries. Although there has been a large increase in international investment, it still forms a relatively small part of the total. Typically only 5 percent of US equity investments go outside the US market; in most of the world's leading financial countries, the vast majority of investments are in domestic stocks and bonds. Even if they have the capacity to be global, most funds are still very local in their investment strategies, being tied to their home markets either because of risk aversion or because local content rules require them to invest domestically.

Globalization in its infancy

Does this mean that globalization is not such a big thing after all? On the contrary, we believe it is a process that is still in its infancy. Non-American companies such as Daimler-Benz are increasingly being listed in New York, and non-British ones on the London Stock Exchange. We will see more and more of such phenomena as NASDAQ – the US-based National Association of Securities Dealers Automated Quotation System – advertising its services in countries outside North America. The German *Neue Markt* is now beginning to attract attention not just for local, German technology start-up companies, but more widely as a source of finance for European start-up companies.

Information

The increased sophistication of telecommunications and computers means, as we know, that money can now travel across the world in a matter of seconds. Two further developments in the information revolution have facilitated the application of shareholder value and at the same time increased the demand for information to create an efficient market.

Firstly, the advent of PC-based modelling software has relieved investors of the need to spend time on the complex calculations underlying SHV methodology. This has enabled them to focus on the quality of a company's strategic thinking, its product and market knowledge.

Secondly, the quantity and quality of information now available to investors are far superior to even ten years ago. Companies such as Reuters and Bloomberg provide online news and market information; the Edgar database provides immediate access to US financial filings; and product and market data proliferate. Many companies also now spend a considerable amount on investor relations and communications, while the amount of information now available for free on the internet is truly remarkable. Further developments in computer internet language (XML) will enable investors and analysts to "slice and dice" even more company information.

The value of disclosing fuller and more comprehensive information is perhaps best illustrated in Switzerland: there, companies that have chosen the disclosure route regularly attract capital at a lower cost than those that remain secretive.

All these trends, taken together, have one message: you can't hide from the markets. Any company that wants to do well – and that means attracting investment funds, and continuing to attract them – will (unless it can sustain its investment need from its own resources) have to submit itself happily to the scrutiny of the people whose money it is using.

WHAT IS SHV?

What then does the investment community understand by shareholder value? One definition of it is simply "corporate value minus debt" – or, to put it another way, a company's SHV is calculated as the present value of future cash flows of the business discounted at its weighted average cost of capital, less the value of debt. But the more fundamental principle is that *a company only adds value for its shareholders when equity returns exceed equity cost*. If an investor is considering buying your company's equity, he or she ought to take account of the *opportunity cost* of having capital tied up there rather than elsewhere. We shall return to this crucial question of the cost of capital in Chapter 3.

You may already be feeling uneasy, however. Sure, the markets want to know the value of my company – there's nothing wrong with that, you will say. But why introduce new methods? What's wrong with looking at the balance sheet and the profit and loss statement? Aren't measures such as EPS (earnings per share – the net income a share will receive in dividends after tax) sufficient for analysts?

Unfortunately they aren't. Economists have looked back over the past and have been able to show that there is little correlation between historical accounting earnings and stock market performance. With GAAP (generally accepted accounting practices) varying markedly from country to country, it is possible for the same company, using the same figures, to declare a profit in one country and a loss in another. Profit, in other words, is an opinion rather than an established fact.

The gaps in GAAP

For this reason, among others, there has been a growing disenchantment with company results as reported. In particular there is a feeling that too much attention is given to earnings per share (EPS) measurements. (The overuse of EPS and anomalous accounting measures is discussed further in Chapter 4.)

But of even more concern to investors is the question of whether accounting measures in Europe – and indeed around the world – are consistent. As one would expect, they are not. The treatment of goodwill, deferred taxation and the valuing of inventory varies from country to country.

There is now a healthy industry in recasting reported accounts for use by investors. But it is questionable whether managements are arriving at their internally compiled figures – upon which they base operating and strategic decisions – in the same way. Without a focus on shareholder value principles, pan-European businesses or businesses that cross different trading blocs could be in danger of relying on internal accounts that have the same fault-lines as external accounts. The result is bad decision-making.

It is no surprise, then, that investment analysts are looking behind the headline figures to find other numbers that can measure more informatively the long-term prospects for a company. Shareholder value analysis based on free cash flow and the cost of capital can produce such numbers. Later on, we will examine the different ways of making the necessary calculations – look out for acronyms such as CAPM, CFROI, EVA and TSR, all of which manipulate the source data on cash flow, capital or its cost to show different aspects of value. The important thing to take on board now is that these are the measures increasingly being used by the market to take investment decisions, and they concentrate on economic or cash flow measures rather than earnings or traditional accounting measures.

WHY IS SHV SO CONTROVERSIAL?

Understandably, boardrooms and middle managers are suspicious of the stock market. A superficial glance at the behavior of share prices in the market might lead you to think that short-termism has priority over long-term evaluation. Companies are convinced that investors are driven by short-term targets and do not therefore understand management strategies. This view has its counterpart in the investment community: many shareholders feel managements take too little account of their needs, in particular for information about companies' future plans and strategies.

Paradoxically, this misunderstanding between management and investor concerning the short and the long term arises because of the enormous immediate effects on value of announcements made by companies, even concerning short-term results, if these change the market's perception of their long-term cash flows.

So perhaps there is less conflict than is at first apparent. An essential component of value-based management is an emphasis on communication, both internally and externally. As our own research at PricewaterhouseCoopers has shown, investors are not simply looking for short-term rewards in the form of dividends and an increasing share price; they want long-term prospects for growth. There is a great deal of evidence that the market evaluates management decisions according to their impact on long-term discounted cash flow.

All the same, it cannot be denied that tensions exist between investor and management. This tension can all too easily be repeated elsewhere: within many companies the culture of the strategist and creative visionary clashes with that of the manager and controller. Shareholder value demands a consistent link between both. Similarly, tension can arise between corporate and divisional management.

In a company structured to maximize shareholder value, the divisional manager will have to be more aware of what the shareholders want – which is nothing but better returns. He or she will have to think much more as an entrepreneur, rather than just as an employee. Accustomed perhaps to carrying out head office's requirements without too much thought, managers may face some difficult adjustments. The quiet life they long for will not be an option as they both become more empowered and also acquire more responsibility and accountability. For many, this will be uncomfortable – as will the scrutiny that comes with the new focus on value creation. With that bad news, however, should come the promise of better things in the shape of rewards for value creation: the measurements that shareholder value brings in its train are ideal tools for the incentivization of management. (We will deal with such incentivization later in the book, in Chapter 7.)

Shareholders and stakeholders

So far we have argued that significant trends at work in the economy and society are pushing for an increased role for SHV. However persuasive such evidence is, it has to be compared critically with a number of alternative approaches. For many people, it is not self-evident that the equity-based approach is the best. Emphasizing the interests of shareholders over those of other groups, they argue, is misplaced. In this "stakeholder" view of companies – perhaps more often encountered on the mainland of Europe and in Japan than in Britain or North America – the interests of suppliers, customers, creditors, employees and the state are at least as important as those of shareholders.

Since this is a widely held view it is worth looking at in more detail. The "stakeholder" view can be thought of at two levels: the national or macro level, and the micro or corporate level.

At the macro level, a stakeholder economy is, in the words of a recent advocate, "one which derives competitive strength from a cohesive national culture, in which the exercise of property rights is conditioned by shared values and cooperative behavior."[1] Within this framework the manager is seen as a "trustee," whose primary responsibility is to balance the demands of different interest groups. Managers, according to this view, become stewards of "social" capital, seen here as "networks, behavioral norms and trust which enable people to work more effectively towards common goals – intangible qualities referred to by legal theorists as relational contracting and known in economics as implicit contracts."[2] People are expected to be nice to each other, in other words, simply because it is in their best general interest to behave that way. Conflicts and differences will be ironed out within the consensus that will rumble on in an untroubled manner. The use of implicit contracts, and the consequent reduction in transaction costs, gives a further lift to the efficiency of the stakeholder economy – or so it is claimed.

As examples, stakeholder advocates take countries like Germany and Japan – in the past, paragons of economic virtue and financial rectitude. But recent experience tells a different story. Both countries have found it difficult to cope with the new, more flexible world we live in: the structures that earlier had seemed capable of delivering social peace and consensus, combined with large dollops of additional wealth and welfare, have been struggling. Consensus decisions have been revealed as having been flawed. Japanese banks have taken a decade to come to terms fully with the excesses of the "bubble" economy. German society has also only gradually realized that its generous levels of social provision will probably not be affordable in the twenty-first century. Rather than being seen as powerhouses of growth and dynamism, both countries have begun to look rather ossified and stagnant. (For more about individual countries' problems, see Chapter 11.)

What about the micro, or corporate, level? Consider the remarks of a former chairman of the Standard Oil Company of New Jersey, Frank Abrams. In 1951, he asserted that "the job of management is to maintain an equitable and working balance among the claims of the various directly interested groups – stockholder, employees, customers and the public at large." Management is supposed to do this by recognizing that there is "value" in a wider set of relationships which go beyond the "principal-agent" model of capitalism, which overemphasizes the role of property rights, the rights of the owners of capital. Both social capital and implicit contracts are "all important elements in the competitive advantage of firms. It is the job of the manager to foster them in the long-term interests of the company and the wider interests of society. The emphasis on the cohesive nature of the relationships between the various economic actors does not preclude shareholders' exercise of discipline over management. But it does imply a different definition of objectives and thus a different approach to monitoring."[3]

Simply focusing on SHV, in this view, will mean that the only stakeholder to get any benefit from a company's success will be the investor; employees in particular will suffer. There is a close correlation in people's minds between companies performing poorly, redundancy programs and share price increases. The stakeholder view, on the other hand, will mean taking a less "callous" view and considering the sometimes competing interests of worker, shareholder, customer and supplier – and indeed the wider community.

This "stakeholder corporation" does, on the face of it, make sense: wouldn't it be fairer if everybody's interests could be weighed against each other and reconciled by management? The trouble is, ultimately, they can't be. The management of a business must have one prime focus: maximizing the value of its equity. If it is accountable to more than one interest, it will sooner or later be faced with the problem of deciding between them, and it can only give preference to one or the other by using some further criterion. This is all the more true in today's decentralized corporation where middle managers are continually taking decisions with value implications: for instance, should an investment that adds value and keeps customers satisfied – but reduces the workforce – go ahead? Corporate paralysis would ensue without a clear, common criterion. When interests conflict, such as those of employees and shareholders, a choice has to be made, and stakeholder theory offers no help in making that choice.

Putting SHV first, however, does. While it concentrates on its one objective, a company managed for value cannot afford to ignore the other stakeholders. Customers will leave if not satisfied; suppliers have to be kept happy. And staff will leave or underperform if under-rewarded or otherwise mistreated – a phenomenon perhaps most noticeable in the high-technology sphere, where skilled workers are often a company's most precious resource. So by adopting the measures necessary to maximize corporate value, a company can advance the interests of other stakeholders as well as its shareholders. It also adds value to the society in which it operates. And whatever else it does, it is of no use to its employees or to the community at large if it fails to make money.

A few years ago, the late Roberto C. Goizueta, then CEO of the Coca-Cola Company, trenchantly argued the case for putting shareholders (or as he describes them, "share owners") first:

> Saying that we work for our share owners may sound simplistic – but we frequently see companies that have forgotten the reason they exist. They may even try in vain to be all things to all people and serve many masters in many different ways. In any event, they miss their primary calling, which is to stick to the business of creating value for their owners. ... [W]hile a healthy company can have a positive and seemingly infinite impact on others, a sick company is a drag on the social order of things. It cannot sustain jobs, much less widen the opportunities available to its employees. It cannot serve customers. It cannot give to philanthropic causes. ...
>
> The real and lasting benefits we create don't come because we do good deeds, but because we do good work – work focused on our mission of creating value over time for the people who own the company.[4]

While at the time of writing the Coca-Cola organization is not riding as high as it has done, the words of its CEO in 1996 still hold true. A focus on one overriding aim simplifies everything, even as it incidentally brings other benefits in its train. Motivation of a company's managers, for example. As Samuel Brittan has remarked, "People function best if they have specific responsibilities for which they are held accountable by means which are transparent, verifiable and respect the realities of human nature."[5] The objective of maximizing SHV affords just such a responsibility, and the means by which it is measured, as we shall see in later chapters, are indeed transparent and verifiable.

A further argument in favor of SHV comes from a perhaps surprising quarter – South Korea. A university professor has been leading a shareholder activist movement, People's Solidarity for Participatory Democracy, that has challenged some of the entrenched *Chaebol*s (conglomerates) that dominate economic life there, in some cases taking them to court. He forced the Korea First Bank, which had lent funds illegally to a bankrupt steel group, to reimburse some £23 million for losses arising from mismanagement and abuse of power. This was achieved with the clear aim of improving matters for shareholders, but others benefitted, too: as he said, "If shareholder's rights are not protected … no other stakeholders will be protected. With shareholder rights, others get a safety net."[6]

A tale of two companies

In this book we try to avoid lengthy case studies, but two examples of recent corporate behavior can, we feel, exemplify the problems of "stakeholder" companies.

Daimler-Benz was quite closely wedded to stakeholder principles. During the late 1980s, flush with cash and success from its auto and truck businesses, the corporate chairman Edzard Reuter embarked on what was to turn out to be an unfortunate series of acquisitions and mergers. As the Berlin Wall fell, so the company greatly expanded its defense interests, attempting to become a German "national champion" as it did so. The subsequent "peace dividend" had not been factored in, and the aerospace subsidiary found it difficult to make money even as it was serving a wider stakeholder interest. Decisions about restructuring the domestic appliance and heavy engineering divisions were also delayed, so that they continued to rack up heavy losses. Stakeholder regulations making it expensive to lay off workers undoubtedly played a role in this – the cost of which was largely borne by the shareholders. Throw in a recession that affected the market for the company's core business areas of cars and trucks, and a management that had taken its eye off the ball in this critical area, and it becomes easy, in hindsight, to understand why Daimler – since 1998, Daimler Chrysler – lost so much money, and why so much shareholder value was destroyed.

Now things are beginning to change. Current CEO Jurgen Schrempp's espousal of SHV principles, the successful de-merger of much of the company's aerospace business and a renewed emphasis on its core businesses have helped to turn Daimler around – and its shareholder value has started to prosper. Decisions to list the company in New York helped Deutsche Bank offload some of its shareholding (stakeholding), and probably made the subsequent merger with Chrysler easier. Germany's largest industrial company survived – but only after it woke up to the rigors of the financial markets and after realizing that shareholders had to be given some additional performance.

In the British equity market, meanwhile, Marks & Spencer was for a long time a stalwart stock – a highly regarded "blue chip" that was increasingly able to take its shareholders for granted. The company had developed what was to some a slightly idiosyncratic formula for its stores, where there were no changing rooms and credit cards were not accepted. Offering good value for money and, for British standards, good service and a generous returns policy was sufficient for many years to attract customers and produce steady growth in revenues and profits. On this basis, Marks & Spencer gradually turned into a "stakeholder company." Senior management were asked to advise UK governments, and were seen as setting the standard in labor relations, in signing long-term contracts with suppliers and providing a meaningful revenue stream for much of the British textile and clothing industry. In his 1997 book, John Plender cites the company as being a clear example of a "stakeholder"-led management, which, while describing the company accurately today, probably belies its earlier origins as a stock market (hence SHV) favorite. Success seems to have bred a growing distance from the consumer.

The arrival of new competitors, some domestic and some of foreign origin, has presented the company with a challenge. Niche retailers offering attractively designed clothes at equally good or better prices started to erode Marks & Spencer's market share. The British public, it seemed, preferred stores that both offered changing rooms and accepted credit cards. A strong exchange rate penalized the company's policy of sourcing clothes from the UK and gave it a price disadvantage compared to the competition. Customers drifted away, increasingly skeptical about the attractiveness of the company's fashions and designs. This stakeholder company initially seemed to take some time to evolve an effective response. Credit cards are now allowed; fashions have been improved, and painful decisions negatively affecting another stakeholder – the stores' UK suppliers – have been made. The company is now making huge efforts to reconnect both with its shareholders and its customers, but it seems to us that Marks & Spencer is a company that strayed a long way from shareholder value.

There are other examples of stakeholder projects that have had little success. Nationalized industries in most countries have had great difficulties in meeting the conflicting demands of stakeholders. One group in particular – consumers – has tended to be neglected. After privatization has introduced shareholders into the picture, it is sometimes remarkable just how large the efficiency gains have been. And if it can be objected that privatizations lead to job losses, there are some interesting counter-examples: for instance, the increase in employment in Britain's telecommunications sector following privatization and deregulation has more than offset the decrease in the size of BT's workforce from the days of state ownership.

SHV HAS ARRIVED

In the longer term, then, neither employees nor customers need fear SHV. Many of the goals and objectives desired by stakeholders can in fact be better achieved by paying close attention to the needs of the shareholders. In our view, the decisive factor will often be organization, and, as we will show in the course of this book, SHV can create organizational conditions under which other broader goals can be pursued. Whereas the stakeholder view will in a crisis attempt a difficult balancing act between competing interests, the shareholder view in a similar situation will opt for a strategy that keeps the financing side on board and ultimately satisfied. The SHV approach, with its one overarching principle, can often react much more swiftly *in extremis* than a strategy that has to take into account multiple, and potentially conflicting, interests before a course of action can be adopted.

All over the world, and in a variety of industries, companies are increasingly recognizing the importance of SHV – as we will see in Part 3 of this book. In Japan the blocs of cross-shareholdings that create families of companies are breaking up, and in Germany most of the large banks have been steadily reducing their "strategic" investments in industry. We see this as further evidence of a shift towards concentrating both risks and rewards more clearly and simply in the hands of shareholders. It is a tacit recognition of the practical problems of organizing and controlling stakeholder enterprises.

In other words, shareholder value is no longer just an option; as a framework for thinking about how a modern economy should be organized, it has arrived.

SUMMARY

In this chapter we have introduced the global context in which companies have to operate as competitors for (among other things) capital. Cash flow, however it is measured, is a better indicator of a company's value than more traditional measures. Consequently, investors increasingly look at cash flow figures when estimating shareholder value, and hence the potential value of an investment. We also looked at the rival claims of the "stakeholder" model and rejected it as a viable way of financing and running a company.

Notes

1. Plender, J. (1997) *A Stake in the Future* London: Nicholas Brealey.
2. Ibid.
3. Ibid.
4. Remarks delivered to Executives' Club of Chicago, quoted in Coca-Cola Company annual report, 1996.
5. "The snares of stakeholding," *Financial Times*, 1 February 1996.
6. "A Big Voice for the Small Man," *Financial Times*, 4 May 2000, p.15.

THE HISTORY
OF VALUE

Value has existed as a concept as long as humanity has conducted trade and accumulated "capital" and "wealth." As economies and societies have developed from subsistence, through agriculture and industry to service, value has been the consistent measurement used by those with freedom of choice to trade or to invest and preserve their capital.

Of course this historical development has taken place against occasional catastrophe (war, disease, environmental difficulties) and a background provided by government, which is involved in value in four ways: war and peace, the administration of justice (particularly property rights), the redistribution of wealth and income, and the provision of infrastructure. On the last, Professor George Stigler argues that:

The propensity to use the state is like the propensity to use coal: we use coal when it is the most efficient resource with which to heat our houses and power our factories. Similarly, we use the state to build our roads or tax our consumers when the state is the most efficient way to reach those goals.[1]

With the global economic development of the last 50 years has come an increasing study of the value creation process. From a political and social standpoint this has concentrated largely on the shareholder/stakeholder debate referred to in the previous chapter, where the superior effectiveness of the capital market approach to creating value is now widely recognized. The argument now revolves basically around how to provide infrastructure in the case of the market's perceived failure to do so (for example, in health and education), how much to redistribute wealth and income, and what legal framework is needed for the operation of the market – what laws are necessary, for example, to deal with monopolies, health and safety, environmental protection and minimum wage levels.

CUSTOMER VALUE

From a business perspective, two main themes are rapidly converging: customer value and shareholder value. On customers and markets, much work on strategy and operations has been done by business schools and strategic consultants who have examined the competitive forces that drive them. Leading thinkers in this area include Michael Porter, who developed the "five forces" model to analyze competition for custom in an industry and identified the generic strategies for achieving competitive advantage (overall cost leadership, differentiation and focus)[2]; and Gary Hamel and C.K. Prahalad, who coined the term "core competencies" to describe those attributes that give an enterprise a competitive advantage.[3]

Clearly we are living in a market economy where what matters is winning maximum share and keeping customers satisfied – by meeting or exceeding their expectations at a price no higher than a product's (or service's) perceived value. This drive to customer value has been accompanied by other processes designed to lower costs and improve quality and performance, such as total quality management (TQM), process and systems re-engineering and change integration.

Customer satisfaction is, of course, only ultimately of value when it produces over time an economic cash return on the investment – a return in excess of a company's cost of capital. Thus the strategic thinking aimed at customers needs to be reconciled with the financial thinking behind shareholder value, which brings us to the development of shareholder value theories.

SHAREHOLDER VALUE

Theories about shareholder value (SHV) have a long and illustrious history stretching back to the 1950s and 1960s, with their intellectual roots in the path-breaking work of Markovitz, Modigliani and Miller, and Sharpe, Fama, and Treynor (to name but a few). Many of these economists have subsequently been honored with the Nobel prize for economics, thus putting what had started out as a "fringe" activity in economics firmly at the center of that discipline's development. Their contributions ranged from effectively describing risk and return trade-offs and the development of efficient market theorems, to the idea of a risk premium for equities and to the idea that the value of a company was a reflection of its expected future development and not a result of its history. All of these ideas and more started to coalesce into what is called the capital asset pricing model, or CAPM.

SHV started to take on a life of its own as a result of work done on CAPM. In essence, this model argues that the returns received by investors are related to the risk incurred by owning particular financial assets. Broadly speaking, the higher the risk, the greater the return should be.

The key insight of the CAPM model – one that is central to the SHV view of the world – is that there is a risk-weighted discount factor which allows you to assess the value today of tomorrow's developments, profits and cash flows. This discount rate is derived from observations of capital markets, and defines what the opportunity cost of equity to an investor in the market is. It states what the company has to earn in order to justify the use of the capital resources tied up in the business.

THE DEVELOPMENT OF A THEORY

It was sometime during the late 1970s and early 1980s that work in applying some of the insights of CAPM to the corporate sector got under way. These efforts first gained prominence with the publication, in 1986, of *Creating Shareholder Value* by Professor Alfred Rappaport of Northwestern University, Illinois.[4] He subsequently went on to found the Alcar group, a company dedicated to the production of software to help executives achieve some of the goals laid out in his book. The Rappaport approach introduced the free cash flow (FCF) model and showed how the normal discounted cash flow techniques could be adapted and put into a shareholder value framework.

This was followed in 1987 by a less well known book, *Managing for Value* by Bernard Reimann, which began to link SHV to the art of running a company and thus was taken up by management consultants.[5] Some of the ideas expressed there have subsequently been developed into the cash flow return on investment (CFROI) approach.

Interest in the SHV approach received a further boost with the 1990 publication of *Valuation* by Tom Copeland and others from the McKinsey Group.[6] This book contained a detailed exposition of the issues and how to deal with them, showing that the application of SHV principles to companies is both feasible and highly desirable. It also argued that such an approach could yield substantial benefits not only to shareholders but also to other "stakeholders" in a company.

The following year, 1991, G. Bennett Stewart brought out *The Quest for Value*, which introduced the idea of economic value added (EVA™). We will have more to say about this later in the book, but for the moment we will just say that it is defined as the spread between the return on capital and the cost of capital in a single period. The important thing is that it focused more attention on the detailed measurement of a firm's balance sheet, and on how certain items need to be treated differently from the way accountants usually handle them.

All these books put particular emphasis on the ability of companies to apply the ideas of SHV analysis in practice, and by doing so to achieve real and sustainable increases in their share values. These ideas have continued to develop subsequently thanks to the emergence of a number of software products which, combined with the skills of consultants and managements, have brought SHV analysis within the reach of companies who had previously never considered it, or had not felt competent or comfortable with the idea of applying it to themselves. Software programs that deserve mention in this context include Alcar, Evaluator and ValueBuilder. These models make it much easier to embark on SHV analysis, since they can look at companies not only from a consolidated corporate view but also in considerable detail for subsidiaries and strategic business units.

More recent developments have enabled SHV models to be linked to internal corporate management information systems, so that executives can now have a continuously updated view as to how well the company is performing in shareholder value terms.

AFTER THE HISTORY, WHAT?

Brought down to its simplest, the SHV approach was well summarized by former Coca-Cola CEO Roberto Goizueta: "We raise capital to make concentrate, and sell it at an operating profit. Then we pay the cost of that capital. Shareholders pocket the difference." This surprisingly simple statement points to new ways of setting and achieving goals and targets.

Let us look at them in terms of three major elements of SHV analysis: growth, risk and return. Traditionally, managements have been encouraged by being set growth objectives. They have also been encouraged to reduce borrowing costs and diversify their enterprises (possibly in pursuit of the growth goal already mentioned) so as to reduce risk, and to increase returns. Looked at from the point of view of shareholder value theory, all three policies can be seriously flawed, not to say destructive. A growth policy can tie up considerable capital resources, which are then applied inefficiently and yield inadequate returns. In SHV terms, this policy will have destroyed shareholder value, even though the company may have grown larger as a result.

Traditionally, too, debt repayment schemes are seen as a way to reduce risk. After all why be beholden to your bank or bond holder when you can maintain control and profits for the shareholder alone? But this course of action can also help to reduce SHV by putting up the cost of capital, and thus raising the threshold rate of return which the company has to reach before it begins to add to shareholder value. (Incidentally, it also overlooks the fact that geared companies often perform better than ungeared ones – see Chapter 8 for more details.)

Finally, efforts to reduce risk by diversifying a company's portfolio and getting involved in extensive mergers and acquisitions activity can also be value destroying. Poorly-thought-out mergers and takeovers have been described by a leading proponent of the shareholder value approach as being "equivalent to charitable contributions made to random passers-by"[7] as the acquirer regularly overpays for the privilege of managing a decidedly mediocre business.

So if businesses and capital markets have to be increasingly value-oriented, what are the implications? What will success look like for companies in the new millennium? If SHV is the new game, how will corporate players win?

Certainly the rules are changing. Product excellence and customer satisfaction is still necessary but is no longer sufficient, nor is it enough to focus on profit alone. There is now a business climate in which success requires both sustainable superior returns on capital and peer-leading growth rates. Combine these with a proactive management of the risks associated with optimizing returns and growth, and you have a whole new set of trade-offs and strategic permutations to challenge the corporate sector.

These challenges may be new, but in a sense they are the same old challenges in a different guise. The three aspects of market activity just referred to – risk, growth and return – continue to be central. The economic reality, that cash is king and investors require compensating returns for the risks they bear, is not new. It has always been the case that investors buy securities based on their expectations of future performance, not merely as a belated recognition of past performance. Growth, too, has always been a good thing, other variables remaining constant. It is on these basics that shareholder value theory is founded.

Paradoxically, then, we are going forward to the past. Although the capitalist system has always appeared to be structured to serve the interests of the owners of equity – the shareholders – it is only now, with the increased global pressures described in Chapter 1 now applying, and with the increased sophistication of software tools, that shareholders' interests are really being considered. Value for shareholders has finally reached the top of the agenda.

SHV IN PRACTICE

The basic SHV approach is a simple one, then – although some aspects of the theory and calculations are complicated, and will be dealt with later in this book. It addresses the relationship between what a company is using in terms of capital resources, how they are allocated throughout the firm, and what the likelihood is of their "earning their keep" over the planning horizon.

Meanwhile, it is worth noting that 65 percent of all large companies in the USA claim that they have adopted SHV as a primary goal. Indeed, they might be slightly offended at any suggestion they had not taken this issue seriously. But it is also clear that only a relatively small number of companies have embarked on detailed SHV programs, let alone had the patience and forbearance to hold on until they are finished.

Companies that are on record as having embarked on, or having signed up to, SHV programs include such names as Coca-Cola, Pepsi Cola, Quaker Oats, Reuters, Lloyds Bank, Veba, General Electric, Briggs and Stratton, ICI, Boots, Novo Nordisk and many more. Many (but not all) of the companies on this list have indeed experienced above-average share price performance – which is one good indication that the companies have really taken SHV seriously.

What then are the reasons why companies adopt a shareholder value approach? There are the external stimuli:

- when they are faced with strong external pressure from investors. This can be because of an actual or threatened take-over situation;
- when incumbent senior management is faced with a new CEO who understands SHV concepts;
- when a new CEO wants to implement a SHV project as part of finding out what is going on in the company.

But there are other reasons, too:

- to "empower" the work of lower management, and encourage them to take steps that will explicitly consider SHV, and match empowerment with accountability and incentivization;
- to give additional focus to other consultancy projects, to ensure that the new systems are aligned with shareholder value goals;
- when there are serious mismatches between corporate expectations and subsidiary performance;
- when there is confidence that the programs can be implemented properly, reliably and within budget.

Companies are less likely actually to implement SHV programs if the conditions above are not met. They may also stall if there is serious disagreement at a senior level about the wisdom of the exercise – which may reach unpleasant conclusions, thereby upsetting a perhaps fragile consensus at board level.

These are general issues that affect many consultants and programs offering change to a corporation. Companies may give up on SHV programs if it is felt that they are not getting anywhere, and if there is too little support from the top to ensure that everyone is cooperating. SHV programs work better if the wider circle of managers and employees can be convinced that they are necessary and that they will yield some benefits over and above the laying-off of staff. Indeed, to be successful, such programs will often have started a lively discourse about where the company is going, and how it can set itself feasible goals that will raise shareholder value.

SUMMARY

In this chapter we took a brief view of the historical context of value. Alongside the development of customer value approaches in business, shareholder value theories have arisen from academic work on the cost of capital. Underlying all these theories is a belief that companies have to earn a certain amount of returns to justify the use of the capital they have tied up in their enterprise. In effect, this belief is a reassertion of one of the basic facts of capitalism – that shareholders have to be rewarded for investing in you.

Finally, we identified the circumstances in which companies in practice have sought to adopt shareholder value-based programs.

Notes

1. Stigler, G. (1986) *The Regularity of Regulation*, David Hume Institute, quoted in Veljanovski (1987) *Selling the State* Weidenfeld.

2. Porter, M.E. (1990) *Competitive Strategy* New York: Free Press.

3. Prahalad, C.D. and Hamel, G. (1990) "The Core Competence of the Corporation," *Harvard Business Review*, May–June.

4. Rappaport, A. (1986) *Creating Shareholder Value* New York: Free Press.

5. Reimann, B. (1989) *Managing for Value* Blackwell.

6. Copeland, T., Kollen, T. and Murrim, J. (McKinsey & Company, Inc.) (1994) *Valuation: Measuring and Managing the Value of Companies*, 2nd edn. New York: John Wiley.

7. Stewart, G.B. (Stern Stewart & Co.) (1991) *The Quest for Value* New York: HarperBusiness.

WHAT DOES YOUR CAPITAL COST?

It sounds so simple, and yet it is probably one of the most commonly overlooked aspects of business. All enterprises require some capital, and it does not come free.

Although capital comes in more than one form – as equity or debt – we are primarily concerned here with a company's shareholder capital, since this is the most common form of corporate finance. When we say capital is not a "free" good, we mean that if it is not adequately rewarded it will migrate into areas where it can earn a reasonable rate of return – equivalent to what is sometimes called the *opportunity cost* (the term we introduced in Chapter 1).

This chapter, then, is all about ways of identifying what a company's share and debt capital actually costs. These calculations have two sides. The suppliers of capital look to a minimum risk-weighted return to compensate them for putting up the money in the first place; while the consumers of capital have to ensure that the suppliers obtain a return at least as high as any that could be earned elsewhere. (Obviously, if a company can achieve a higher return, so much the better.) Afterwards, we will link the cost of capital to a general shareholder value model and introduce the concept of the drivers of shareholder value.

HURDLE RATES

The cost of capital is a very important concept – indeed, it is a concept that is central to this book. In simple terms, it is not unlike the situation described by Mr Micawber in Dickens' *David Copperfield*: "Annual income twenty pounds, annual expenditure nineteen shillings and six pence, result happiness. Annual income twenty pounds, annual expenditure twenty pounds ought and six, result misery." Cost of capital calculations are similar: there exists a figure which marks the boundary between misery and happiness. This is the hurdle rate, or the rate of return that a company should realistically be able to earn on a risk-adjusted basis.

Suppose the hurdle rate is set at 10 percent a year. If this represents the cost of capital – a concept to which we will return in more detail below – then a company is creating shareholder value if the return on capital is greater than this (say 12 percent a year). It is destroying shareholder value if its return on capital is lower that this, at say 8 percent a year.

In our experience, corporate hurdle rates can vary considerably. One rate might be very low because the investment is regarded as strategic, and hence will not be obliged to earn a realistic rate of return. This approach is often adopted by governments, and to a degree by nationalized companies. It reflects what might be termed the social rate of time preference, or the willingness of society to postpone consumption today in order to receive higher consumption tomorrow. A low hurdle rate might also be used if the investment is regarded as intermediate to the production process, with the money to be recouped elsewhere.

On the other hand, a company might use a more "realistic" approach, perhaps using an apparently arbitrary number established during the days of high inflation, and never subsequently adjusted downwards in the light of new circumstances. You might find a 25 percent hurdle rate being used, irrespective of the actual risks incurred.

The use of global hurdle or discount rates across an entire group of activities in a company gives rise to some odd results. Not only does the firm's internal planning process become clogged up with various draft proposals all managing to pass the conditions set by senior management; it can also seriously bias the direction of investment policy. Discount rates that are uniformly too high will generally push the company into taking bigger risks than are justified – even though the actual probability of reaching the rate set may be quite low. By the same token, the use of the high discount rate will rule out many apparently unprofitable projects that might have earned the company a respectable addition to its SHV. We favor using a hurdle rate as close to the market rate as possible, since by definition this will be close to the opportunity cost we mentioned above.

The key weakness of the "conventional" hurdle rate is that it fails to adequately include any market risk component in making a calculation. The SHV approach, on the other hand, will include a risk factor in assessing what the appropriate rate of return for investors (and hence management) should be. It thus provides a more satisfactory way of measuring the return a company should be achieving on the capital resources it uses.

CAPM: THE KEY RISK EQUATION

You will have come across the phrase "risk-weighted discount factor" in Chapter 2, when we introduced the capital asset pricing model (CAPM). As we said then, this discount factor states what a company has to earn in order to justify the use of the capital resources tied up in the business. We call this the *cost of equity*. Let us now look at this model in more detail.

There is a key relationship in the CAPM. Expressed as a formula, it looks like this:

$$r_i = r_f + \beta r_m$$

Here, r_i refers to the return on an individual security, r_f is the risk-free rate of return, and r_m represents the market risk premium. β (beta) describes the systematic risk attached to investing in that security – a concept we will return to later in this chapter. This is saying that the return on an individual security r is a function of β, a risk-free rate of return r_f and the market risk premium r_m. This describes the opportunity cost of capital to an external investor and describes both what the borrower, the firm, must deliver, and what the investor can reasonably expect. Let us look in more detail at these components starting with r_f – the risk-free rate of return.

ELEMENTS OF THE CAPM EQUATION

Risk-free rates of return

The notion that there is something called a "risk-free" rate of return may bring a smile to a bond trader's or fixed income investment manager's face, since they are confronted by quite large swings in the yield and value of a bond during its lifetime. But we are not primarily concerned with this aspect, but rather with the fact that, unlike an equity, a bond offers the holder two promises: to pay a regular coupon – the interest on the debt – and to repay the bond holder in full when the bond reaches maturity. "Risk-free" here refers to the risk that the debt issuer might default on repaying the bond, or possibly skip some of the interest payments. Generally it is only governments that can reasonably claim to be "risk-free," and so we use the yield on their bonds as the basis for the "risk-free" rate, in the sense of zero default risk. Sovereign governments (with one or two exceptions) can generally be counted on to repay their debts. What we are saying, then, is that the interest offered by government bonds is the current ruling market rate, and an investment decision made today must be able to achieve those rates.

You may already begin to see that we are inserting a different view on the cost of capital – a market-based view that will change with market conditions. It will always be up to date and will reflect what the current opportunity cost of lending and borrowing is. Since we are looking ahead, however, we will want to know what the "risk-free" rate is over the length of time used for the forecast cash flows. In many cases it may be convenient to use the yields on ten-year government bonds as a benchmark. These bonds are attractive for several reasons.

Ten years corresponds to a feasible planning cycle; some would argue that it is very similar to the duration of the equity market. Ten-year bond yields are also less volatile in the face of unexpected changes in inflation than those with a longer maturity, such as 30-year Treasuries in the USA. For shorter cash-flow forecasts of, say, five years we would use bond yields over this maturity. This yield is preferable to whatever interest rates short-term deposits are currently able to attract; short-term deposits have to be rolled over, and it is not easy to say whether these roll-over rates will stay constant over the life of a project. Generally they will not – so we prefer using the longer-term bond rates.

Incidentally, when we talk of interest rates available on the market, we may sometimes have a problem deciding which market. In our view, SHV analysis should try and keep everything as local as possible, at least to start with. We look at where a company is paying its dividends – its home country. The returns on investment will have to be made in that currency and bear some relationship to current interest rates available on that market. The situation can become much more complicated when a large corporation has multiple borrowings in multiple currencies, or is registered in several countries. Best practice here is to try and bring everything back into the domestic currency at what looks like a reasonable estimate when allowing for currency conversion factors.

There are other situations where there is no obvious long-term risk-free rate that can be used. This can be a problem in high-inflation countries and in emerging markets where no long-term bond has yet been issued. We take the view that since all interest payments are in nominal terms, as indeed are all other flows in the SHV model, it is generally best to use nominal rates, and not real rates. There are two objections to using real rates, and these are that there is little consensus as to what the real rate of interest should be, and that it becomes a very tricky exercise to link historical nominal numbers to future real forecasts. There are some circumstances where, in the absence of any reliable local information, it might be better to shift the whole analysis over to a hypothetical "hard currency" case like the euro or the dollar.

Betas (βs)

Why are betas important? Why have economists discussed them so much? The beta measures the association between changes in an individual share price and the changes in an underlying share index. It measures the systematic risk taken on when an investor buys that share, and gives an idea of how much the share will move in line with the market. This is important because while investors can offset specific risks associated with individual shares by holding diversified portfolios, they remain exposed to systematic risks associated with the market as a whole which cannot be diversified away.

The higher its beta, the riskier the share: thus a share having a beta greater than one will move more than the market, and is sometimes described as being a volatile share. A share having a beta of less than one moves less than the market, and is sometimes thought of as a defensive investment (see Fig. 3.1).

This has several implications for the returns expected from a share. Broadly speaking, the higher the beta, the higher the expected return of the share, and so the higher the cost of capital for the firm issuing the shares. Obviously, though, the beta relates to both upward and downward volatility: most investors are looking for the "good" (i.e. positive) volatility that is associated with a share that rises faster than the market. The investor's expectation is that the company can continue to outperform the market, and although there is

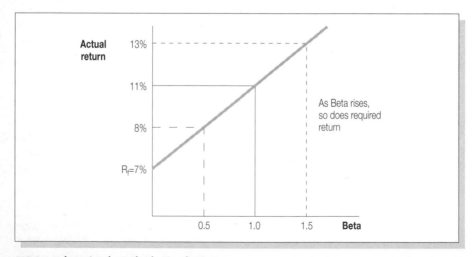

FIG 3.1 ● **Investors' required rate of return**

some associated risk, it is of a benevolent kind. There is another side to the coin, however: volatility in the negative sense. In this case the share falls more than the market, and under such circumstances a high beta is the signal for a downwardly risky investment, something to avoid rather than seek out. All of which means that the company's management is faced with having to provide a higher return to compensate for the higher (negative) risks associated with investing in the company.

There is a link between a share's beta and its subsequent performance, as has been demonstrated by Friend and Blume.[1] They looked at the betas on shares (here aggregated into portfolios), and their returns: the results are summarized in Table 3.1, where the most risky portfolios are at the bottom of the table.

TABLE 3.1 ● **More risk means higher returns – but less than the CAPM predicts**

Portfolio No	1939–69		1948–69		1956–69	
	β	Mean return %	β	Mean return %	β	Mean return %
1	0.19	0.79	0.45	0.99	0.28	0.95
2	0.92	1.26	0.94	1.35	0.91	1.17
3	1.29	1.53	1.23	1.33	1.3	1.18
4	2.02	1.59	1.67	1.36	1.92	1.10

Source: Friend and Blume (1973)

As you can see from Table 3.1, the average returns of a number of portfolios increased with their riskiness. Interestingly, however, after a certain point mean return did not rise commensurately with risk, so that not much is gained from taking on riskier portfolios. Another interesting feature is that the gap in performance between the most risky and the least risky portfolios appears to have narrowed over time – supporting the idea that markets have become more efficient.

Other work by Black, Jensen and Scholes,[2] which looked at the risk/return characteristics of different US stocks over a 35-year period, concluded that the average returns on the stocks increased by 1.08 percent a month (13 percent annually) for a one-unit increase in β. While providing good evidence for CAPM, the strength of the observed relationship was only about three-quarters of what had been expected. The authors concluded that their tests "provide substantial support for the hypothesis that realized returns are a linear function of systematic risk value. *Moreover, it shows that the relationship is significantly positive over long periods of time.*"

What this research suggests is that less volatile, low beta stocks will on balance perform less well than their more volatile competitors. In other words, as an investor you can only achieve a higher performance by exposing yourself to higher risk.

Betas beaten?

However, this is not the end of the story. Table 3.1's figures raised some questions about the validity of beta. If the relationship between betas and stock performance was not as strong as the theory suggested, is the theory flawed, and should beta be buried?

After conducting extensive empirical tests, Fama and French concluded in 1992 that betas and average stock returns were not positively related.[3] They suggested that the size of companies was important in determining a portfolio's performance. Smaller companies seemed to perform better, while those that had a high market-to-book ratio also did rather well. Some observers have suggested that these two additional measures should be used instead of the CAPM-based betas.

Other writers and researchers have variously indicated that financial leverage (gearing) is important in determining stock return, while others have found seasonal effects that influence stock returns.

While these findings have weakened the CAPM theory, in our view they have not destroyed it. As Josef Lakonishok has stated: "Based on available data, no clear-cut evidence supports the interment of beta. Fama and French probably went too far when they said no relationship exists between beta and returns." Fischer Black of the famous Black-Scholes model[4] also came out on the side of the theory, arguing that there was sufficient power left in the beta to merit continuing its use. We are sympathetic to this view and continue to use the CAPM approach in our work.

All the same, readers should be aware that there are alternatives. They are rather more complicated and it is not entirely clear whether at the end of the day a lot more is gained by using them. The arbitrage pricing theory (APT) is one that seeks to divide up the single beta into a series of smaller effects, mini-betas if you will, all associated with a specific effect. Factors that have been found to have a regular association with stock performance include things like the industrial production index, the real short-term interest rate, unexpected changes in inflation, measures of default risk and estimators of longer term inflation such as the slope of the bond yield curve.

Measuring betas

The measurement of betas is a relatively straightforward matter of using data from the past. We start with the assumption that the relevant beta for investors will measure a share's volatility relative to the main market index where the share is quoted. In most cases this is clear cut, and follows the principle adopted for identifying the risk-free rate of return. Using a historic measure, we can take a five-year (60-month) moving average. We think this provides the best estimator of the future beta, which is what we are actually looking for. It may not always be a particularly good estimator, though: the variance (or degree of dispersion) of the estimates can sometimes be quite large, meaning that we cannot always attach a high degree of confidence to them. But tests we have done suggest that on balance a five-year period is better than most others at providing a long-run and relatively stable estimate of betas over a business cycle.

There are several published sources for betas, however; how do we decide between them? This is a perfectly reasonable question, and it is worth bearing in mind that not only do betas change over time, even when keeping the sample time constant, but also they will vary markedly with the frequency of observation – whether they are measured using daily, weekly or monthly data. The more frequent the intervals, the more likely it is that there will be bigger swings in the betas –another reason why we favor the five-year betas. They are more stable.

A few additional factors need to be considered. The first is that a share may not be traded very frequently, thus giving rise to deceptively low beta values. This can be adjusted for by using more detailed benchmarking and peer group analysis (more on benchmarking later, in Part 2). Secondly, in some circumstances differences in the debt-to-equity ratio can also impact on the beta. On occasion, it is more suitable to adjust for leverage levels to find a "truer" estimate of what the underlying volatility of the share is.

Finally, a company may change what it actually does. It may have been through an extensive re-structuring process, making it no longer the same company it was a few years ago. In this case it may be useful to take a shorter time period. Remember, the main object is to find the best estimator of what the beta is likely to be over a forecast period taking into account likely business cycle changes.

All this serves to underline the point that while the basic mechanics of a CAPM-related SHV approach are not particularly complicated, its actual implementation can be, and is full of pitfalls.

Market risk premia

The shareholder value approach is all about comparing future outcomes with each other. One of the most important ways of doing this is to establish the opportunity cost of capital in general, and the opportunity cost of equity in particular. This is done by estimating what are called market risk premia. In other words, the additional return an average investor can obtain from investing in equities (which are risky investments) as compared with "risk-free" alternatives such as government bonds. As with betas, we have to rely primarily on history to help find the best estimator of a future risk premium.

There are two basic ways to calculate market risk premia: *ex post* (backward looking), based on the actual performance of equities as compared to bonds, and *ex ante* (forward looking), based on the expected future performance of equities, or what is realistically needed to get an institutional investor to give up the relative security of the bond market for the more uncertain pastures of the equity market.

Ex post: *looking at history*

The *ex post* method relies on identifying a historical period likely to give a good estimator of future market risk premia. Within this, two calculation methods can be used: an arithmetic average of the excess equity returns, which assumes a re-balancing of the portfolios after every year, or a geometric average which assumes a long-term buy-and-hold investment strategy (often used as a benchmark for investment performance comparisons in asset management). Many of the numbers quoted for market risk premia use arithmetic rather than geometric calculations, and tend to be larger.[5] (Note that the arithmetic return is always higher than the geometric return: the spread increases as a function of the variance of the return and the interval chosen.)

How can we be sure of identifying the right time period for an *ex post* estimate? How relevant will it be? There are several answers, frequently coloured by the amount of information available. In the USA, where equity market performance has been long and reliably documented, the approach has often been simply to put as much information as is available into an analysis and calculate an average number. Doing this provides a figure of around 7 per cent a year "extra" equity performance.

Simple though it seems, this approach has a number of difficulties. The first is that, as Table 3.2 shows, there are some striking differences in the market risk premium on a decade-by-decade basis. Indeed, the performance achieved by equities in one decade has very little correlation with that of the next. A cursory examination of US economic history can provide plenty of reasons why this should be; indeed, the apparently high overall number is buoyed up by two very exceptional periods – the 1920s and the 1980s. Generally we do not expect to see such good bull markets as we saw then.

Table 3.2 throws some light on other issues too. It is often asserted that equity markets are the best hedges in times of high inflation; but the figures show that this is not generally the case. During the 1960s, when inflation was beginning to accelerate, and more noticeably in the 1970s, when even the US suffered from relatively high rates of inflation, equity performance was modest. The market risk premium virtually disappeared in the 1970s.

Let us look at the history another way, then. Table 3.3 adopts a moving average approach to the issue of the market risk premium. Here you can see how the numbers look year by year when the geometric mean of the excess returns is taken over a constant 30-year period.

TABLE 3.2 ● **Market risk premia (USA)**

Period	Percentage
1920s	7.0
1930s	2.3
1940s	7.8
1950s	17.9
1960s	4.2
1970s	0.2
1980s	7.9
1990s	12.1
overall average, 1920s–1990s	7.4

Source: *Stocks, Bonds, Bills and Inflation Yearbook 2000* Ibbotson Associates, Chicago

TABLE 3.3 ● **Longer-term average MRP (30-year) – S&P compared to US Treasuries**

Year	Percentage
1986	4.4
1987	4.2
1988	5.0
1989	4.4
1990	3.7
1991	4.6
1992	3.8
1993	4.4
1994	3.6
1995	4.1
1996	4.4
1997	5.8
1998	5.9
1999	6.2

Source: *Stocks, Bonds, Bills and Inflation Yearbook 2000*, Ibbotson Associates, Chicago and authors' calculations.

So when we try to use a constant length of historical time to estimate the market risk premium, the values look substantially more conservative than the shorter-run average figures shown in Table 3.2.

We must remember, of course, that so far we have been dealing exclusively with the USA. As soon as we look at other countries, it becomes increasingly clear that the USA is more an exception than a rule. On the basis of our research, countries like the UK, France, Switzerland and the Netherlands show a positive market risk premium more often than not, with the UK taking the premier position. The ability of equities to consistently deliver superior investment performance in other countries is more questionable. In Germany, equities under-perform bonds for substantial periods of time, thus giving lie to the idea that the riskier investment is always the better one in the longer run. In countries like Canada, Australia, Italy and Spain the outcome is also more uncertain.

Why is this? Part of the reason is that all these countries have experienced lengthy periods of high inflation and high government deficits. Government investment needs tend to "crowd out" those of the private sector, simply because the government is generally able to offer investors a positive real rate of return, which equities sometimes find difficult to emulate. In all the countries mentioned, equities under-performed bonds for substantial periods of time, and although a positive equity risk premium has returned recently, it is probably too early to say whether this will become a truly permanent feature of equities.

As for Japan, it offers an extraordinary spectacle of sustained equity outperformance until the late 1980s, after which it has been virtually downhill all the way for the stock market. If a reminder is needed of how risky equities can be, then you need look no further than the land of the rising sun. (More on Japan in Part 3.)

Ex ante: *looking to the future*

Establishing a market risk premium by selecting the "right" historical period can seem too complicated – or maybe too arbitrary – a task. In any case, the MRP measures observed actual returns, not required or expected returns which is of interest to us in looking forward. Perhaps then we should look at current market opinion about the extent by which equities are expected to outperform bonds in the future. That is what we have done – and have found no hard and fast opinion. A recent PWC survey came up with market risk premium estimates ranging from a low of 2.7 percent to a high of 4.5 percent. Answers varied not only according to the time period under consideration, but also in relation to who we were talking to. People more closely associated with equity trading tend to be more optimistic about equities' chances in the future, while people actually involved in managing funds – the asset managers and strategists – tend to be more cautious about future equity performance.

There is also some evidence that estimates of the market risk premium can vary over the business cycle, as Fig. 3.2 shows. It also emphasizes how important the investment horizon is. It is highly likely that market practitioners' views on the risk premium vary over the cycle. Towards the top of the cycle, perceptions of further outperformance on the equity side are tempered by the fear of downturns and a negative twist to interest rates and bond yields. When asked, analysts will probably give estimates at the lower end of the range, say between 3 and 4 percent. At the bottom of the cycle, though, the same analysts could be much more sanguine and see several years of extra performance, with MRPs in the upper range, between 6 and 9 percent, entering the picture. It is fair to add that analysts' powers of prediction in this area are weak, and we prefer to rely on a judicious interpretation of the past as providing the best guide for the expected MRP.

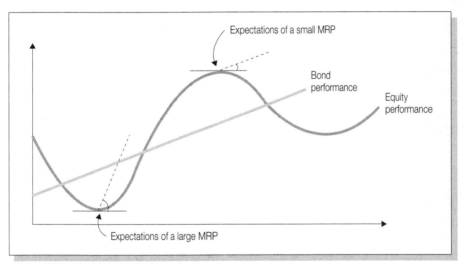

FIG 3.2 ● **MRP expectations over the business cycle**

As with the *ex-post* analysis, shareholder value practitioners need to realize that judgement is needed. The aim should always be to provide the best "estimator" for a firm's market risk premium over the period being considered; which will typically involve combining estimates about the future with evidence from the past. But, once a figure has been arrived at, it should be open and transparent, and should come close to most analysts' and other observers' opinions of the underlying market. We would argue that this ultimately is less arbitrary than other approaches.

We have dwelt on the subject of the market risk premium at some length because it is crucially important. All discounted cash flow (DCF) approaches are very sensitive to the choice of discount rate, and so great care has to be exercised to get it right. Inevitably, estimates will contain errors. As we have seen, market risk premia shift substantially from one decade to the next, and observers in one period may not be all that good at accurate predictions of the next period's risk premium.

THE COST OF EQUITY

After identifying the components of the CAPM formula, it is relatively easy to calculate the cost of equity. It cannot be stressed too much that this is an *expectational* cost, and differs from what some would argue is the actual cost of equity. The cost of equity combines the risk-free rate of return, the market risk premium and the beta factor, or

$$R_e = R_f + MRP \times \beta$$

This represents both the expected cost to the borrower (the company) and the expected return to the investor (the shareholder).

For traditionalists, the cost of equity is something that is limited to dividend payments made to shareholders, with an eye being kept on dividend yields that are currently available in the market. But in the SHV view of the world, the message of the cost of equity concept is different. It is telling both investors and managers that while dividends are important they are only part of the picture. The investor is concerned with the overall rate of return, which in addition to the stream of dividend payments also includes capital appreciation – any increases in the share price. We think of this as total shareholder return (TSR);[6] over a period of time investments in the equity of a company have to minimally attain the cost of equity target. How it is done is of secondary consideration for the time being – it could be all capital appreciation, as in the case of start-up, venture-capital types of enterprises; or it could be entirely dividends as in the case of more established companies. The investor is concerned with the overall rate of return, not just with the stream of dividend payments.

THE COST OF DEBT

We also need to calculate the cost of debt for SHV analysis. Companies use both equity and debt in their operations, and just as equity has a "cost" to management – and a return to investors – so does debt. However, debt differs from equity in one important respect. Interest charges on debt are normally tax deductible, so that the effective cost of debt to management is lowered by the extent of a "tax shield." From the corporate perspective, this tends to make debt costs lower than the cost of equity. As with establishing the cost of equity, so we try and use a market-based view where possible.

The starting-point for estimating the cost of debt is the risk-free rate mentioned above. This is based on the investment horizon, or on the maturity of the outstanding debt. As we shall see later, it is probably easier to take the first of these approaches, which avoids the question of whether the debt structure is likely to go forward. We then try to add an appropriate debt risk premium based on market conditions. In estimating the cost of debt there are two angles to consider: the value of the tax shield and the value of the debt premium.

As we have stated, the advantage of using debt for finance is that it is cheaper. This is an entirely tax-driven effect, and the degree to which a company enjoys a tax shield on its debt will depend on its overall tax position – which can vary tremendously from country to country as well as over time. In the absence of any other information, it is probably best to use the statutory tax rate as the marginal tax rate for investment and tax shield calculations. But where there is evidence that the company is not in a full tax paying position, and is unlikely to return to this state within the investment horizon, then another approach should be considered. Here a view on the likely future effective tax rate needs to be made. This should then form the basis for the marginal tax rate used in the cost-of-debt calculations.

The tax shield argument does not apply to investors themselves, however, or at least not in the same way. Investors may be interested in their post-tax rate of return, where their individual tax positions will have to be taken into account. This is one aspect dealt with by the cash flow return on investment (CFROI), which we will look at in more detail in the next chapter.

Where a company already has some publicly quoted debt – corporate bond issues, for instance – an idea of the current cost of debt can be obtained directly by looking at market price and yield quotes. This approach is entirely consistent with trying to link calculations to actual market experience. Where this information is not directly available, then an estimate of the cost of debt has to be made. Here we are once again looking at debt from the outside, from a market-based point of view, and asking what value the marketplace would put on this debt at a particular point in time. Rating agencies such as Moody's and Standard & Poor's are useful in this context, since their ratings allow us to estimate a credit risk premium based on the current market yield structure. Obviously, we need to establish the right peer group for comparison purposes. Since the US corporate debt market is much better developed than those elsewhere, you may well find that the yield spreads there factor largely in any calculations. But as the European debt market develops with the advent of the euro, so more information from the debt rating agencies in Europe will become available.

Following the previous logic of the risk-free rate of return, we can use the rating agencies' figures for competitors and the relevant sector, and add a risk premium for the specific company. This may sound simple, but in practice it can involve some judgement, especially where the company has extensive borrowings in different currencies over different maturity periods. Various forms of hybrid financing such as warrants and convertibles introduce further complexities. This means that a view has to be taken about how the debt structure could evolve, especially if we know that certain debt instruments will be retired at some point during the period for which we are forecasting.

It is worth remembering, however, that outside the select group of triple-A-rated bonds, there is a tendency in the medium term for companies bond ratings to slip, and for the risk premia associated with their debt to rise. Again, it is worth stressing that this approach derives from a market-based view of the world and is trying to assess what the opportunity cost of debt is, in just the same way as was done with the cost of equity. This need not coincide with the existing interest rate structure the company is actually paying, and it is worth assessing how the actual interest rate payments made compare to the "market" rates to establish whether there is any overall benefit in SHV terms.

THE WEIGHTED AVERAGE COST OF CAPITAL (WACC)

The point of calculating the cost of equity and the cost of debt is to bring them together to create the weighted average cost of capital (WACC), as in Fig. 3.3. Having, in this hypothetical example, established the "risk-free" cost of debt currently ruling in the market as 5.5 percent, we use that figure to determine both the cost of equity and the cost of debt for this particular company. For the

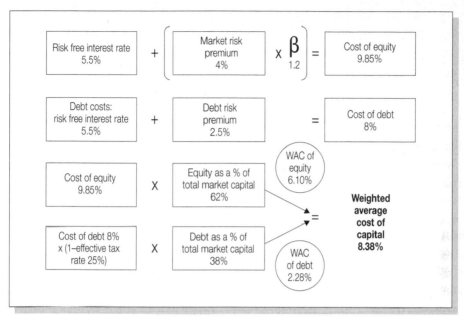

FIG 3.3 ● **Cost of capital calculation**

cost of equity, we add to that 5.5 a market risk premium of 4 percent, which is then multiplied by the beta of the company's share price – in this case it is 1.2, indicating some share price volatility. The cost of equity, then, is 10.3 percent. For the cost of debt, we simply take the same figure of 5.5 and add a company risk premium of 2.5 percent to reach 8 percent. However, the cost of debt for the company is offset by the tax shield, which in this case is assumed to give relief at a rate of 25 percent. The total capital of the company is made up of 38 percent debt and 62 percent equity, so we reduce the costs of the debt and equity by the relevant percentages and then add them together to arrive at a figure of 8.66 percent.

We need to be aware of some important features of the WACC. As with the other measures, you can use a historical approach, or think about an expected WACC. If we are using the latest market rates, then we cannot change the interest rate side of the calculations, nor can we change the betas, assuming that we are using what we think is a reasonable estimator of the future beta for the investment horizon. But we can change the relative weights of equity and debt in the capital structure.

It is possible to use a company's most recent debt and equity figures but, before accepting them, it is worth checking to see if the most recent year is reasonably typical of the recent past – it might not be.

Another approach is to use a target capital structure for the WACC calculation. This is an assessment of what the likely debt/total capital and equity/total capital ratios will be. Estimates can be gained from looking at industry averages or from benchmarking against competitors.

The importance of the WACC cannot be stressed enough. SHV models require a steady WACC to operate, and therefore careful consideration has to be given to the number chosen. All the questions about expected future changes in capital structure mentioned above play a role here. It may be worth taking a view as to whether your company is likely to run out of capital in the forecast period – a distinct possibility if a steady cash outflow is predicted. In that case, it might be wise to assume that another visit to the capital market is necessary, and to establish whether it will be the equity or the debt side that will be topped up. As with other components of the SHV approach, what looks simple at first glance turns out to be quite complex in implementation. But before looking at these issues, let us consider just what the WACC is telling us.

A measure of success

The WACC is an expression of what return a company must earn if it is to justify the financial assets it uses – in other words, the opportunity cost of the assets in use. It is entirely market-driven: if the assets cannot earn that return, then investors will eventually withdraw their funds from the business. Share prices will fall relative to the market, and the company could then become a take-over target. Pushed to its extreme, the failure of company to earn its cost of capital could result in the management being replaced by another.

From the manager's point of view, the WACC establishes the *market relevant hurdle rate against which success has to be measured*. It is a risk-weighted measure, since it specifically includes a measure of the riskiness of the investment. Since we are saying that the costs of both equity and debt have to be exceeded if the business is to survive in the longer term, it is important to realize that these differ from other ways of measuring financial success. The cost of equity is different from the cost of dividend payments, and the cost of debt is different from the apparent interest rate actually charged on outstanding debt.

Indeed, the SHV approach is saying something even more serious to managers. It is not just a question of ensuring that the business earns returns that are equivalent to its WACC. If the business is to prosper in the longer term, it has to earn more than that WACC. It is only when this condition is met that we can talk about the creation of shareholder value.

Finally, we need to remember that everything mentioned so far has concerned publicly quoted companies, and our analysis has been assumed to be of entire quoted companies or entities. This approach can also be fine-tuned to accommodate subsidiaries and divisions of companies. It's a more complex matter for private or state-owned companies, since the information we need is not directly available. Rather it is necessary to "proxy" what the capital structure might look like if the company was in the hands of shareholders. Occasionally capital structures can be found, and even if the current management has not paid them the slightest attention they may provide a good basis to start an analysis. But, although more complex, the approach ultimately comes down to finding the best estimators for the risk-free rate of return, beta and the market risk premium for the unit being analyzed.

SUMMARY

Having emphasized the importance of calculating the true cost of your capital – not the same as the conventional hurdle rate – we then looked at the elements that contribute to such a calculation: risk-free rates of return, market risk premia, and betas, which measure the volatility of a share. These are all part of the CAPM formula which is used to determine a company's WACC (weighted average cost of capital), the market-relevant hurdle rate against which you measure success.

Notes

1. Friend, I. and Blume, M. (1973) "A New Look at the Capital Asset Pricing Model," *Journal of Finance*, 19–33.

2. Black, F., Jensen, M. and Scholes, M. (1972) "The Capital Asset Pricing Model: some empirical tests," in *Studies in the Theory of Capital Markets* Praeger.

3. Fama, E. and French, K. (1988) "Permanent and Temporary Components of Stock Prices," *Journal of Political Economy*, 246–73.

4. This model provides a way of calculating the value of options and has been important in the development of derivative markets (see Chapter 10 for more on options).

5. Cooper, I. (1995) *Arithmetic versus Geometric Mean Risk Framed: Setting Discount Rates for Capital Budgeting*, IFA working paper 174–95.

6. Total shareholder return represents the change in capital value of a company over a one-year period, plus dividends, expressed as a plus or minus percentage of the opening value.

PROFIT IS AN OPINION; CASH IS A FACT

Having a good estimate of the cost of capital is a fundamental first step for conducting SHV analysis. However, against what cash flow should it be used to measure value creation? In Chapter 1, we drew attention to weaknesses in conventional accounting measures: here we want to consider them in more detail. We also examine here how large institutional investors in the equity markets are assessing the market value of corporates.

ACCOUNTING PROFIT

Figure 4.1 shows the main flows and definitions used in arriving at a profit figure. As can be seen, there are many factors that influence the profit, or earnings, that will come out at the end of a calculation. Even in the best of circumstances, movements in profits and earnings will be hard to understand unless you know something about how profits are defined.

Profit figures are, of course, used to arrive at earnings per share (EPS) figures, which have long been recognized by investment managers as a con-

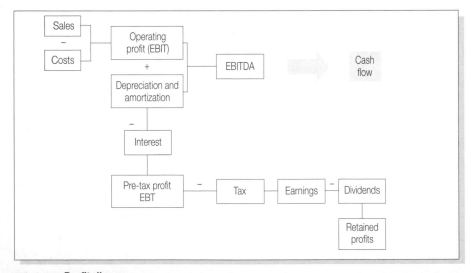

FIG 4.1 ● Profit diagram

venient shorthand for valuing stock. The difficulty is that the EPS calculation is inconsistent with shareholder value measures, and is rather poorly correlated with share price movements. Being based on accounting profit, which is arrived at using different accounting methods in different countries, it has the disadvantage of making earnings comparisons difficult.

TABLE 4.1 ● Accounting profit can vary from country to country

	Most likely net profit	Maximum net profit	Minimum net profit
	(Ecu millions)		
Belgium	135	193	90
Germany	133	140	27
Spain	131	192	121
France	149	160	121
Italy	174	193	167
Netherlands	140	156	76
United Kingdom	192	194	171

Source: Henley Management College

Consider Table 4.1, compiled as part of a management training exercise in the early 1990s. For this, managers were given a basic set of data about a company, and were then asked to disclose a profits figure using their own local accounting conventions. There are several striking things about the results shown. The UK is particularly generous in its view on profits. The most likely number struck is close to the feasible maximum. This is due in part to the different basis on which UK and US accounts are constructed, independently of the tax calculations and more oriented towards investors. Nevertheless, seen from a Continental European point of view, UK accounts may be too ready to declare as profit items which are more prudently held in reserve elsewhere – even if the main motivation for the reserves is one of tax efficiency.

Another striking feature is that the range of profits in other countries is very wide, and hence the most likely number struck is an arbitrary one. At the extreme, for German managers and analysts anything between 27 and 133 is a feasible profits number – undoubtedly calling into question the usefulness, and credibility, of much profit- and earnings-based analysis and information.

Considerable effort is going into trying to produce a more level playing field in the area of accounting practice. It looks increasingly likely that the two most commonly used standards for international investors will be either the IAS (international accounting standards) approach, or the USA's GAAP (generally agreed accounting principles). International investors will find some of the details and idiosyncrasies permitted by individual countries' accounting systems more and more archaic as we move into the twenty-first century. But there remains a substantial number of areas where further work is needed to allow the various systems to converge.

OTHER INDICATORS: ROI AND ROE

In addition to the earnings-based ratios based on profit figures, there are two other indicators that are still used to assess company performance: return on investment (ROI) and return on equity (ROE). These too are not consistent with the SHV methods we will be developing below. ROI suffers from the problem of identifying the investment. This can be measured in several ways, and it can be looked at as either gross or net. Gross investment includes all spending on fixed assets and all depreciation "spending" on capital assets. Net investment is a function of accountancy and tax-driven depreciation rules; depreciation is not a "cash" item. There is also some variation in the way leases and other items are capitalized. All of this means that the ROI ratio can be manipulated by driving down the effective value of the investments.

ROI is also frequently used as a single-period measure and thus tells us little about the future. Even using several years of prospective ROI ratios can give misleading results. When ROI and DCF measures are compared with each other, there is little systematic relationship, with ROI alternately either over- or under-shooting the DCF valuation.[1]

Return on equity (ROE) also suffers from some disadvantages, the principal one being that it is affected by the gearing levels within a firm. Broadly speaking, the higher the gearing the higher the ROE, a rule that is rarely corrected for. The degree of asset turnover can also effect the ROE, so that the faster assets are "turned over," the higher the ROE.

In our view, then, changes in earnings, or measured changes in either ROI or ROE, are unlikely to be closely associated with changes in SHV. Earnings figures fail to take into account the levels of business and financial risk, and they do not take account of the amounts of fixed and working capital needed to run a business. ROI, ROE and earnings measures can all be affected by differences in accounting conventions, which by and large are not cash flow based. So these measures do not reflect a company's SHV.

CORRELATING SHARE PRICE MOVEMENTS AND CASH FLOW

Even if an underlying earnings figure could be defined reasonably accurately, it would still be of little help in establishing a share price or in calculating SHV, surprising though this sounds. Figure 4.2 dramatically shows the wide disparity between earnings per share (EPS) data and share price movements in Germany.

The dots in the chart represent combinations of changes in company share prices and changes in earnings per share. The EPS changes are prospective forecasts for 1994 made in January, while the change in share price is what actually happened over the year. The diagonal line gives an idea of the preferred relationship. Ideally, a positive expected move in earnings should (all things being equal) be associated with a positive change in share prices along the 45-degree line. The cloud of measle-like spots shows that there was a very poor relationship between EPS changes and share price changes that year in Germany.

This result is confirmed in other studies, and if there is one thing about which there is agreement it is that the earnings-based view of the world is a poor predictor of share prices and share values. If this is the case, why do so many people continue to hold to their earnings per share methods?

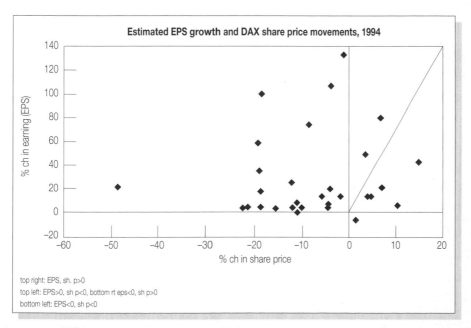

FIG 4.2 ● **EPS is a poor predictor of share prices**

There is no simple answer to this question. However, to summarize briefly a lot of views and experience, we would concede that earnings continue to be used because they are relatively simple to calculate, and for relatively short time horizons are still quite likely to help in the difficult art of stock selection. It is notable, though, that since the first appearance of the SHV approach, an increasing number of leading investment banking houses now use SHV methodology. Most analysts in the major financial centers use cash flow techniques in valuing companies. Their results may still be expressed in earnings terms, but frequently there are batteries of models, including cash flow models, supporting these forecasts.

Cash flow models are still very good at distinguishing between companies that are growing both earnings and cash flows, and those that are not. The latter tend to have shorter lives, particularly in times of recession.

What, though, is the link between the cash flow models and SHV? Again, there is no simple answer, since we have to decide what we mean by shareholder value. One measure that we favor is the total shareholder return, or TSR. This is also a key indicator for the fund managers whose own performance is frequently assessed by applying this metric to their portfolios. The TSR has the benefit of being easy to understand, and is more "dynamic" in that its values are constantly being assessed by the market. After all, share prices are exposed to a constant flow of information and views, both about the individual share and more generally about the market as a whole. At any moment in time the TSR will be influenced by an amalgam of factors, some of which will be company-specific, and among these company specific-factors are those that relate directly to an ability to generate cash flows.

To relate the fast moving world of the stock market to the slower moving world of accounts – a task that has been attempted many times – is by no means easy. The information used to calculate SHV is mostly historical, and crucially many of the tests used in the academic literature have drawn extensively from this pool. The difficulty here is that if we are to successfully show that the SHV approach works, we need to have a time series of past forecasts to compare with actual outcomes. In the absence of such data, we are left with the correlation of various SHV measures with changes in the market/book ratios of companies.

Work in the 1980s by Rawley Thomas and Marvin Lipson[2] looked at correlations between the share prices (proxied by the market-to-book ratios) and several explanatory and often used accountancy-based performance ratios. The results, set out in Table 4.2, show that cash-flow-based figures (specifically, CFROI, or cash flow return on investment) provide a superior explanation for the market-to-book ratios on the US stock market. (For ROE and ROCE, see Chapter 6.)

TABLE 4.2 ● What best explains the variance in market/book ratios of the S&P Index? (1982–4)

Variable	R^2
EPS	<0.1
ROE	0.19
ROI	0.34
Real CFROI	0.65

Other studies that are worth mentioning in this context include the work by CSFB on the retail sector that showed a r^2 of .94 between the ratio of economic value (equity + debt) to invested capital and the spread between the return and the cost of capital;[3] while Copeland *et al.* report a study where they also have a r^2 of .94 after taking 35 companies and regressing the market-to-book ratio to the DCF/book value of assets.[4] Interesting though these studies are, they tend to give a partial view of what is happening, since they don't explain how the share price reacts to developments in cash flows or other shareholder measures such as the spread. Here the evidence is still rather mixed.

Academics continue to debate whether cash flow or earnings-based information provides a better explanation for share prices and company values – but neither side seems capable of delivering a knock-out blow to the other. There is one school that broadly thinks that cash flow measures are superior to earnings and accrual-based methods. Others are not so sure, or rather think that it is very difficult to empirically distinguish between earnings and cash-flow-related measures.

Our experience has shown that our cash flow models are quite good at linking market expectations to the share prices of companies using the shareholder methodology. Interestingly enough, they can also pick up instances when the market has got it wrong, and where a mispricing has occurred: looked at on a three- to six-month horizon, there have been many occasions when the market has converged with the prices indicated in the model, and not the other way around. We have also found that the models are particularly accurate in a whole range of what might politely be called "mature" industries. They can also perform well in areas of great structural and commercial change. Nevertheless, the link between a spread measure and TSR is sometimes less clear-cut than we would ideally want it to be.

All the same, we are persuaded that cash-flow-based measures are more closely aligned with share price movements, and indeed can more satisfactorily explain them, than alternative measures.

THE INVESTOR'S NEW FOCUS

How, then, are large institutional investors assessing companies' economic value? They are clearly moving from earnings-based return calculations to a more sophisticated assessment based on risk, growth expectations and cash flow returns on invested capital. PricewaterhouseCoopers commissioned independent market research on 50 of the largest global investment managers and their approach to stock valuation, and the research has confirmed this trend. For these firms, cash-flow-based economic models have become vital valuation techniques.

As one US investment manager put it, "We feel that when push comes to shove, it all comes down to cash." Another commented: "We think that the market is influenced by things that we don't tend to look at in the short run, but in the long run [it] is influenced by precisely what we look at – real cash-on-cash returns on investment." The focus on cash was emphasized by a third, who said: "Cash is what you actually have. You can take your cash and you can reinvest it. You can reinvest earnings, but if your cash is in excess of your earnings then you have the ability to make more investments or pay down more debt."[5]

In response to the changing focus among institutional investors, equity analysts at securities firms have also been revising their approaches to value analysis. For example, the equity research group at Credit Suisse First Boston (CSFB) commented: "P/Es may have value as a rough proxy for expectations, but do a poor job of explaining the fundamental determinants of value. How much, how well and how long capital can be successfully redeployed in the business are considerations explicitly addressed in a free cash flow model."

In other words, free cash flow (FCF) is the key. Clearly it is now time to introduce our basic cash-flow-based shareholder value model – and this is what we will do in the next chapter.

SUMMARY

Using data from the recent past, we have shown how accounting measures such as earnings per share are no guide to share values. Instead, investors are increasingly using cash flow as a measuring tool to predict future company performance.

Notes

1. Solomon, E. quoted in Rappaport (1986) *Creating Shareholder Value*, Ch. 2 (New York: Free Press).

2. Thomas, R. and Lipson, M. (1985) *Linking Corporate Return Measures to Stock Prices*, Illinois: Holt Planning Associates.

3. CSFB report, May 1998.

4. Copeland, T., Koller, T. and Murrin, J. (1996) *Valuation*, 2nd edition (New York: John Wiley).

5. From "Value Transformation: Driving Shareholder Value Throughout the Organization," *PW Review*, June 1997.

SHAREHOLDER

VALUE:

A DEFINITION

I n the last two chapters we have established three basic things: the importance
of understanding your cost of capital, the relevance of cash flow approaches
for explaining developments in the share price and corporate values, and the
trend among investors towards using cash-flow analysis in evaluating
companies. It is important, then, to focus on the key components that contribute
to your company's success in achieving a positive cash flow and thus a return on
invested capital.

For this, we draw inspiration from Alfred Rappaport's seminal 1986 book,
Creating Shareholder Value, introduced in Chapter 2. Our free cash flow (FCF)
model of SHV uses and develops the seven value drivers originally put forward in
that book – drivers that provide the framework for analyzing the economic value
of a business. They are set out in Fig. 5.1 below.

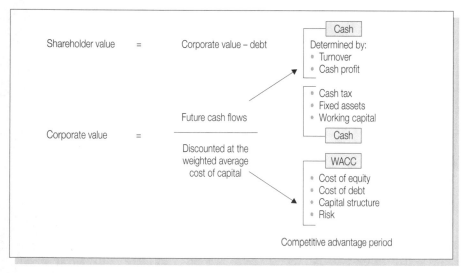

FIG 5.1 ● Free cash flow model of shareholder value

RISK, GROWTH, AND RETURNS,
AND THE SEVEN VALUE DRIVERS

Shareholder value is therefore defined as the difference between corporate value and debt, where corporate value is the sum of the future (or free) cash flows discounted at the WACC. In other words, after all the claims of a company's debt holders have been taken care of, it is the value that can be claimed by the shareholders. The free cash flows themselves are made up of the individual cash flows for each year of the competitive advantage period and the residual value and details of its derivation are shown below in Fig. 5.2. (More on residual value in Chapter 6.) The cash flow is "free" in the sense that it could be used to add to the value available ultimately to shareholders, thus giving the free cash flow model its name. As Fig. 5.2 also shows, there are further refinements to cash flow definitions, which can be made to be more and more specific.

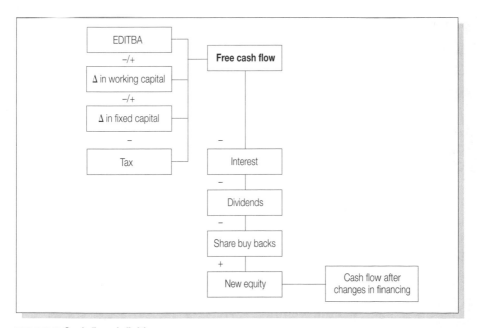

FIG 5.2 ● Cash flow definitions

Let us consider three general aspects of this SHV model. It can be thought of as looking at three things – growth, returns, and risk. These aspects can be explained by seven "value drivers," which feature in Fig. 5.1. The seven, to which we will return in later chapters, are:

- Sales growth (or turnover growth);

- Cash profit margin (EBITDA – earnings before interest, tax, depreciation and amortization);

- Cash tax rate;

- Working capital (to grow the business);

- Capital expenditure (or fixed capital), also to grow the business;

- WACC – the risk- and inflation-adjusted weighted average cost of capital;

- Competitive advantage period.

Growth

Growth is analyzed by three drivers: *sales growth* and investments in *working capital* and *fixed capital*. Revenue growth is all about growing the top line of the business, and the free cash flow model focuses attention on this. As we will see in later chapters, we can break the revenue growth driver out into a large number of industry-specific micro-drivers, as well as allowing for the impact of changes in price, volume and product mix.

Growth can have a significant affect on shareholder value. As Fig. 5.3 shows, SHV can be significantly improved by increasing the efficiency of investment, which in turn is all about assessing and exploiting different investment and growth strategies. The diagram shows that, where a return on invested capital (fixed and working capital) of 20 percent can be achieved, under similar investment conditions the company will be worth substantially more than if it was achieving an ROIC of only 10 percent. The usefulness of this approach is largely associated with being able to distinguish clearly between such different investment strategies.

As the business grows, so additional *working capital* is required, which is a deduction from the free cash flow. Similarly, any shrinkage of the business will release resources. This raises important questions about the marginal conditions needed to create SHV. There are cases where the investment in working capital needed to finance subsequent sales is too high to make the strategy worthwhile. On the other hand, efforts to diversify a company's portfolio into areas where the working capital becomes "positive" – money is received more quickly than it is paid out – can have a dramatic impact on the overall fortunes of a company.

Fixed capital investment is another very important driver. In one sense, all spending on plant and equipment is a deduction from a company's free cash

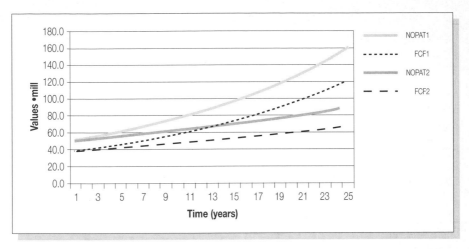

FIG 5.3 ● Impact of different investment efficiencies on net operating profit after tax (NOPAT) and FCF, showing return on invested capital (ROIC) of 20 percent (NOPAT1), and 10 percent (NOPAT2)

flow, and so the smaller this sum is, the higher the funds available for share-holders. But all businesses require investment to prosper into the future, so the question of the right amount of investment becomes one of the most crucial decisions managers have to make. Too much investment can lead to a waste of resources and lower overall efficiency levels. Too little investment, though, can starve a company of funds and prevent it from taking full advantage of the opportunities it has. SHV models have a lot to say about what the right rate of investment should be.

We also need to bear in mind that we are moving into a "knowledge economy" where investments in intangibles such as R&D and intellectual property are becoming increasingly important value creators. Our concept of what we should include within the investment category is being continually revised and expanded, and new definitions here have an important role to play in what we call "value reporting." (We shall return to this topic in Part 3.)

Returns

For returns, there are two drivers. The *cash profit margin* driver is of great importance, and will often make the largest contribution to shareholder value creation. It is defined as earnings before interest, tax and depreciation, or EBITDA. As this definition implies, it is a driver that is focused on the pre-tax cash margin earned in the business before any financing or depreciation charges, thus eliminating any accounting distortions. This makes it much easier to make international and cross-sector comparisons between companies.

The margin is a function of pricing policies and product mix strategies on the one hand, and cost structures on the other. Increasing the EBITDA margin is not an excuse for cost-cutting; rather, a balance between efficiency improvements and more effective exploitation and penetration of markets should be sought.

Also associated with returns is the *cash tax* driver. Although it may not always appear important, it is a direct deduction from the free cash flow and so impacts on the return. Since we are interested only in the amount of cash flowing into and out of a corporation, the tax driver specifically concerns cash taxes paid. In other words we should ring-fence the tax payments, and try to identify only those flows occurring at a particular point of time. Our preference is to try to undo the impact of provisioning and delayed tax charges by attributing them to the time when they are incurred. It is at this point that deviations between value-based reporting/accounting methods and more traditional accrual-based accounting occur; sometimes traditional tax figures have to be substantially adjusted.

It also has to be appreciated that the tax driver is also intimately connected with the whole question of corporate financing. While the impact of tax deductions on free cash flows often looks relatively small, the most powerful driver is that of the weighted average cost of capital (see below), which is strongly affected by tax considerations, and is also a very strong driver of shareholder value.

Risk

Finally, there is risk – often described as "appropriate risk" to distinguish it from other kinds of hazard or chance. Here we have the *WACC* (cost of capital) driver, crucial for bringing financial market perceptions into SHV assessment. This driver is not only affected by market expectations of likely performance in the future, but is also influenced by the financing structure of the company. Tax shield effects arising from debt interest play a major role here. Risks also vary across business lines and geography, and more detailed analysis of a company can often reveal interesting ways of reducing costs of capital with consequently favorable effects on company valuations.

Additionally, there are other aspects of risk that need to be considered. Some can be identified and analyzed by looking at the variance in a company's cash flows and their volatility. Estimates can be made of the probable outcomes of certain strategies, and these can then be developed into a series of decisions which at the end can be used as a basis for the real options valuation approach (see Chapter 10 for more details on real options).

The other driver to be considered under the heading of "risk" is the *growth duration* or *competitive advantage period*, which covers the important question of the dynamics of corporate behavior and its interaction with competitors and other macro-economic factors. Before looking at this in more detail, however, let us look at the conditions a company needs to satisfy if it is to achieve a particular goal. SHV models are particularly good at identifying what these conditions have to be.

Growth and corporate planning

As we have already stressed, a company is only creating SHV when its return on capital exceeds the cost of capital. The FCF model can help us to understand what is needed in order to maintain a particular spread over a period of time and, in so doing, start to solve some of the puzzles that can affect corporate performance. Figures 5.4 and 5.5 plot out the different re-investment and capex (capital expenditure) rates that are needed to maintain a constant spread for a range of revenue growth rates. "Reinvestment" here refers to the proportion of NOPAT (net operating profit after tax) that has to be reinvested in order to maintain a given spread (difference between the return and the cost of capital).

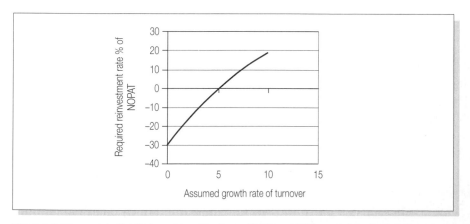

FIG 5.4 ● **Changes in the "reinvestment" rate needed to maintain a constant spread**

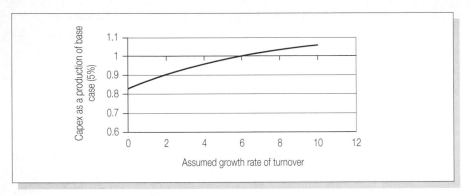

FIG 5.5 ● Changes in capex needed to maintain a constant spread

The initial case shows a 5 percent growth in turnover, which requires around 5 percent of NOPAT to be reinvested. As the turnover growth rate rises, so the proportion of NOPAT that has to be re-invested starts to rise quite rapidly; this is the rate that is "required" if a given positive spread is to be maintained. Figure 5.5 shows the same situation, but this time by expressing the capital spending rate as a proportion of sales. Here too, a rise in turnover growth rate requires a further increase in capex if the spread is to be maintained. The corollary to this is that a failure to step up capex will inevitably result in a fall in the spread as the ROIC starts to decline.

Figures 5.4 and 5.5 also show what happens in the case of a shortfall, where growth in turnover comes in below target. In terms of the re-investment rate, this can release resources as the amounts required fall away very quickly. If growth becomes negative, resources will have to be sold if the spread is to be maintained. In terms of capital expenditure this is the same as steadily reducing the rate of capex, and could also be associated with an absolute decline in assets. This model highlights the phenomenon of a company that continues its investment program in the hope of better days to come. If these days don't appear, the company is left with a capex program too large to be compatible with maintaining a positive spread – a recipe for the destruction of shareholder value.

We can already start to see that, looked at over a period of time and with different turnover growth rates, the creation or maintenance of SHV may require different treatment for different parts of a business. In the case of faster turnover growth, the company will have to step up investment even more if the given spread is to be maintained. When growth is below expectations, quick decisions will be needed to ensure that wholesale SHV destruction does not begin. History is replete with examples of companies that have persisted with capital spending programs even though positive returns within an acceptable time frame have been unlikely. Similar exercises can be done for the other drivers in the model.

The competitive advantage period

We now return to the last of our seven value drivers. The *competitive advantage period* is normally defined as the time during which a company has a competitive advantage – the period during which it has a positive net present value when discounted at the WACC. One way of thinking about this is shown in Fig. 5.6. Industry studies have shown that these competitive advantage periods are often much shorter than managers think. As we shall see later, in Part 3, sectoral and industry differences in growth duration can make a material difference to how shareholder value models are applied.

The competitive advantage period is fairly complex. When thought of in terms of an individual project, or perhaps for an individual product, Fig. 5.6 makes a lot of intuitive sense. The situation becomes much more complicated with bundles of activities – which is what describes most large companies. Interestingly, however, while companies may be involved in many areas, their overall success or failure is often determined by their comparative performance in a much smaller sub-set of their activities. In our work we have been analyzing different types of companies by means of the *market implied competitive advantage period* – a slightly different concept that enables us to look at them as a whole and assess their SHV-generating properties.

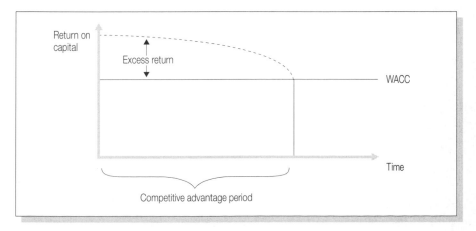

FIG 5.6 ● **The growth duration or competitive advantage period**

The market implied competitive advantage period compares the pattern of valuation over time as you extend the investment horizon forward. It is a function of this spread, or the returns in excess of capital costs and the rate of growth of the business. We start by comparing the company's estimated value with its current market value, and simply ask how many years of free cash flow and residual value (minus debt) are needed until we have a value that is the same as the current market capitalization. The period of time is not exactly the same as the competitive advantage period defined above, but is close enough to it to lead to some interesting conclusions.

To illustrate, let us take the competitive advantage period of four different companies, shown in Figs. 5.7 to 5.10. (These are adapted from real life, but are used here simply as examples.) In the first case, shown in Fig. 5.7, the company's initial valuation is greater than its market value, and for the first few years its valuations continue to increase. However, at some point competition starts to bite: the company's excess returns trickle away. Estimated values will converge with the current market valuation in 21 years, suggesting that this company could enjoy a competitive advantage for most of this period. We think of companies like this as being "stayers" since their initial estimated valuations are bullish and greatly in excess of the current market value. The market is perhaps considering the longer-term implications of the company's estimated strategy.

More classically, we can describe a second situation (see Fig. 5.8) where, although a company's initial estimated valuation is higher than the market value, as with the "stayer" company, the forecast strategy is never likely to create a situation where there are excess returns. Rather, marginal returns will

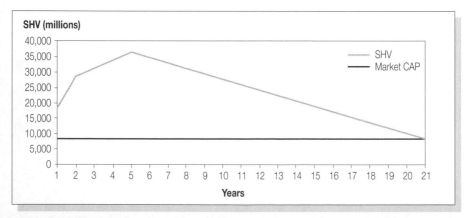

FIG 5.7 ● **"Stayer" company: market implied competitive advantage period extends over 20 years**

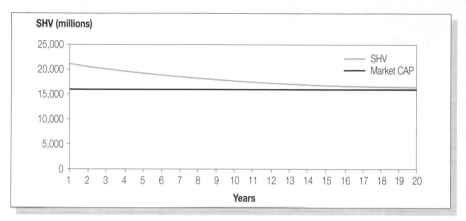

FIG 5.8 ● "Slider" company's market implied CAP diminishes

be below the cost of capital, with the result that over time there will be a steady convergence of the firm's value with its current market value. Although Fig. 5.8 shows a steady convergence, it is quite likely that, in the absence of any other changes, this company's competitive advantage period could be shorter than shown. We could call such a company a "slider," whose situation could arise because it is under-investing.

We can compare these two with what we can call a "riser" company. Here the forecasts suggest a huge increase in valuation over time, although its calculated initial value is less than the current market valuation. In this example, forecasts suggest that the company's intrinsic value will equal current market values in six years, and thereafter rapidly increase. This is a situation we encounter in some information technology (IT) areas or with internet stocks.

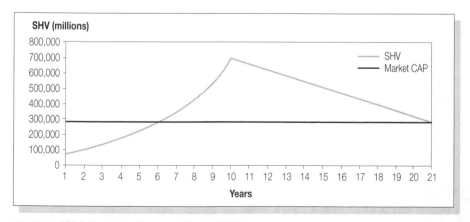

FIG 5.9 ● "Riser" company's market implied CAP

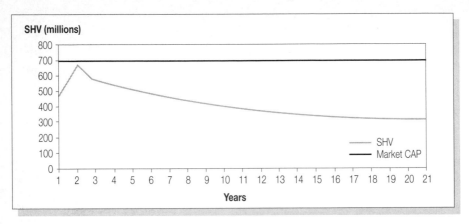

FIG 5.10 ● "Loser" company's market implied CAP

We take the view that the forces of competition will eventually come into play, and so introduce a "fade" period where returns on investment start to fall below the cost of capital – seen here as the period when the estimated value converges with market value.

Finally, there is the "loser" or "depressive" company shown in Fig. 5.10. Its initial estimated valuation is already below current market values, but there is little in its forecast strategy to suggest that the company is ever going to earn an excess return. Rather, it is locked into a position where the costs of capital remain obstinately above the returns on capital, and value is continuously destroyed over the investment horizon. There are more companies of this kind in existence than one might think, and they can greatly benefit from the application of SHV methods.

A common framework

Taken together, then, the seven value drivers – sales growth, cash profit margin, cash tax rate, working capital, capital expenditure, WACC and competitive advantage period – provide a common planning platform from which to review the variety of business units to be found within a typical corporation. The linkage of financial planning to business operations and decision-making requires that these drivers be mapped on to the business-specific measures which drive success with markets, customers and production. For example, a customer services business will focus on highly valued customer segments through market penetration, customer acquisition, product extension and business retention measures; whereas an innovation-driven business will focus on research and development, intellectual property and time-to-market measurement.

In both cases the business-specific measures are mapped or translated into their anticipated effect on the financial value drivers, providing a clear linkage between the operational and the financial value drivers, and enabling a reconciliation from these through the shareholder value framework to the market price.

COMPARISONS AND SENSITIVITY ANALYSIS

Using historical and forecast estimates of the value drivers based on consensus market estimates – or industry forecasts where available – it is possible at least to understand the derivation of the existing market capitalization and current share price. It is essential to compare this market-derived estimate with the company's own estimate of its intrinsic worth, using the same shareholder value framework. This comparison between intrinsic and market value – the "market mirror" – will clearly indicate where the market is more bullish or bearish than the company's own management. The results can sometimes be both surprising and alarming to managements who have not used the SHV framework before, and often speak volumes about communication between company and market, or about confidence of the market in the company's management.

Finally in this chapter, we should mention that the SHV approach has the advantage of showing how sensitive the share price can be to changes in the underlying value drivers over the duration of the forecast period – see Fig. 5.11, which shows the likely affect on a hypothetical company's share price performance of a 1 percent change in each value driver. Understanding these sensitivities can help management develop more useful forecasts while building better insights into where they should concentrate their efforts to increase value.

This technique, known as sensitivity analysis, offers a bridge between the world of finance and the world of management, in that the SHV model can provide an agenda for change within the company and an idea of the effect of such a change. Even at relatively general levels of analysis, the combination of sensitivity analysis and the market mirror can provide considerable insights into what is going on inside a company, thus acting as a very useful lever for subsequent strategies. We shall return to this kind of analysis in Part 2.

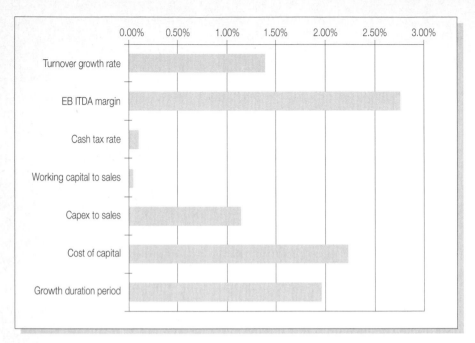

FIG 5.11 ● **Effect on share price of 1 percent favorable change in value drivers (example)**

In essence, any substantive idea put forward to improve a company's performance can, and should, be measured by the value yardstick – measured, in other words, against the cost and availability of capital employed to make it happen.

SUMMARY

In this chapter we have looked at the free cash flow (FCF) model of shareholder value with its seven main drivers of value, and have discussed their relationship to the measurement of risk, growth and returns. The seven drivers – sales growth, cash profit margin, cash tax rate, working capital, fixed capital, WACC and competitive advantage period – provide a framework for analyzing company performance and, through sensitivity analysis, judging the effect of future strategies. Further, in discussing the competitive advantage period, we identified four different types of company – the stayer, the slider, the riser and the loser – to illustrate the concept of a market implied competitive advantage period.

SHAREHOLDER VALUE:

A SINGLE METRIC

OR A COMMON

FRAMEWORK?

So far we have concentrated on explaining the rise of shareholder value and its basic economic elements – cash flow and cost of capital. Many corporations and some advisers have sought to reduce this whole theme to a specific single metric in order to simplify the process of introducing SHV across a whole organization. They have tried to align all operating and investment decisions, performance measures and compensation using one measurement.

In addition to the FCF model already discussed, the two other main metrics used are economic profit, branded as economic value added or EVA™ by the US consulting firm of Stern Stewart, and cash flow return on investment (CFROI). There is also a third, less well known, approach called CVA or cash value added which concentrates attention on the quality of the investment decisions. We will examine each of these in turn in this chapter.

In our experience, senior executives who have been exposed to these various SHV metrics understand that each is built on a common economic foundation and each plays a useful part in the value creation process. Economic profit, for example, can be employed to track overall corporate and business unit performance; CFROI is used in evaluating a company's longer-term strategy and resource allocation; and FCF provides the bridge linking the core strategic and operational objectives to the overall goal of maximizing value via the financial value drivers. CVA is useful for examining the impact of strategic and non-strategic investment on corporate value.

THE FCF MODEL

In the FCF model we look at how a company is going to develop, based on forecasts and opinions, over the next few years – a "multi-period" model. This has the advantage of enabling us to link the company's likely growth path with other observable macro-economic and sector trends. It also makes it easier to subject these forecasts to some consistency checks. The FCF model is entirely future-oriented, assumes no opening capital or balance sheet and discounts the future free cash flow at the WACC. If we start by establishing the market's perception of a company's competitive advantage period – the seventh value driver – we will establish what period of time should be considered for the cash flow forecast in the first place. We can supplement this with our analysis of the market implied competitive advantage period (MICAP) outlined in the previous chapter. As we have said, the FCF model looks primarily at the impact on shareholder value. Incorporated within this is a view on the total value, the sum of debt and equity or economic value (EV), of the company, but this is not the main focus.

Finally, it should be said that the FCF model is probably the most efficient and "economical" with the data. As we shall see later, it can also be adapted to take into account adjusted present value (APV) and real option valuation approaches.

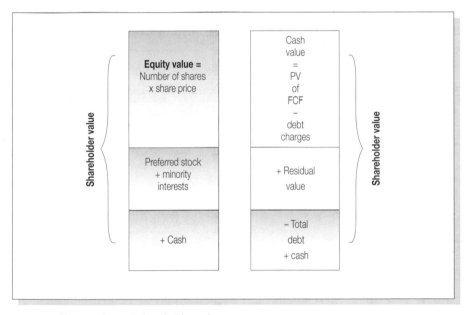

FIG 6.1 ● **Two versions of shareholder value**

THE SVA MODEL: CAPITAL AND CALCULATIONS

The key concept behind the SVA (or EVA™) model is the idea of a spread between the economic return a company earns in a single period compared to the cost of the capital resources used in the business. Rather than looking at the situation over several years, however, SVA models are built on a close analysis of a company's position year by year. The sum of the spreads between the return and the cost of capital for all future periods will of course be equivalent to the positive net present values achieved in the earlier "top down" multi-period model.

The SVA or economic profit model requires a starting balance sheet based on an estimate of the capital resources needed in the company, and this is not identical to the historical financial balance sheet – "value" adjustments are needed.

The definition of SVA is expressed in the formula:

$$\text{SVA} = \text{total capital} \times (\text{return on total capital} - \text{WACC})$$

where total capital is defined as equity plus net debt and other capital.

SVAs are calculated on an annual basis. So in order to arrive at an estimate of market value added (MVA), we take a discounted stream of SVAs and add a residual value to it. We do this to take account of a firm's continuing value after the end of the forecast period; it is a shorthand for assuming that the company would have a resale value. (We will return to this point later.) In other words,

$$\text{MVA} = \text{SVA} + \text{Residual value}$$

and

$$\text{Shareholder value} = \text{MVA} + \text{Opening capital}$$

The example in Fig. 6.2 provides another way of thinking about the SVA for a given year. "Stacking" these up over several years generates a company's MVAs, which can then be used to calculate the shareholder value.

The position with respect to a longer period of time is shown in Fig. 6.3. As you can see the difference between the market and the book values of the assets is made up of the present values (PV) of the SVAs, the MVA. The difference in value that has to be explained will also be affected by the book values assigned to the assets. What is shown here is the financial balance sheet, but there is an equivalent operating balance sheet, and some care is needed in maintaining equilibrium between them.

The important thing in the SVA approach is to establish the spread between what a company earns and what it has to pay for the capital it needs to run its business. For this we use what is known as an economic return on capital employed, or economic ROCE, which is:

$$\text{ROCE} = \text{NOPAT} - (\text{Capital employed} \times \text{WACC})$$

NOPAT (the net operating profit after tax) is a function of the value drivers introduced in Chapter 5. A company should aim to direct all of its strategies

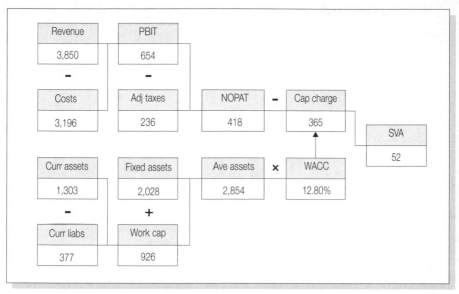

Source: Evaluator/Valuad

FIG 6.2 ● **Example of SVA (Shareholder Value Added) calculation**

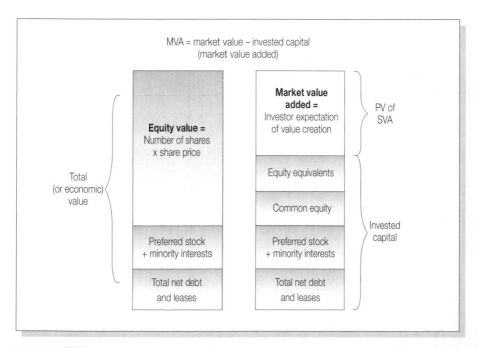

FIG 6.3 ● **MVA**

towards increasing such a spread. An idea of how effectively a company is doing can be obtained by using an economic index, which is:

$$\frac{\text{Economic ROCE}}{\text{WACC}}$$

This ratio is closely correlated with the market-to-book ratio.

The SVA approach is relatively data hungry – in other words, it requires a lot of information about the company that is being analyzed. As we noted earlier, the model needs opening balance sheets and profit-and-loss statements, but not simply in their customary form: they have to be adjusted to allow for various distortions found in normal statutory accounts, and to a lesser extent in management accounts. Let us consider a few of these adjustments.

Inflation and asset adjustments

One of the first things to look at is the impact of inflation, and the age mix of assets. To establish whether a company is producing any SVA, it is important to get a good "fix" on the current replacement value of assets. The SVA approach depends very much on the opening balance sheet of a company, which will typically include a variety of assets with different useful lives and with different ages. These assets will, for the most part, be included at their "book" values, with their age profile playing a significant role. Even with relatively modest inflation, old assets will have book values that are significantly below their replacement value.

Since it is this asset base that is going to have to earn a return, the lower it is, the more likely it is that a firm will earn a high rate of economic return. One of the first steps in any analysis, therefore, will be to adjust the asset base and put it on an equivalent replacement cost basis. This can be quite difficult: making an *ad hoc* adjustment to an asset to calculate its new replacement value can raise an important issue – namely, that you might not want to replace this particular asset in the same form at all. Technical progress might mean that, were you to start again, you would choose a different process or technology.

Bear in mind that, under current performance measurement systems, businesses with old assets may be earning highly respectable rates of return – which will change dramatically if these assets are revalued. What was formerly a good money earner can now turn out to be a business that has to work much harder to justify its existence.

A further consequence is that the SVA approach requires a more detailed analysis of a company's balance sheet. Again, this can be difficult. SVA analysis works very well when a corporate balance sheet can be allocated across different divisions or business units. The analysis also benefits from sensible forecasts concerning changes in balance sheet requirements both for the business as a whole and for its various subsidiaries and divisions.

Other adjustments

Other distortions from the SVA point of view are caused by accrual accounting methodology, which for prudential reasons sometimes brings forward expected losses and makes other timing adjustments. As we have noted earlier, our cash-flow-based approach is primarily interested in seeing what flows across the corporate "border" and really in little else. This means that timing adjustments have to be either eliminated or added back in.

One such adjustment would be in the calculation of the "economic" equity involved in a business, which is defined as the sum of ordinary equity adjusted for tax effects. So we would have to add back deferred tax provisions into the equity pool, while deducting future tax benefits. Similarly, changes might be required in the calculation of NOPAT. This would typically involve adding back the tax shield effects to operating profits estimated as part of the firm's borrowing costs. Other adjustments would be needed for research and development (capitalized rather than expensed), for goodwill (likewise), and for inventory valuation methods among other items.

As if this is not enough, the careful SVA practitioner must beware of expected changes in the capital structure following the issue of warrants and convertible bonds, as well as having to incorporate a lot of off-balance-sheet items that accountants spend so much time excluding from the picture. If nothing else, a company can find that simply running through such a list can help define – possibly for the first time – just what the common value-based accounting framework is going to be before it starts using SHV models.

The resulting figures are bound to be different from those generated by a typical accounts department. We would view this as being a matter of "horses for courses;" for an interim period, SHV calculations and statutory accounting calculations will continue down parallel tracks. Looking further ahead, however, we believe that the changes needed for what we will term value based accounting or value reporting ought anyway to become part of the mainstream of accountancy practices – a topic that we shall return to at the end of this book.

THE CASH FLOW RETURN ON INVESTMENT
(CFROI) MODEL

A third approach, called cash flow return on investment (CFROI) and associated with the Holt Value company, has been developed using the internal rate of return technique. The internal rate of return (IRR) represents the rate of return that would make the present value of future cash flows equal to the initial investment. The interplay between this and a market-derived discount rate representing investor interests is what lies at the heart of the CRFOI process. Where its CFROIs are greater than the market discount rate, and we have a positive spread, a company prospers; where this spread is negative, value is being destroyed.

CFROI measures can assess the rate of return on all investments made in a company, including those made by debt-holders. They can therefore be utilized in any investigation into the financial viability of a company overall rather than just its viability as seen from the shareholder perspective. (Although, as we say throughout this book, the two are closely related.) CFROI aims to allow for the effects of inflation, and to subject any possible strategies to a stringent comparison with what companies on average in a particular industry or sector can achieve by way of returns to investors. It takes a top-down view of total corporate performance, treating the company almost as if it were one large "project."

CFROI has some notable differences from other shareholder value approaches. Let us start by introducing – and defining – one of its elements: the operating cash flow after taxes (OCFAT). If

$$\text{Revenues} - \text{costs} - \text{cash taxes} = \text{NOPAT}$$

then

$$\text{NOPAT} + \text{depreciation} + \text{other adjustments} = \text{OCFAT}$$

We will have to make a distinction between depreciating and non-depreciating assets, since the non-depreciating assets must be adjusted by the rate of inflation in order to keep everything, initially at least, measured in nominal, but inflation-adjusted, terms. This means we have to take

$$\text{Non-depreciating assets} - \text{current liabilities} = \text{Non-depreciating assets (adjusted)}$$

If we add in an estimate of depreciating assets – which includes plant, property and equipment, intangibles and accumulated depreciation, all adjusted for inflation – we will create a term called gross assets. We can then reach the following simple definition:

$$\text{CFROI} = \frac{\text{OCFAT}}{\text{Gross assets}}$$

Since we know what the gross asset value is for each period, we can calculate the CFROI to be the internal rate of return on that investment – which is the discount rate needed (or calculated) to ensure that the net present value of future cash flows, minus the initial investment, comes to zero. These rates are then compared to the WACC and calculated to produce a spread, which is similar to that used in the SVA analysis.

But there are further complications. Firstly, this analysis looks at the return to all capital holders, so there are no tax shelter effects on debt, and debt is more expensive relative to equity in this model. Tax has relevance to the capital side only through the tax position of the investor, rather than the tax position of the enterprise borrowing the money. The second complication is that we want to look at the spread referred to above in real terms, making it relevant to the perceived period of time over which a company can be expected to achieve an IRR higher than its WACC. Again, this is similar to the idea of the competitive advantage period used in the SVA and FCF models.

There are two crucial aspects of this process that need to be considered, though. These are the time period over which the forecast is being made, and the asset base of the company. Since this is a calculation that can be rolled forward, running updated totals on the asset side becomes very important.

Defining the asset base requires making a distinction between depreciating and non-depreciating assets and takes us into the area of value-based adjustments. Some assets such as property can be expected to appreciate over time, while others will depreciate. However, the question of depreciation is crucially dependent on the time period over which the assets are operated, the so-called economic life of the assets.

For a given investment, and assuming positive cash flows, IRRs will generally be higher the longer the forecast time period is. In order to control for this, the CFROI approach invokes what is called a "fade" period, or the period over which the return on the assets is assumed to move towards the market discount rate. This has been calculated for different sectors and results from the normal forces of competition as new entrants drive returns down to a long-term average. The basics are shown in Fig. 6.4. It is important to distinguish between a "hold" period, when excess returns can be maintained, and the "fade" period which represents the time period over which CFROIs are expected to decay.

The "hold" period is similar to the competitive advantage period discussed in earlier chapters. The "hold" assumption tells us the number of years that a company can maintain a rate of return in excess of the WACC. This is based on

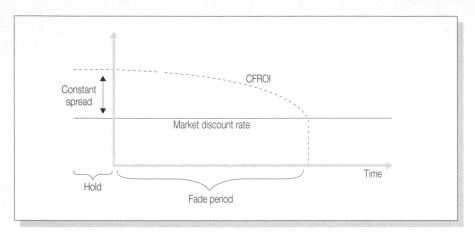

FIG 6.4 ● **Hold and fade in CFROI**

close observation of the US equity market, and the perception that on average companies are not able to "beat" the market for more than seven or eight years at the most. The estimated real return on investment is around 7 percent a year (this figure is just for the USA – see Chapter 3's discussion of market risk premia), with a real asset growth of around 3 percent a year.

After this seven- or eight-year period, performance will gradually decay until eventually the return on investment will equal the WACC. This decay rate is known as the "fade" period, which can be considerably longer than eight years – over 20 years in some cases. This links the analysis of cash flows to observable behavior in the equity market, and has the benefit of pointing out just how transitory periods of competitive advantage can be. The "fade" period serves a rather similar function to the residual value used in other models (see below for more details on residuals).

The actual calculation of hold and fade periods, as well as the adjustments needed to the capital base, can be complex. In principle, though, it is possible to analyze the drivers of CFROI in a similar manner to those used in the other models – see Fig. 6.5.

This approach has some following among institutional investors who are interested in understanding what impact their forecasts will have on expected rates of return. While it has a neatness to it for those who are simply interested in the financing side, experience has shown it to be an approach that is quite difficult to implement. Many factors are by their nature external to the firm and so hard to influence. The CFROIs are highly sensitive to the parameters chosen and so results need to be scrutinized carefully.

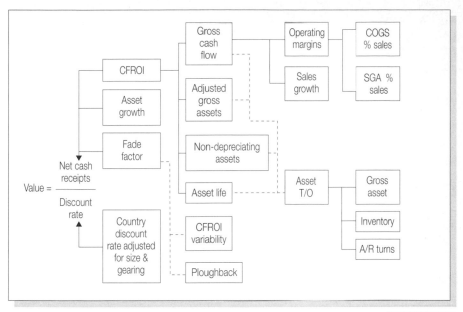

FIG 6.5 ● **CFROI driver tree**

THE CASH VALUE ADDED (CVA) MODEL

Finally, we come to another shareholder metric that shares some of the features of the earlier models, but is designed to throw more light on the details of an investment decision. In particular, this approach develops a method of assessing the impact of individual investment projects on the development of SHV.

We must start with some general definitions, shown in Fig. 6.6. A firm's total value can be divided into three parts: cash surplus value, replacement value and strategy value. The cash surplus value is the NPV of the future cash flows from the continuing business assuming that nothing more is done to it and no further major investment takes place. (It is as if a plane's engines are turned off and it continues to glide for a while before finally landing.) Cash surplus value simply considers the future cash flow from the existing asset base.[1]

Of course, normally, investment does occur in companies. Here CVA makes a distinction about the type of investment. Replacement value in Fig. 6.7 is the cash flow generated by new investment that is needed to keep the business going. It is the marginal cash flow generated by investment that essentially equals depreciation. (This is depreciation in an economic, not an accounting, sense.) One important practical point this distinction picks up is that technical progress can alter the relation between the marginal investment and marginal cash flow output from it, and this relationship is not necessarily the same as that calculated for the existing capital stock.

Another key point is that the replacement investment is defined as not increasing output or capacity. It can, however, reduce costs: which means that the marginal profitability or efficiency of the replacement investment can differ from the rest. Operationally, it is often the case that the "pre-strategy" value of a company – i.e. before any changes take place – is made up of the continuing and the replacement value.

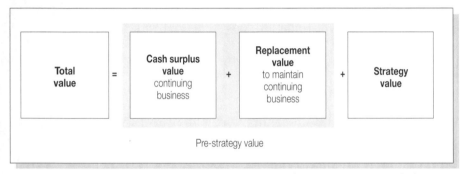

Source: Frederick Weissenrieder and Eric Ottosen, Anelda

FIG 6.6 ● CVA valuation scheme

Finally, we have the "strategy" value, which considers the marginal cash flows arising from investment that actually changes output in either revenue or in volume terms. The sum of all three parts defines total intrinsic value, which may or may not be equal to the economic value of the company. The approach provides a means of assessing the impact of individual investment projects on the development of corporate SHV.

Operational cash flow demand and CVA

When a company invests, it wants to know of course whether the investment is going to create any "value." The operational cash flow demand (OCFD) is one way to calculate the financing and cash flow requirements that a new investment places on an organization. The OCFD is a function of the sum invested, the expected economic life of the asset and the rate of inflation. It is the amount of cash flow needed each year to ensure that at the end of its life the NPV of the investment is zero. It is the same as the internal rate of return used in the CFROI approach above, but applied to the investment side alone. This can be contrasted with the operational cash flows, which is what the investment is capable of producing and forecast to produce. The situation is described graphically in Fig. 6.7, where we have a situation where the strategic investment is generating cash (OCF) more rapidly than is required by the OCFD. The ratio between the OCF and the OCFD is the cash value added (CVA) – which in this case is greater than one. This also means that the project will have a positive NPV and so will be creating value. When the CVA index is equal to 1 then the NPV will be zero, and the estimated rate of return will equal the internal rate of return of the project.

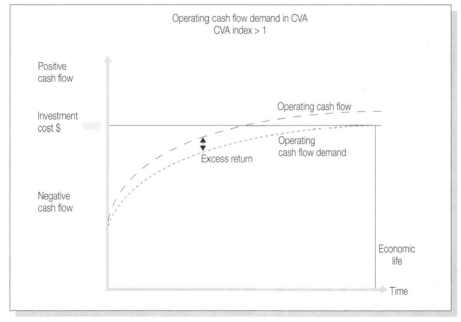

Source: Frederick Weissenrieder and Eric Ottosen, Anelda

FIG 6.7 ● **CVA and OCFD**

The CVA approach can be useful in looking at what sort of return has to be generated by future investments in order to generate SHV. It also focuses attention on the minutiae of the investment process and helps management decide on which investments are important for adding to the long-term survival of the company and which are more oriented towards maintaining current output levels. Practically, it requires a lot of information on the company's asset base and, under some circumstances, this can be difficult and expensive to acquire. Its general applicability will be improved when it is allied with a more effective explanation of the economic life of assets.

ASSESSING STRATEGY DECISIONS

How, using any kind of SHV analysis, can the impact of different strategies be looked at before you take any action? In our experience, applying the SHV approach can be beneficial simply by virtue of the fact that companies have to sort out what kinds of information their internal control systems currently produce, and what is actually needed to answer the question as to who and what is creating or destroying value. At the same time, though, you can easily get lost in the detail. Business history is replete with examples of semi-finished home grown spreadsheets all aiming to demonstrate the impact of different policies and strategies on SHV. Such approaches frequently fail to create the bigger picture that is so necessary before strategies to increase SHV are adopted. We find there is some benefit in starting with more standardized approaches to shareholder value before entering the do-it-yourself school.

One way of keeping a focus on the bigger picture is to use Pricewater-houseCooper's ValueBuilder 1.4™ – a "top down" model – in order to compare the outcome of prospective strategies with the current market value of the company. Indeed, we can also compare various future strategies with each other by this method. Another very good, detailed and stable model for analytical purposes is Alcar which, like the ValueBuilder model, is closely aligned with the Rappaport approach.

These models have a number of advantages: they focus on cash flows and it is easier to link analysis to share price movements. They also focus attention on the growth and capital expenditure drivers. By using fairly large numbers such as EBITDA, it is easier to make internationally interesting comparisons. Their disadvantages include too high a level of generality, and a great dependence on one fixed discount factor, the WACC. The calculation of the residual value can also play a disproportionately important role in the valuation.

Switching to the SVA view of the world, the Evaluator™ model is another very useful tool with which to make comparisons and look at the impact different strategies will have. Its main advantage is that it allows more detailed focus on single time periods, and a more detailed examination of balance sheet informa-tion. The SVA targets can be sensibly implemented and used to incentivize management, which makes it a good approach for any value-based management exercise. It is relatively straightforward to build interfaces with internal manage-ment information systems and so get a rapid update on the SHV implications of recent performance. The main disadvantage is that it is highly dependent on the accurate measurement of adjusted balance sheet information, which is very often not available for anything other than the consolidated or parent company. The single-period analysis is also a weakness, in that it is less straightforward to project broader dynamic trends into the analysis.

The other two approaches, CFROI and CVA are also helpful for understanding the impact of different investment and growth scenarios, as we have explained above.

Value return on investment

There are a number of other techniques we can use to judge whether a prospective strategy is on course or not. The aim here is twofold. Firstly, to find out what the impact of any incremental investment and associated return is going to be – in short, is it going to create any value? Secondly, to work out whether the market is likely to value the overall strategy positively. For the first question we are going to use what is called the value return on investment (VROI), and for the second we are going to look at the Q ratio. Details of both can be seen in Table 6. 1.

We start by estimating what is called the "pre-strategy" value of the company, achieved by capitalizing the existing free cash flow. In Table 6.1's example, for year 0 the value of 106.7 is arrived at. Sometimes you might want to correct for short-term distortions in the latest year's figure, so you could use an average based on the last five years of cash flow performance. This is then compared with the "post-strategy" view. The post-strategy view is made up of the sum of the present value of the incremental cash flows (52.6 in Table 6.1) and the residual value (80 in the example), totalling 132.6. The difference between pre- and post-strategy is 25.9 (132.6 minus 106.7), representing a gain from the strategy. The last piece of the puzzle is to work out the present value of the incremental investments needed for the strategy. In Table 6.1 this comes to 24.5; the calculated VROI ratio is

$$\frac{25.9}{24.5} = 1.1$$

or

$$\text{VROI} = \frac{\text{post-strategy value} - \text{pre-strategy value}}{\text{present value of projected investments}}$$

The decision rule is relatively straightforward: where VROI is greater than 1, SHV is being created, while a VROI of less than 1 implies the opposite – the destruction of SHV – since the incremental value added is smaller than the incremental value of the resources being used. In our example, the VROI ratio is 1.1 over the five-year forecast period – indicating that the net investment is just contributing to shareholder value.

Like all systems of measurement, however, VROI has to be used with care. The numerator (the top half of the equation) can be quite unstable, particularly if a company's pre-strategy value is very small – if for instance it was making losses in the previous year. The ratio also requires there to be meaningful capital spending. If this is likely to be rather low, then the ratio will become unreasonably and misleadingly high.

TABLE 6.1 ● Example of VROI and Q ratios

At a WACC of 15%	Year 0	Year 1	Year 2	Year 3	Year 4	Year 5	Year 6
Profit after tax (PAT)	16.0						
Assets employed (nominal)	80.0						
Incremental cash flow		12.0	14.0	12.0	14.0	18.0	12.0
Discount factor		0.9	0.8	0.7	0.6	0.5	0.4
Present value		10.8	11.2	8.4	8.4	9.0	4.8
Residual value							200.0
Present value of residual							80.0
Present value of cash flows							52.6
Total present value pre-strategy	106.7						
Total present value post-strategy							132.6
Total assets employed inflation adjusted. (3% inflation assumed)							95.5
Incremental net investment		5.0	8.0	6.0	7.0	8.0	3.0
Present value of incremental investment		4.5	6.4	4.2	4.2	4.0	1.2
Total present value of incremental investment							24.5
VROI calculation (post-pre) strategy value							25.9
VROI = (post-pre) strategy/PV of incremental investment							1.1
Q ratio = (post-pre) strategy value/total assets (inflation adjusted)							1.4

Q ratios

The second part of answering the question as to which strategies generate value, and which do not, is based on the Nobel prize-winning work of the economist James Tobin. The now famous Tobin's Q ratio is the ratio between the market value of the physical assets in an economy and the replacement cost of those assets measured in current currency units. From the macro-economic point of view a Q ratio of greater than 1 means that the stock market is valuing a company's (or an economy's) assets at more than their actual cost, while a ratio of less than 1 implies the opposite. A high value of Q means that corporations have a good incentive to invest in new plant and equipment since the market values each unit of investment at more than it is worth. A low value of Q reduces the incentive to invest but encourages acquisitions via the stock market, since investors are paying less for an asset on the financial markets than it would cost them to replace it on the goods market.

The same kind of thinking can be applied to individual companies. Company value can be thought of in two ways, the first being similar to the way bond yields are calculated. An investor has a bond price and a pattern of coupon payments: if the bond coupon rate exceeds prevailing interest rates, then the bond will sell at a premium to the market. Conversely, where the coupon rate is lower than prevailing interest rates, the bond will sell at a discount to the market. Similarly, in the cash flow return on investment model, if the future CFROI exceeds an investor's required return (the cost of capital), then the company will be priced above its book value; if CFROI is lower than the investor's required rate of return, then the company will sell below its book value. In other words, companies with a positive CFROI "spread" will have a Q ratio greater than 1, and companies with a negative CFROI "spread" will have a Q ratio of less than 1. Market price and the CFROI price (current inflation-adjusted book value) will only be same – in other words, Q will be exactly 1 – when the anticipated future CFROI is the same as the investor's discount rate. These relationships are summarized in Fig. 6.8 below.

The second way that the CFROI approach can put a value on a company is by looking in nominal, rather than real, terms at the discount rate that will discount the cash flows back to the company's current market price. This spot valuation therefore will relate all the various assumptions about inflation rates and assets' life expectancies and use them to generate a figure for the return on the invested resources that would justify today's observed market value (debt plus equity).

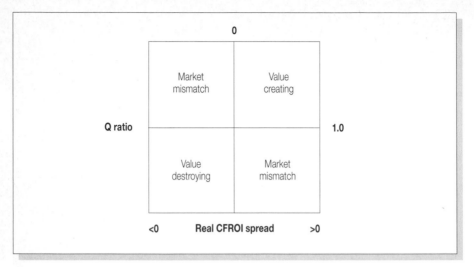

FIG 6.8 ● Q ratios and CFROI spreads

The one great attraction of the CFROI/Q approach is that it can explain a lot of the movements in real market to book ratios, which themselves are derived from share price movements. The combination of real growth and the real ROI spread (i.e. real ROI less real WACC) explains over 80 percent of the variance in the Q ratio of the S&P 400 in the USA.[2] The link between the Q ratio, real ROI spreads and SHV creation is shown in Fig. 6.8, and this can be used to assess the usefulness of different strategies, in a similar manner to the value map (see Chapter 7). The CFROI approach also avoids some of the problems of accrual-based accounting methodologies, as well as specifically allowing for inflation.

If it is not a perfect measure, then neither are the others. What are the drawbacks of the Q ratio approach – and how far are they true for the other approaches as well? In our Table 6.1 example, we calculated not only the post-strategy return to the company but also the replacement cost of the assets used in the company, which we assumed to be inflating at 3 percent a year. After making this value adjustment to the company's asset figures, we arrive at a Q value of 1.4 – which suggests that the stock market should be willing to pay a handsome premium on the price of assets used in the business. This Q ratio also suggests a strategy that is adding to shareholder value.

Such analysis may also reveal "mis-pricing" situations where the current Q ratio as seen in the market is not compatible with the cash flow spreads. In our experience, the market ultimately responds to cash flows rather than the other way around.

RESIDUAL VALUE

Residual value, which we introduced in Chapter 5, is a shorthand term for any estimate of the continuing value of a company at the end of a forecast period. Residual value calculations are needed for the assumptions that have to be made about a business's value at the end of a planning period. They are an important feature of the entire shareholder value approach – indeed, there may be occasions when one of the main conclusions of an SHV analysis will be that almost all of a firm's value rests on its residual worth.

Another way of looking at it is to assume that the business could be sold at the end of the planning horizon; in which case we need an estimate of what its value should be. Some SHV practitioners argue that one should try to value the different parts of the business, then add them together to achieve a sale value – an approach that could be misleading as well as time-consuming. It is often based on today's earnings multiples, begging the question as to what these multiples might be in ten years' time, or whenever the envisaged "sale" takes place. More seriously, there will have been several years of inflation between current values and those in the future. Inflation does not proceed smoothly through the economy; some assets appreciate or depreciate noticeably faster than others, making a significant difference to the sort of re-sale values calculated.

More problematically, it is not clear whether a sale of assets would achieve a premium or a discount over the estimated "book" value. Premia are sometimes paid for control of an asset or a group of assets, on the grounds that the value of the whole is greater than the sum of its parts. (This is the matter of synergies, to which we will return in Chapter 8.)

The residual value calculation, then, is a way of trying to avoid these difficulties. It implies that the business is still a going concern, and that it has settled down into an equilibrium after the end of the forecast period. It is traditionally calculated as an "equilibrium" cash flow divided by the weighted average cost of capital (WACC), with the WACC now based on some "ideal" long-term capital structure. This is also known as a perpetuity calculation.

Much, of course, can depend on the residual value being correctly calculated. As Fig. 6.9 shows, its impact on the total value calculated varies with the investment horizon or planning period. The shorter this is, the more important the residual value.

Some SHV practitioners regularly include a growth factor in their residual value calculation. Reasons given for this include an expectation of continuing inflation, continuing GDP growth, or some other "advantage." A reason less

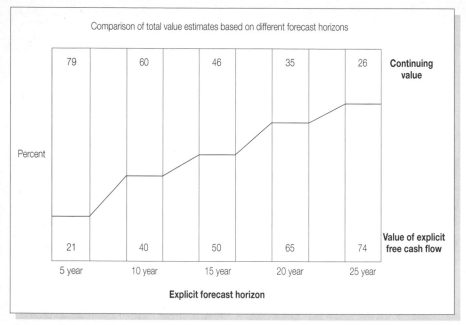

FIG 6.9 ● **Relationship between residual values and investment horizons**

often given, but all the more true for that, is that the residual values are sometimes manipulated to get a valuation to come closer to a target, often the current stock market price. The impact of effectively lowering the cost of capital this way is highly significant, as Fig. 6.10 shows. In the example, a growth factor of 5 is sufficient to raise the residual value by 50 percent, which is to add a lot to what is already a large number.

Given our earlier views on the competitive advantage period, we think that it is better to think of the residual as being based on some kind of steady-state equilibrium. If this is not reached in the chosen investment horizon, then it is probably better to extend the investment horizon until it can plausibly be thought to "settle down," rather than inject an arbitrary growth factor. Our preference, then, is to avoid growth factors where possible, and be very cautious in introducing them.

Other interpretations of residuals

If the residual value offers a shorthand way of understanding the continuing going-concern value of an enterprise, it also offers a number of new opportunities. One is that we can look more closely at the determinants of this residual,

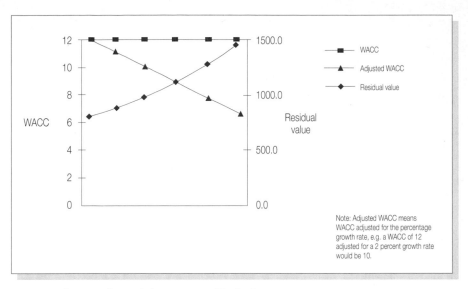

FIG 6.10 ● **Impact of growth factors on residual values**

and include features specific to a particular industry or sector. In the financial area, residual value might be related to the years to maturity of various loans and other obligations, for instance insurance policies. With resources, it might be an adjustment based on depletion rates and the estimated years of life of provable reserves. In both cases, we can adapt the residual calculation to take into account the extent an organization's resources are more or less committed after the end of the planning forecast period.

In the high technology area, the treatment of residual value differs again. At PricewaterhouseCoopers we are looking at ways of linking the perception of a value gap – where market valuations are far higher than either the enterprise or the residual value would justify – to the value placed by the investor on a firm's flexibility in the face of rapid technical change. Work is continuing on including real options valuations as an additional factor in establishing how high-technology firms create shareholder value.

DRAWBACKS AND ADVANTAGES

All the methods we have looked at so far are good at identifying strategies that could increase shareholder value – which of course is the point of the whole exercise. We have to consider, though, whether in some circumstances our criteria might be too rigorous – whether they might be too harsh to some projects that fall just outside the charmed circle of value creation. The CFROI approach, for instance, risks penalizing mature and basically profitable businesses simply because their assets are old and have been given a relatively high "real" cost. The same problem exists for the SVA models, where one-off adjustments have to be made to those businesses with old assets. Although these businesses still have a positive cash flow, with assets that may still have many years of useful life, it is possible they do not measure up in either CFROI or SVA terms.

Another issue is that strategic choices about investing and divesting are not always as clear cut as we could wish for. For instance, when the alternatives are either to divest or to add investment in a mature business, the Q ratio approach may not always lead to the best choice. The excessively high investment needed in the denominator of the VROI fraction on page 85 requires an unreasonably high cash flow to produce either a Q ratio greater than 1, or a positive SHV. Management could then decide to sell the business only to find that the cash received will not generate as high a value for the shareholders as the old business would have done. Here some of the insights of the real options approach (see the high-technology section of Chapter 10) can be useful in trying to put a value on flexibility.

So when we pull all these insights together, the best benchmark against which to value different alternatives is the market value of the business, which is what we do in the free cash flow approach. In many cases there is no reason to conclude that an inflation-adjusted figure (or indeed a value-adjusted figure) is better than the market for assessing the value of assets.

Let us end this chapter, however, by dwelling on the advantages of all the approaches we have dealt with so far. The important thing is that they simulate actual investor behavior, particularly with their emphasis on expected future performance. They offer a decisive break with more backward-looking, accrual-accountancy-based, methods. They also offer sound ways of linking companies' cash-generating capacities, the expectations of their shareholders and the creation of SHV.

The SHV approach can be thought of as a large filter through which a lot of statistical and financial material has to pass. What gets through that filter is the information that can throw light on, and be aligned with, the creation of value. SHV is all about ensuring that external metrics – those of the financial markets – are extended internally within a company, and recognizing that the strategies it adopts internally will have an impact on the way it is viewed by the external market.

At this stage we do not want to say categorically that one SHV approach is superior to any other. In our experience we have found uses for most, if not all, of the approaches described above; we are not particularly interested in representing one view or another in some kind of "metric war." But, as you may learn, in certain situations some models can be more successfully applied than others. Economic profit, for example, can be used to track overall corporate and business-unit performance; CFROI is increasingly used in evaluating a corporation's longer-term strategies and resource allocation; and free cash flow methods can help implement core strategic objectives by using the financial value drivers to specify each business unit's operational objectives. In Part 2 of this book we will look much more closely at how you can go about applying the approaches outlined here.

Complex they may be, but in expert hands some SHV approaches can provide highly relevant insights into what management needs to do to satisfy investors, as well as helping investors see what they should be asking management to do. All of which should keep their clients, the pension funds and other institutional investors, which means ultimately you and me, happy.

SUMMARY

In this chapter we have examined several variations on the SHV theme – in particular, the SVA, CVA and CFROI approaches. We have seen how, with help of concepts such as value return on investment (VROI), operational cash flow demand (OCFD) and Q ratios, we can relate the different strategies a firm might follow to the use of resources this involves, and establish whether such strategies are likely to add to or detract from SHV.

Notes

1. Weissenrieder, F. and Ottosen, E. (1996), "Cash Value Added: A New Method for Measuring Financial Performance," Gothenburg University Working Paper, 1996:1.
2. Reimann, B.C. (1989) *Managing for Value* Planning Forum/Blackwells.

PART

2

PUTTING IT INTO
PRACTICE: THE
VALUE MINDSET

THE
TRANSFORMING
POWER OF
SHV

In Part 1 we explained why shareholder value has moved center stage around the world – you will have recognized increasing market liberalization, the simultaneous rise in influence of global institutional investors, and the enabling power of computers as factors in this process. We looked at how the concept of value has developed; introduced the key elements in measuring value, cash flow and the cost of capital; and examined in some detail the three main but differing techniques that are used to derive measurements of economic value from these basic elements: FCF, EVA™ and CFROI.

But what does all this have to do with the corporate executive? Why, you will ask, should your company make shareholder value the focus of its strategy? One answer was provided in 1999 by Jack Welch, the chairman of General Electric:

Managing in the last ten years has been made easier by the equity markets, let's not even kid ourselves about that. That's reality. If you perform well and you are victim of a bad market I think morale is easy to keep up. What has an impact is if you have a lousy performance in a good market.[1]

Corporate executives increasingly have to ensure that the shares of their company are keeping up with those of competitors. Failure to do so can result in the company itself becoming a bid target.

Another answer is simply to point to the organizations that have taken the initiative to manage for shareholder value – companies such as Lloyds Bank, General Electric, BP and Novo Nordisk. All companies that have outperformed their competitors in terms of share price – see the diagrams in Figs. 7.1 to 7.4. There are also many other companies that have embarked on implementing shareholder value strategies.

Part 2 of this book will look at what it means in practice for an organization to adopt a shareholder value focus. We aim to explain how SHV techniques are in practice used in corporations for analysis and planning, for action and implementation and for communication, investor relations and value reporting. This will demonstrate how the shareholder value framework integrates the core processes underlying the creation, preservation and realization of value.

We will also, in this part, be looking at how these SHV techniques should be applied not only in the ongoing business of a company, commonly called value based management (VBM), but also in the circumstances of mergers and acquisitions and value re-creation in business turnarounds. Finally, we will reflect on the lessons we have learned as practitioners in this field and explain the issues that will need to be confronted as well as the pitfalls to be avoided.

Our approach in these chapters will not be a matter of examining case histories: rather, it will be to provide a route map for a company's journey into the world of shareholder value. In drawing up this map, we will of course be utilizing PricewaterhouseCoopers' experience of advising companies on the introduction of shareholder value systems. You can be assured, therefore, that the following chapters are grounded in the practicalities of management, not in theory – except insofar as we have found the theories of professors and consultants to have useful applications in the real world.

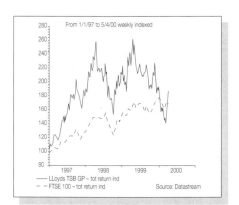

FIG 7.1 ● **Creating SHV at Lloyds-TSB**

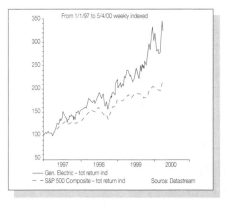

FIG 7.2 ● **Creating SHV at General Electric**

FIG 7.3 ● **Creating SHV at BP Amoco**

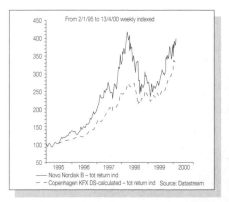

FIG 7.4 ● **Creating SHV at Novo Nordisk**

VALUE AND ITS TRANSFORMATION

Let us return to the five-letter word that we began this book with: value. Put behind you, if you can, the apparent complications of calculating your SHV outlined in Chapter 4 and elsewhere. Deciding between methods to use – SVA, CFROI or whatever – should not obscure the basic fact underlying the theories of SHV: that the markets require invested capital to provide returns that are equivalent to, or exceed, its opportunity cost.

Warren Buffett, chairman of the very successful US investment company Berkshire Hathaway, thrives on finding investments in which value is not yet reflected in the share price. "What counts is intrinsic value, a number that is impossible to pinpoint but essential to estimate" is how he explained his priorities in a letter to shareholders in Berkshire Hathaway's 1994 annual report. He went on to emphasize that

> Understanding intrinsic value is as important for managers as it is for
> investors. When managers are making capital allocation decisions ... it's
> vital that they act in ways that increase per-share intrinsic value and avoid
> moves that decrease it. This principle may seem obvious but we constantly
> see it violated. And when misallocations occur, shareholders are hurt.

If "understanding intrinsic value" is paramount, SHV analysis, as long as it is applied properly, should ensure that "misallocations" do not occur. But it's more than a matter of avoiding the negative: when you adopt SHV you are taking positive action. Applying the insights from shareholder value theory to a company is a powerful way of improving performance at all levels within it; turning the theory into practice can make it easier to meet apparently demanding shareholder performance targets. In our view a careful application of the methodology will result in a dramatic transformation in the way your company is run.

What it all amounts to, in fact, is the triple process expressed graphically in Fig. 7.5: *analysis* (Warren Buffett's "understanding intrinsic value") should be followed by *action* – the transformation of your company to align it with shareholder value goals – and then *communication* to the market.

This trio of abstract nouns reflects the fact that if your overriding aim is to maximize shareholder value, every aspect of your business has to adopt an approach consistent with that imperative. What's more, by really committing yourself as a management to the SHV concept, you can make it an energizing force for change throughout your company. Value-based management – which

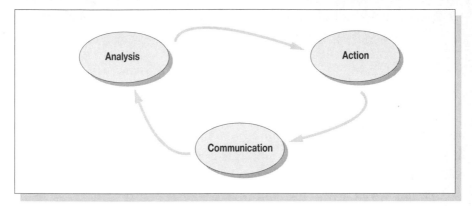

FIG 7.5 ● **The triple transformation process**

is what this chapter is about – is all-embracing: it aligns strategies, policies, performance measures, rewards, organization, processes, people and systems to deliver increased SHV.

To succeed with a value transformation initiative, management must understand the linkage of strategy to operations and the importance for that linkage of focusing on the value drivers introduced in Chapter 4. That is *analysis*. But creating and sustaining value is not merely an analytical or planning exercise. To build long-term sustainable value in your organization you must transform its people, culture, and processes to drive for shareholder wealth. In other words, *action*. Finally, you will require excellent *communication* at all levels internally and with the outside investors and other stakeholders.

How then does a CEO with a team committed to shareholder value start the process of institutionalizing it in his or her business's strategic and operational decision-making? There is another threefold process that we believe is essential for any company that is serious about introducing value-based management. Its components, shown in Fig. 7.6, are *value creation*, *value preservation*, and

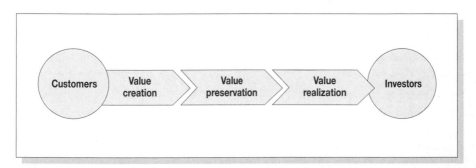

FIG 7.6 ● **SHV links customers to investors**

value realization; the triple requirement of this process – which begins by developing value with your customers and ends by delivering that value to your investors – should be borne in mind throughout this chapter. Dealing effectively with these three steps will enable you to complete the SHV mission and ensure that your promises to your investors can be delivered.

The question of measurement

While we believe the shareholder value approach is consistent with the way that managements want to run their businesses, there is more to these three steps than might at first be apparent. Take the question of metrics – in other words, how corporate performance can connect with things that can be measured. To quote Robert Kaplan and David Norton, "What you measure is what you get."[2]

Oddly, although total shareholder returns can be measured to the third decimal point, attempts to link these figures to behavioral changes within a company have been very limited. Indeed, the quest for a more balanced approach to measuring performance has in most cases left managers wondering just how to decide, among all the various "factors," "indicators," and so on that can be measured, what they should concentrate on. The purpose of this chapter is to simplify things by arguing for the primacy of an external, shareholder-based view – to suggest that, if earlier financial measures emphasized a more backward-looking, accountancy-based approach, it is now more appropriate to adopt a way of looking forward at the financial parameters within which a company is going to have to operate and survive.

Shareholder value analysis, like Warren Buffett's "intrinsic value" approach, judges a company on the basis of what it can produce in the future, rather than concentrating on what it has done in the past. This way, we believe, it is possible to pinpoint the elements that will contribute to the way the fundamentals of your business might develop – elements on which you can base a valuation that can be compared to the current market value.

Well-run companies, among them GE and others referred to above, have done just such analysis. All of them, at various times, have embarked on specific SHV projects whose aim has been to shift management's attention to the raising of share price. In order to do this they have taken steps, some of them radical, not only to raise performance, but to go on doing so over a period of time. For instance at GE, senior executives are expressly asked to suggest ways in which insights from their business line can be applied to another part of GE – thus helping to bring out the synergies within the group that might otherwise remain hidden. Management generally have looked at shareholder value from both a corporate and from a divisional point of view, and have adopted strategies whose outcome has been an improved share price.

THE THREE STAGES OF VALUE

What then is the formula for SHV success? Let us return to the three steps of *value creation*, *value preservation* and *value realization*. The first, value creation, is the process whereby a company can maintain a return on capital greater than its cost of capital. This positive "spread," which can be retained in the business or distributed to shareholders, represents the value shareholders are looking for when they make their decision to invest in a company.

Value creation involves being able to offer something, either a product or a service, to your clients and customers at a price that satisfies the condition of earning this positive return. (This is the customer value discussed briefly in Chapter 2.) Your enterprise will need to be able to earn this positive return for a period of time – the growth duration period – and the longer this is, the greater the shareholder returns will be. Companies that do this will very often develop *competitive advantages* using proprietary technologies and favorable cost structures, or by exploiting efficiencies in manufacturing or in selling. (More on competitive advantages below.)

Value creation alone does not ensure success, however. It is just as important to work towards value *preservation*, to make sure that what is created is not simply wasted or lost through inefficiency and poor management. You may therefore need to take steps to secure the appropriate management, resource allocation, cash and tax management systems. Companies need to be able to effectively manage risk, knowledge and human capital across their strategic business units. Risk, in particular, is an important area. Many companies operate from a narrow concept of risk management and as a result miss opportunities. They need to be able to consider risk in three categories – hazard, opportunity and uncertainty which can be planned for[3] – and actively manage their businesses around each of these areas.

Regrettably, there are several recent examples of firms – particularly financial services companies – that have lost money through poor management controls or inadequate risk management. As corporations become increasingly global, many are discovering additional pitfalls in tax and currency controls that trap value in certain countries and actually destroy value through poor management of the country or currency in which cash flows are generated.

The final step, *value realization*, is often neglected by corporations. Investors realize value through capital appreciation of their stock and dividend payouts. In most cases the bulk of shareholder returns comes through capital appreciation. Since markets are only as efficient as the information available, investors will not benefit unless the market understands the value created by your company and the strategies in place to build and preserve that value. Companies that deliver credible and relevant information to the market in a timely fashion, and are recognized for effectively managing value expectations, are much more likely to maintain a market value that reflects the company's true value than businesses with poor communications programs.

In recent years, there have been several companies which, in response to the market's failure to perceive their value, have fundamentally restructured themselves. To increase transparency, they have taken steps such as issuing special-purpose stock on individual business units, "tracker stocks" within their organization, or spinning off those businesses through stock flotations or IPOs. The main effect of such initiatives has been to make the communication path from business unit to the market cleaner, crisper and less cluttered. These initiatives are examples of how written communications (what the company says) can be combined with actual restructuring of ownerships (what the company does) in a value realization program.

It is doubtless this kind of restructuring that Jean-Pierre Tirouflet, CFO of Rhône-Poulenc, was referring to when he told a Conference Board survey of European CFOs that "we must change our organization in order to use [SHV] measures effectively. This means we may need to redraw the company into profit centers, which make sense with their own working capital, equipment, and an economic meaning."[4]

Challenges in achieving value transformation

Three phases

Success in applying and implementing a shareholder value program is not at all easy. Businesses that set out to enhance their shareholder value vary widely in their levels of understanding, involvement and, ultimately, effectiveness. Normally, in our experience, large organizations pass through three distinct phases as they move towards implementation of value-based management.

Firstly, there are the *talkers*. These are firms whose managements are aware of such things as valuation methodologies and performance metrics. They will probably refer to shareholder value as a desirable goal, but without having any clear idea of how they can move closer to it. Frequently, companies in this phase talk about shareholder value in the boardroom, but have found it very difficult to take the discussion any further. Indeed, some of them will argue strenuously that it cannot be done. And so, with virtually no real transformation, a first-phase company cannot expect any true value growth.

Secondly, we have the *partial adopters*. They are the managements that are persuaded to move cautiously down the shareholder value road, and have perhaps identified one area for improvement without considering the broader implications – taking an *ad hoc* approach to value transformation that frequently ends without much success.

In the final phase, a company becomes a true *value transformer*. Here, a company's management will recognize the need to integrate value across all aspects of the business and drive this philosophy down to the lowest levels; it will accept that value transformation is a broad undertaking that will require extensive education and several business cycles to implement completely.

The task, then, is to move your organization through these three phases of value transformation – to take the company from value-awareness, through adopting a few value elements to the final goal of transforming all its major processes.

Essential requirements

There are great challenges in moving from the "talking" phase through to value transformation. Success will mean planning and implementing a series of closely related and linked initiatives. For this process, we would like to outline what we think are the essential requirements.

Firstly, since this is a multi-year process that affects all of the organization's central processes, your corporation needs CEO *sponsorship* of the change effort, with the support of senior management and the board of directors. Given the importance of value communications programs, the internal communication of a value philosophy should be a major item on the agenda of your CEO and CFO. Without such endorsement from the top, the effort will fail.

A value transformation program also requires a *value transformation team* that includes representatives from all of your major businesses. The existence of such a team encourages the building of "ownership" and consensus to support the shareholder value approach among people at all levels and locations of the organization. This team can also serve to educate management and business units about measuring and managing economic value throughout the organization.

An additional challenge in the value transformation process is *motivation* – inspiring people to make decisions and take actions that support the value philosophy. Mostly this will be done by systems of compensation (see below), but it almost goes without saying that a corporate culture where the focus is on highlighting success rather than "scapegoating" failure is one where motivation levels are likely to be higher. We shall return to this subject towards the end of the chapter, where we will suggest ways of dealing with obstacles that may lie in the path of a value transformation initiative.

FIVE CORE VALUE PROCESSES

In order to achieve the three goals of value creation, preservation and realization, there are five key processes, laid out in Fig. 7.7, that we have identified as being helpful. They are: the establishment of corporate value strategies and goals; resource allocation and planning; performance measurement; compensation; and value communication and reporting – in five words, goals, plans, measures, rewards and communications. These five processes are critical. They ensure that the value link from customer to shareholder is created and solidified.

You can achieve substantial improvement in your company's ability to create value by integrating shareholder value into any of your five processes. However, if these core processes are to be aligned to produce long-term sustain-

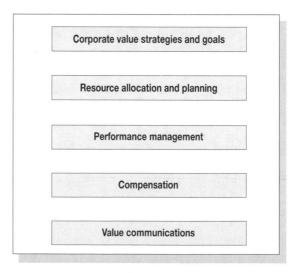

FIG 7.7 ● Five core value processes

able value, you should focus on integrating SHV into each of them. It is these five processes that the rest of this chapter will be mostly concerned with. We will take them one by one.

Corporate value strategies and goals

This is where your shareholder value analysis begins. Corporate strategies define the businesses in which you are competing; they map the course for creating value across a portfolio of companies. Strategy answers four questions – all of which, you will observe, have great relevance to the processes of value creation, value preservation and value realization:

● What goals do you have as a corporation?

● What businesses are you in?

● How will you win – i.e. achieve your goals?

● How will you ensure that you obtain the positive returns with which to reward your shareholders?

There has to be a very close link between the strategy the firm intends to follow, and the creation of shareholder value. Unless SHV is integrated into the strategy development process, a company is unlikely to meet the long-term challenge of creating value with customers and delivering it to investors.

Often, strategy is taken to be exclusively a matter of markets, customers, products, technologies, and competitive dynamics. While these are essential inputs, they are not enough: the question of value creation has to be addressed for each of these areas. In other words, for a strategy to be effective, your company will have to integrate shareholder value into the formulation and development of that strategy. At this level, value is driven by three basic imperatives:

● investing to achieve a return in excess of the cost of capital (return)

● growing the business and the investment base (growth)

● managing and accepting appropriate business risks (risk).

As you contemplate major strategy choices, assessments of return, growth and risk can be used effectively to weigh up the implications for shareholder value of these choices.

A company must set specific long-term value goals; for instance, "delivering total investor returns in the top quintile of our peers over the next five years," as has been done at Lloyds Bank for example. Externally, these goals must satisfy the expectations of the competitive markets for capital – in effect, your investors' expectations. Internally, these same goals should be used to challenge, refine and prioritize the potential strategies of your individual businesses. When used in the strategy development process, they can help identify real constraints and priorities, and ensure that resource allocation among businesses and initiatives will be consistent with creating and delivering value.

This is where economic modelling and cash/capital/returns analyses must begin. The development of strategy will have to focus on markets, technologies, competitive dynamics and customers. Here you will need to establish what your company's critical success factors are and clearly define them. You will also need to go back to two terms we mentioned briefly in Chapter 2: core competencies and competitive advantage.

Core competencies and SHV

It is important to establish what your firm's core competencies are, and more important still to relate them to the creation of shareholder value. Sometimes described as "integrated bundles of skills that enable a company to deliver a particular benefit to customers,"[5] core competencies harness the total learning in an organization, and in particular involve commitment to "boundaryless" working that may involve many levels of management across all the organization's functions. A core competency should be one that competitors find difficult to copy, and should make a perceptible contribution to customer benefits. In this way, it should also materially contribute to the formation of shareholder value.

Core competencies need not simply be a matter of technology; they can also be defined as market understanding and know-how, strength of business process or speed of delivery. Translating these elements into products will allow you to build brands, customer loyalty, distribution channels and corporate image. Most world-class corporations will have three to six core competencies. Canon, for example, has "precision mechanics" (e.g. cameras and colour printers), "fine optics" (e.g. videos and laser imagers) and "micro electronics" (e.g. still video cameras and calculators).

At the same time you need to ensure that your interpretation of what your company is good at is neither defined too narrowly (is too product-specific) or too broadly. As we point out in the next chapter, synergies may be claimed in merged businesses that are not really there. As the originators of the core competency concept, C.K. Prahalad and Gary Hamel put it: "In the long run, competitiveness derives from an ability to build, at lower cost and more speedily than competitors, the core competencies that spawn unanticipated products.'[6]

As we have said, your core competencies must be related to the creation of shareholder value: to put it plainly, it is no use your company being good at making something for which there is little or no market demand. Your core competencies must therefore be capable of creating and sustaining a competitive advantage.

In order to compete, all organizations must demonstrate some form of real or perceived competitive advantage or unique selling point. This goal is often achieved through product and/or service differentiation linked to customer benefits. Of course, over time these advantages may well be eroded by competitors – a likelihood that is usually taken into consideration in any calculations relating to the growth duration or competitive advantage period value driver. As a conscientious manager you will have to tackle this risk head on with a stream of new products developed out of your organization's core competencies to meet customers' wants as they evolve.

While establishing core competencies is an essential element in determining strategy, it is not enough. At this point, a company needs to take its articulated strategy and link it to the other four value processes to serve ultimately both owners and customers in the effort to maximize shareholder value.

The risk factor

Before we leave this section on corporate goal setting, it is worth going back to the risk/growth/returns imperatives of the previous pages to take another look at risk. This can be a neglected area. In developing and evaluating their strategies to improve total shareholder return, many corporations have concentrated on manipulating just two strategic value "levers" – economic returns and growth. With sufficient information about a specific initiative's potential growth and economic return (net cash flow return on investment less the cost of capital), companies have thought themselves able to forecast future shareholder value. If economic returns are positive, growth contributes to value; if economic returns are negative, growth will reduce value.

Using these two levers, however, has at least one significant limitation: it fails to incorporate adequately the impact of *risk* in creating and realizing shareholder value. Some SHV practitioners do adjust cost-of-capital estimates used in economic return calculations in accordance with their judgement about total enterprise risk, but such adjustments seldom reflect the full range of risks among the businesses and initiatives being considered. More importantly, however, the two-lever approach fails to consider the relationship between growth and risk.

Many companies are now struggling to fulfill aggressive growth and value agendas, but not so many recognize that taking risks is essential to both growth and return. Enterprises must integrate explicit measurements of risk into their strategic planning in order to identify the possible organizational, cultural and financial changes that will be needed to achieve their SHV and growth goals.

Resource allocation and planning

Once strategy has been established, resources – human, intellectual and financial – must be allocated to implement the strategy. As a manager, you must make decisions about where to allocate resources to support strategies and maximize returns overall, not simply because individual projects are expected to deliver higher returns.

By adopting SHV as the standard for implementing plans and allocating resources, both the corporate parent and its business units will be operating under a common framework and thus, we believe, will make better decisions. Nevertheless, management should assess performance regularly and objectively: if investments are not performing against value-based objectives, the capital should be freed for a high-return strategic investment elsewhere. In this way, capital can be invested efficiently in the most productive initiatives.

Using the value drivers

Issues of resource allocation can be analyzed using a number of techniques. These include sensitivity analysis, benchmarking, and value mapping. At this point we need to go back to the seven drivers of the SHV model introduced in Chapter 5. Any shareholder value calculation will incorporate these seven value drivers – often described as macro drivers, to distinguish them from operating or micro drivers, which we shall deal with later.

In effect, these drivers can provide a common planning tool for a variety of departments, product lines and business units. By using the historical performance of the value drivers to compute your company's return on invested capital for each business or product, and comparing this computation against the company's cost of capital, you can determine where shareholder value has been created or destroyed in the past. To reach a true understanding of value, however, both management and investors must focus on likely future performance.

Sensitivity analysis

There are definite relationships between business decisions, value drivers and cash flow. By analyzing them, you can gain insights into how it might be possible to enhance shareholder value. Likely changes to any of the drivers can be analyzed to determine their impact on value; for example, different assumptions of risk, reflected in higher or lower cost of capital requirements, can be tested. Similarly, you could study the likely impact on your enterprise's current value of a strategy to generate increases in revenues, decreased selling or marketing costs, or different required levels of working capital investment. In essence, *any substantive idea put forward to improve a company's performance can be measured by the value yardstick, against the cost and availability of capital employed to make it happen.*

This, then, is sensitivity analysis: as we saw in Chapter 5, the seven value drivers can be "flexed" in a computer model to see what the effect on a company's share price might be – in the case of the example in Fig. 5.11, it was a variation of 1 percent in each of the drivers. Such analysis can establish priorities in your management decision processes.

Once you have discovered the power of each value driver to affect the share price, you must then take a long hard look to see how possible it might be to move the relevant value drivers in the appropriate direction. If it is possible, the next question to be asked is: could this strategy be communicated to, and be believed by, the market? Whatever the answer, sensitivity analysis will illustrate how much shareholder value it may be possible to add if best practice can be achieved.

Benchmarking: the external scorecard

By "benchmarking" we mean systematically comparing your own organization, its structures, activities and functions, to others. The others will often be your competitors – but here we are using a wider than usual definition of who is a competitor. Most managers see themselves competing against a clearly defined group of companies, probably offering a similar series of products or services. Investors, however, take a rather different view: their main interest is in the return yielded by their investments. Stock markets are places where by definition all the companies participating compete with each other for capital. Such competition, as investors see it, takes place on a field much wider than most managements envisage. Were managers occasionally to look at the way investors group companies, they might find themselves compared with some surprisingly unlikely companies – perhaps even companies they do not for a moment take seriously as competitors.

We dwell on this point because it throws some light on what investors are looking for in the way of corporate performance. We know that often their main concerns are what other companies in the top "quintile" are achieving, rather than what a particular company's immediate competitors are doing.

Benchmarking can obviously be extended along other lines too. For instance, it may be of interest to know what the performance characteristics of your customers, suppliers, or business partners are. But to benchmark your company against the competition, particularly the "best in class," is a helpful starting-point in any analysis.

We recommend you start such an exercise with an "external scorecard" approach. By employing the same techniques as those used by market analysts, the external scorecard – see Fig. 7.8 for an example – can offer a management useful insights. Competitors are identified and all available information on their strategy carefully analyzed; each of their value drivers is compared to your company's value drivers percentages. Such analysis will reveal performance gaps – some in favor of the company and some showing stronger competitor performance and possible best practice. It may also be possible to join an international benchmarking alliance (for instance the PricewaterhouseCoopers Global Benchmarking Alliance) to gain further insights as to what is the best practice among competitors.

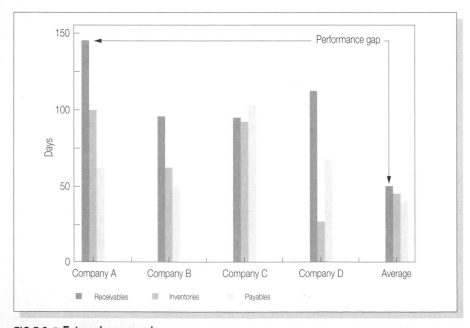

FIG 7.8 ● **External scorecard**

However it is done, the point of benchmarking is that you will gain an understanding of best practice, be able to set out with confidence to improve the performance of your own corporate value drivers, and thus to enhance shareholder value.

The value map

Another useful tool in the resource allocation stage of value-based management is the "value map," examples of which are shown in Fig. 7.9. This is a way of showing graphically which parts of your business are contributing to the creation of value and which are not. To do this, you need to be able to divide your organization into its constituent value centers, each representing a division or business unit with responsibility for the management of revenues, costs and capital.

Assuming this is possible, you can then plot each unit's position on the first "map" according to the value it has created (measured on the vertical axis) against the capital it has employed (the horizontal axis). Often, different business units will be positioned in different markets – in which case for each unit a cost of capital will be applied which reflects the systematic risks to which it is exposed.

Of course, we have to be careful to define our terms, since there can be different value maps designed to answer different questions. One map can be concerned with the value creation possibilities of a division to all asset holders,

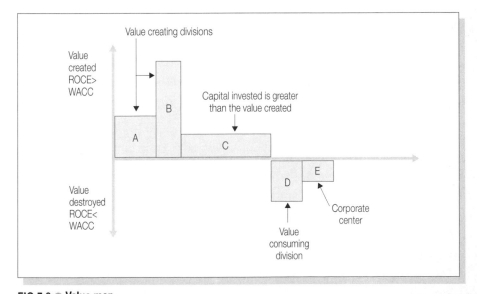

FIG 7.9 ● Value map

in which case we might plot the present value of a free cash flow and look at the total capital employed (drawn on the horizontal axis). Alternatively we could look at it more narrowly from a strict equity point of view. Then we could look at the present value of the future cash flows accruing to the equity holders, and deduct the interest payments to debt holders, and compare this to the equity held in the business. As with other aspects of SHV metrics, it's a matter of selecting the right methodology for the right circumstances.

In the value map in Fig. 7.9, we have four different divisions performing in different ways. Division A is creating value equivalent to the resources it uses. Division B is creating proportionately more value than it is using in resources. C is a user of capital and produces a relatively low spread. Division D, on the other hand, is destroying shareholder value while consuming resources. The total value created by the business is the size of rectangles A+B+C–D.

Whatever measurement gets used in the value map, and whatever map is used, it is easy to see that your high risers will be the most valuable parts of your business; anything that turns out to be a square is "breaking even," while there will have to be a question mark over the future of the "bungalows," the flat value destroyers that are wider than they are tall. The important point is that, in drawing the map, you and your advisers will have had to undertake a thorough assessment of the cash, however defined, that is flowing into and out of each business unit. Without that knowledge, any SHV analysis can be flawed.

This kind of analysis is bound to lead to questions about what action to take and where to target investment. While some divisions that are operating less than efficiently will need additional capital in order to create value, other value-destroyers will remain value destroyers whatever you do – so you will be better off without them. Equally, it may be worth investing in a high-value division, or it may not; if it is operating in a mature, saturated market, further investment may result in excess capacity and thus value destruction.

What's more, your value map can be further enhanced by benchmarking the divisional or business unit figures you have calculated – in other words, going outside the company to identify performance gaps and best practices in a group of companies. Here again global benchmarking alliances can be called upon.

Performance management

Setting the targets

As we have said, corporate analysis must be followed by the setting of targets based on share price goals. Having established what is possible at the corporate level, and having identified which businesses divisions are creating or destroying shareholder value, the next step is to convert your global targets into something much more localized and achievable at an operating level within your company. You must assess the impact of these goals on the seven value drivers as they apply to your company, its action plans and budgets. Performance measurements and incentive systems – two of the main themes of this chapter – must then be agreed and introduced. Many of the high-profile global companies that have introduced shareholder value programs have started with a share price goal – an objective that is easy to understand and communicate.

For example, a management may set a goal "to increase its company's current share price from £20 a share to £30 a share over the next five years." In order to achieve this, a 50 percent increase in price, it will use the cash flow approach outlined in Part 1 to calculate that the following movements must be achieved in relation to the seven macro value drivers:

Revenue growth rate	increase from 12 to 15 percent
Operating margin growth (EBITDA)	from 8 to 9 percent
Cash tax rate	reduce from 33 to 31 percent
Working capital to sales	reduce by 10 percent
Fixed assets to sales	from 12 to 8 percent
WACC	from 13 to 11 percent
Competitive advantage period	increase from 8 to 10 years

In this way companies can translate capital market investment metrics into future performance targets for their managers.

Linkages and metrics

Following on from this, you will need to link these goals to a series of other more localized value drivers. The connections between strategy, operations and compensation systems need to be identified to ensure a single consistent focus internally. These linkages are particularly important in that they can institutionalize targeted changes in the management process and galvanize management action. Performance metrics serve a crucial role in providing these linkages. Indeed in many respects they form the heart of the implementation strategy.

Without a set of relevant value-focused measures, your organization could find it almost impossible to correlate progress in attaining results tied to its strategies. But if these areas are properly linked through a balanced set of performance metrics, senior executives and managers will find themselves with their hands on all the controls required to implement strategy and achieve objectives. At this stage, it is important to spend time ensuring an effective consensus as to what needs to be achieved.

Performance measurement (and performance management) links value from the top to the bottom of an organization. It takes top-down-driven targets and connects them with company-specific, operational drivers. By identifying these operational, or micro, drivers – examples of which are given in the bottom "level" of Fig. 7.10 – and linking them to shareholder value, most companies will develop new insights into their business and new tools to test alternatives.

One of the key messages of value-based management is that shareholder value is created or destroyed at the point where management decisions are made. So you should be aware, as a member of front-line or middle management, of the SHV implications of every decision that you make – which means that performance measurement and reward processes should reflect and reinforce the creation of shareholder value.

As Fig. 7.11 illustrates, different kinds of decision are made at different levels in an organization. Matters of strategy, such as the question of which market your company should actually be in, are dealt with by the chairman, CEO and CFO; at the next level down, in strategic business units, decisions about capital expenditure and investment in (for instance) product development or new distribution networks are taken; while at operating unit level it's a question of detailed planning and budgeting. We think of this as "cascading"

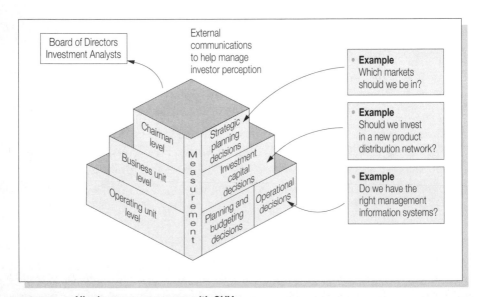

FIG 7.10 ● Aligning your processes with SHV

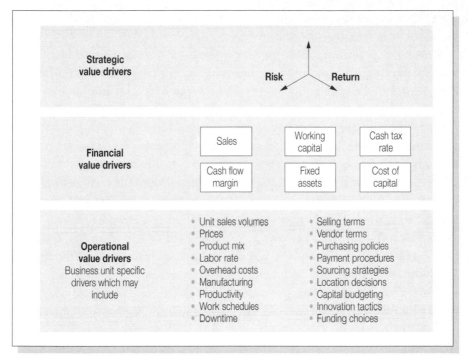

FIG 7.11 ● **From macro to micro SHV drivers**

the strategy down into the organization. But at whatever level you are working, the principles of value-based management apply: you should establish strategies that are clearly understood, and monitor them by being able to measure efficiently – and reward effectively – the creation of SHV.

These different levels of decision are reflected in Fig. 7.11, where the levels are identified as strategic, financial and operational, and a number of operational drivers (sometimes referred to as "micro drivers") are linked with the basic risk/growth/return requirements of the market by six macro drivers. The diagram starts with some broad corporate-level (strategic) goals, which could be the three basic "imperatives" of risk, growth and returns outlined above (corporate strategies). The important thing, though, is to go beyond this and establish a link between the macro drivers and a series of more micro or operational value drivers of the sort described at the bottom of the diagram.

Using the micro drivers

It can be difficult sometimes to see how the seven value drivers relate to the day-to-day business of your company. As Tom Copeland and his colleagues put it in their book *Valuation*,[7] "Generic value drivers lack specificity and cannot be used well at grassroots level."

One way to deal with this is by using econometric business modelling which enables managers to evaluate the shareholder value impact in individual business units of changes to key operating parameters. This is where you can introduce into your calculations factors such as prices, staffing levels, maintenance, marketing costs, debtors and capital spend.

These operating value drivers can be used to make projections for each business unit's financial status before being consolidated to determine the macro value drivers at a corporate level. Figure 7.11, with its examples of operational value drivers, may have already suggested to you some ways in which the two kinds of driver – micro and macro – provide a structure for evaluating business units. Let us take a closer look to see what action can be taken at the "micro" level under the heading of each macro value driver.

Here, then, are some examples of initiatives we have observed being undertaken by global corporations to generate SHV. We have listed them according to which of the macro value drivers they affect. (Some of these initiatives will have an impact on more than one driver.)

Revenue growth rate

- Ensure profitable growth that will add value.
- Consider new market entry.
- Develop new products.
- Globalize the business.
- Develop customer loyalty programs.
- Offer pricing advantage with new distribution outlets.
- Develop focused advertising based on differentiation.

Operating margin growth

- Modernize working practices.
- Restructure including introduction of multi-skilling.
- Cut costs by sharing services and outsourcing.
- Centralize and consolidate back office and finance functions (treasury, tax, corporate finance, financial systems).
- Introduce business process re-engineering with IT systems initiatives including consolidation and integration of billing, customer care, activity-based costing, data warehousing, network management and configuration.

Cash tax rate

- Consider international holding structure.
- Locate and exploit intellectual property and brands.
- Minimize withholding taxes.
- Use coordination centers.
- Customs duty and transfer pricing planning.
- Minimize foreign and withholding taxes.

Working capital

- Implement working capital reviews.
- Improve debtor management.
- Introduce supply chain management systems and just-in-time inventory methods.

Capital expenditure

- Develop capital appraisal and utilization reviews and project finance techniques.
- Weigh up lease versus buy decisions.
- Develop treasury, hedging and risk management systems.

WACC (weighted average cost of capital)

- Build management understanding of cost of capital.
- Calculate gearing/leverage optimization.
- Calculate business-unit-specific WACC.
- Consider share buy-backs and demerger of non-core business.

Competitive advantage period

- Improve investor relations by providing predictable and sustainable financial performance.
- Improve business unit cash flow information.
- Return to core competencies.
- Develop executive performance reward schemes linked to share price improvement.
- Give all employees the opportunity to have an economic stake in the company.
- Incorporate strong risk management procedures.

Once you have been able to break out of the corporate goals into much more specific quantitative (and qualitative) goals such as those listed above, you will have built a bridge between operational decisions on one side, and contributions to shareholder value on the other. As Fig. 7.11 illustrated, decisions are best taken within organizations at the level where they can make the most difference.

Understanding the value chain

An important step in introducing an effective performance measurement system is to record the processes which your company goes through to deliver value. This is your corporate "value chain" – see Fig. 7.12 – which should show the key value functions of your company, each of which must be capable of individual performance measurements. Once you have an agreed value chain, key strategies can be developed and decisions taken to link these strategies to a shareholder value improvement program.

The five-stage value chain in a pharmaceutical company, for example, may start with R&D, move to inbound logistics, then to production, outbound logistics and to marketing and sales. In a service organization the five stages may be to identify and develop new services and products; recruit, train and retain professionals; attract clients; run effective marketing and sales operations; and service and retain clients effectively.

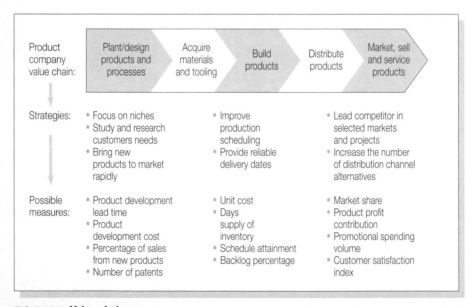

FIG 7.12 ● Value chain

Practical implementation

In your initial implementation of value-based performance management, you may focus on a short-term improvement program that allows quick wins to be realized at the earliest opportunity. But in the longer term, value management must be implemented through a well executed change program – see Fig. 7.13.

In summary, you must tailor performance measures for improving shareholder value to suit each business unit in your organization, and these measures must be ones that the business unit can itself have some control over. At the same time, these measures must be tied in to the short- and long-term targets of the business unit – which in turn will be linked to corporate strategy and targets. The performance measures are based on the key macro and operating value drivers of the business unit and combine both financial and operating measures in the value scorecard. We will return to the use of "scorecards" in our final chapter.

Some performance measures can serve as very valuable early warning signals: customer reports, market share and sales trends, for instance, can be very useful. Other financial measures, however, may only track the past – in which case you may find corrective action will take some time to implement.

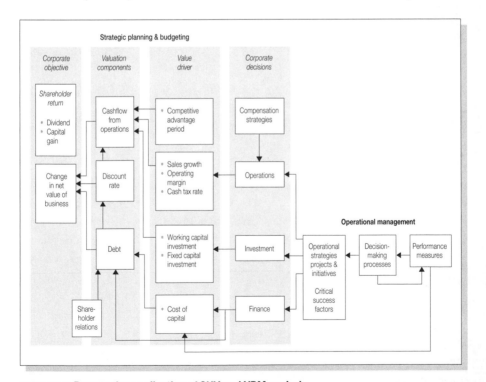

FIG 7.13 ● **Progressive application of SHV and VBM analysis**

Compensation

Two elements of Fig. 7.13 have yet to be dealt with: compensation strategies and shareholder communication. For an effective value-based management program to be fully implemented within a corporation, you will need to incentivize – to link your compensation system to value creation. A successfully directed value-based management program will, we recognize, make big demands on a management: if you respond to the challenge, you deserve to be rewarded. The linkage of remuneration to value creation will, we believe, promote a culture of performance and ownership that rewards shareholder value maximization and empowers employees to manage the business as if it were their own. Such a system will ensure that the interests of shareholders and employees are aligned.

The importance of the right kind of corporate culture is emphasized by the anonymous CFO of a large US company:[8] "In 1995, we established a pay-for-performance plan that went right down to the lowest-level employee and was based on earnings growth and return to the shareholder," he reports. "So everyone in the company became interested in what was happening to the share price."

Once senior management has identified the measures that can be managed to create shareholder value, both executives and employees must be rewarded according to the extent they meet their targets.[9]

No one measure is appropriate for all employees at all levels, nor is one time frame applicable to all people. But any incentive compensation system based on value creation will have certain key features distinguishing it from more traditional plans found in the corporate community today. It will be based on economic performance, which emphasizes cash flow, the amount of capital invested to generate that cash flow, and the cost of the invested capital. It will also use different periods of time to motivate both short-term and longer-term results that collectively lead to value maximization. It may be appropriate for senior managers to address SHV with a longer-range perspective and long-term goals, while people in middle management or on the shop floor will view value through a short-term lens.

By carefully designing a value-based incentive plan that contains an appropriate level of risk and reward, a company can motivate and inspire all employees throughout an organization to work for value creation – to make decisions and take actions that support the value philosophy. (See Fig. 7.14 for an example.) With the right kind of performance metrics, individuals at all levels who are responsible for delivering value should understand what is

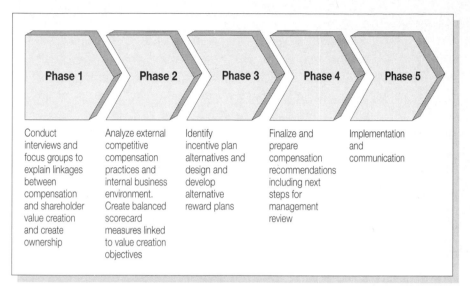

FIG 7.14 ● **Five-phase compensation program approach**

required of them. To ensure they are strongly motivated, their objectives should:

● relate directly to executives' and employees' day-to-day responsibilities;

● be balanced between short-term and long-term objectives;

● contribute to reaching the organization's strategic goals and shareholder value objectives.

There is not the space to go into great detail about the variety of compensation schemes that have been devised – from LTIPs (long-term incentive plans) and share options to performance shares and phantom stock plans – and to what extent they meet the three criteria listed. Suffice it to say that the concerns that have been expressed, particularly in the USA and the UK, over "excessive" executive pay awards are resulting in changes to the way compensation packages are put together. Rolls Royce, for example, in 1997, replaced its executive share options scheme with a long-term incentive plan under which shares worth up to the value of 60 percent of salary would be granted if a shareholder return comparable with "at least" 19 other leading engineering companies was achieved.[10]

Value communications and reporting

Although your company may create and preserve value, your investors will not realize this value unless an effective communications program is in place. Such value communications programs have both internal and external purposes. Internally, they educate the entire workforce about corporate strategies and goals, and have clear linkages both to operations (what they do) and compensation (what they are paid). This education process will teach everyone to think and communicate in the same terms – once again aligning goals with actions.

Your education process also needs to be able to demonstrate to managers and others within your company why the market matters. As Barry Romeril, CFO at Xerox, has said,

> It's good for investors to meet a broader spectrum of management, but it's probably more beneficial for the broader spectrum of management to understand who are the people making decisions to buy, what's driving their decision, and what their thought processes are.[11]

Equally, investor communications must aim at ensuring that investors understand your company's value-based strategies and goals, and are confident in management's ability to implement those objectives and deliver on them. With the right information, investors can develop an informed view on growth, return, and risk assumptions in assessing value. If investors do not understand or do not believe in management's ability to deliver on these strategies and goals, then your market value will reflect a less informed – or a more pessimistic – view of your company's prospects.

In other words, if you want to ensure that market value reflects the real intrinsic value of your company, you must clearly communicate your strategy and implementation plans. Such communication, combined with a good track record of management delivering on expectations, is critical for investors.

Not only in the USA and the UK, but also in continental Europe, successful companies are beginning to recognize that they must actively spread the news about their targets and achievements if their shares are to be properly valued. Daimler-Benz, based in Germany, saw the importance of investor relations when it sought a listing on the New York Stock Exchange in 1994: it was only then, after meeting US analysts, that it saw that good investor relations could not only raise its profile but also thereby reduce the cost of its equity capital.

Analysts and institutional investors agree that regular access to the highest levels of management is essential. A survey by the Investor Relations Society found that more than 60 percent of CFOs and 45 percent of CEOs spend a "significant" amount of time on investor relations. This kind of effort is not likely to decrease as company managements find that developing their presentation and communication skills is essential in today's corporate environment.

In the words of one investor relations specialist,[12] "In Germany and elsewhere in Europe, there is a new generation of managers who know exactly what the international capital markets expect of them. ... They are embracing all the established investor relations techniques – from roadshows to teleconferencing and market research – and are receptive to new ideas."

LINKAGES AND OBSTACLES

All the five core value processes of Fig. 7.7 must be addressed if a company is to create long-term sustainable value – and addressed in a way that provides strong linkages between each of them. Compensation structures, for example, must be closely tied to performance management objectives; and investor communications must link directly to corporate value strategies and goals. Strong linkages across the five core processes will ensure that value is created, preserved, and realized just as in Fig. 7.8.

All the same, attaining value transformation is not easy. Throughout the course of a major initiative, a wide variety of issues, challenges, and problems will surface which can sidetrack – often irrevocably – value creation. These obstacles do not generally arise out of any negative intentions, but simply reflect the fact that people initially resist, rather than embrace, major change. You will need to address such organizational and cultural inertia promptly whenever it occurs in the life cycle of a transformation program. Table 7.1 shows the major stages in a transformation initiative, the typical challenges that may have to be addressed, and the approaches that can be used to overcome resistance.

TABLE 7.1 ● **Major stages in a transformation challenge**

Major transformation stages/challenges	Successful approaches
Evaluate/envision	
● Project does not have support of senior management	● Reset priorities, have CEO sponsorship
● Transition management activities ignored in work planning	● Include in project planning
● Limited communication of project objectives	● Formal internal/external communication programs
● Full impact on shareholder values not determined	● Embed value analysis in management processes
● Performance metrics addressed as afterthought	● Use value drivers to define metrics
● Perceived as the consultant's product	● Joint project teams
Empower	
● Users are reluctant to participate in the change	● Joint project teams
● Users have not bought into the value creation process	● Compensation/incentive program based on value creation
● User acceptance is not occurring as rapidly as possible	● Focus on quick wins, showcase victories
● Decision and issue resolution is not timely	● Have identified sponsors/decision makers
● Turf battles among different teams	● Install issue resolution system
● Team members not pulling weight	● Dedicate best people
Excel	
● Continuous improvement team meetings are addressing broad/general issues	● Revisit team charter – focus on specific issues
● No systematic approach to problem solving being followed	● Use common language, tool kits, training etc.
● Unfounded assumptions made about what the customer wants or what drives value	● Refocus team on customer service and/or the key value drivers

SUSTAINING VBM

Whatever happens, the market overall, and institutional shareholders in particular, will continue to act as judge and jury in determining how the senior management teams of public companies perform. How well or poorly you and your colleagues develop, implement, and deliver value-creating strategies will be critical to the verdicts that these investors render. This is why an increasing number of CEOs and CFOs are seeking to ensure that all decision-making in their organizations is aligned towards an overall shareholder value objective.

In this chapter we have been talking about value-based management (VBM), which closes the gap between strategy and implementation, the standard mode of business for the entire enterprise. Shareholder value theory provides the framework within which each of the five core processes listed above can be examined, changed, and linked together.

The kind of change envisaged will drive your company's strategy, resource allocation, performance management, compensation, and communications in new directions. For even the most successful companies, implementing this transformation will ensure the institutionalization of decision-making processes that enhance SHV.

AND THE FUTURE?

Technology marches on, and recent developments in the area of information technology and the internet are having their impact on SHV and its implementation within the corporation too. Looking ahead, we can speculate that the current uneasy mismatch between a variety of controlling systems within an organization will look increasingly quaint and odd in the new century. In our view, the corporation of the future will look considerably sleeker than it does today, as a variety of systems are integrated to help create the "virtual" company.

At the moment, companies often have very discrete and separate systems in place for budgeting, planning, statutory accounting and performance measurement. These systems have typically grown up at different points in their history, and little thought was given to how they could be integrated, or even whether they should be integrated.

In the future, a successful organization may no longer have the luxury of being able to support a whole range of incompatible and non-integrated systems. As decision and planning horizons shorten, and more and more real-time information becomes available, so it will become increasingly necessary to ensure that this information is successfully integrated to create an accurate, up-to-the-minute picture of how the company is performing. In our view this will mean ensuring that the management information systems, the statutory accounting information and other tools for planning and budgeting are organized to provide a continuous "read-out" that registers whether the company is creating or destroying shareholder value.

These trends will become the more apparent as accounting systems become more closely harmonized, and as investor demands for more current information are met. Standards of quarterly reporting, common in the USA, may become a requirement in Europe and Japan as well – all of which will speed up reporting cycles and make it more and more necessary to compile and interpret the available material quickly. As this happens, so those companies more attuned to the needs of investors will find ways of ensuring that it is passed on, in an appropriate form, to the financial markets. What we could see is something like Fig. 7.15 below.

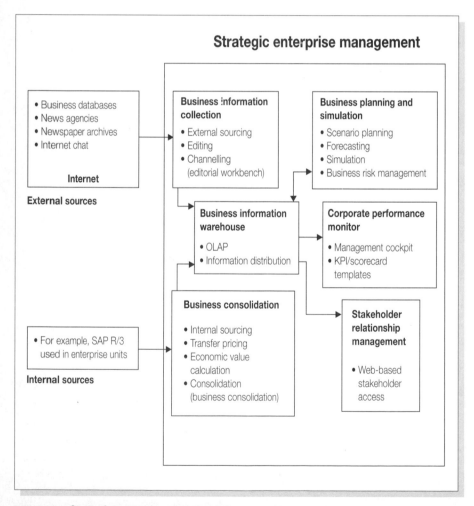

FIG 7.15 ● Strategic enterprise management

What can be termed strategic enterprise management systems will become practical solutions to handling the flood of information as more and more enterprise processes are digitalized. As more and more information becomes available, so it is increasingly likely that we could see the creation of special executive information rooms, or cockpits, which will give the CEO and his immediate staff access to all the important components of their organization.

This in turn will underline the importance of a better understanding of the stock systems and flows within the corporation, and their dynamic context. Areas that were previously the domain of operational research departments and highly trained systems dynamics experts are now becoming accessible to a wider audience. More sophisticated modelling of different processes is possible along the lines shown below in Fig. 7.16.

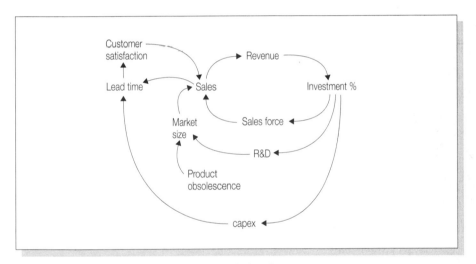

FIG 7.16 ● **Dynamic modelling of processes within a firm**

As these techniques become more widespread, and our understanding of them increases, so it will be easier to draw up strategies that draw on recognized synergies, and which show where there are increasing returns from pursuing a particular course of action. Conversely, we will be able to better understand how the achievement of certain other goals can be mutually exclusive and leave the organization little better off as a result. In all these processes, the SHV metric will be highly useful as a means of unambiguously describing the major benefits a particular strategy should create.

SUMMARY

In this chapter we have looked at how a shareholder value approach concentrates on sustaining and increasing value at the creation, preservation and realization stages. We did this by focusing on the five core value processes, and showed how it is possible to move from a very macro level of analysis into a very detailed agenda of quantitative and qualitative targets which can be applied and implemented at an operational level. We also commented on several obstacles that can prevent the implementation of such an approach. Finally we outlined how SHV will tie into ideas of the "virtual" corporation of the future.

Notes

1. *Financial Times,* 9 November 1999, p.27.

2. Kaplan, R.S. and Norton, D.P. (1992) "The Balanced Scorecard – Measures that Drive Performance," *Harvard Business Review*, January–February.

3. For more detail see Puschaver, L. and Eccles, R.G. (1996) "In Pursuit of the Upside: The New Opportunity in Risk Management," *PW Review*, December, 7.

4. Quoted in *CFO 2000: The Global CFO as Strategic Busines Partner.* Conference Board Europe 1997, p.14.

5. Price Waterhouse Change Integration Team, *The Paradox Principles: How High-Performance Companies Manage Chaos, Complexity and Contradiction to Achieve Superior Results.* Chicago: Irwin, p.46.

6. Prahalad, C.K. and Hamel, G. (1990) "The Core Competence of the Corporation," *Harvard Business Review*, May–June.

7. Copeland, T., Koller, T. and Murrin, J. (McKinsey & Company, Inc.) (1996) *Valuation: Measuring and Managing the Value of Companies*, 2nd edition. New York: John Wiley.

8. Quoted in *CFO 2000: The Global CFO as Strategic Business Partner.* Conference Board Europe 1997, p.17.

9. In 1999, Jack Welch vetoed the idea of rewarding staff according to the profits made on investments: "If we are trying to maximize collective intellect we can't have people in separate rowboats." Defending the priniciple that all GE compensation should be tied to GE stock, he said, "They can have more compensation but everyone should be tied to one currency ... There's no single business and no single person that's going to change the company, including me." *Financial Times*, 9 November 1999, p.27.

10. *Financial Times*, 11 April 1997.

11. *CFO 2000: The Global CFO as Strategic Business Partner*. Conference Board Europe, p.11.

12. Bill Stokoe, investor relations specialist at Brunswick.

SHV AT WAR: MERGERS AND ACQUISITIONS

One of the most compelling reasons for taking the concept of shareholder value seriously is that investors already do. In other words, as we have argued, it is in your interest to see your company the way the market sees it. This is especially true in cases where one company seeks to take over, or merge with, another.

In this book we have already made several references to takeovers – mostly looking at them from the point of view of the victim. When (in Chapter 3) we discussed the importance of ensuring a return for investors above the cost of capital, we implied that it was important to avoid becoming a takeover target – which you could do by delivering consistently high returns to your shareholders. But if your assets cannot earn a return higher than the cost of capital, we argued, then investors will eventually withdraw their funds, making your company a takeover target.

This is certainly true in markets where SHV (and value-based management) is taken seriously. But here we want to take a different angle and look at the whole business of mergers and acquisitions (M&A) from the point of view of the shareholder and of the potential acquirer.

As investors adjust their expectations in the light of how a company is performing, so opportunities may arise for buying companies "on the cheap." Using the Q ratio introduced in Chapter 6, both investors and managers can establish which is less expensive: to invest in new assets or to buy up undervalued assets from someone else.

In this chapter we want to show in more detail how you can use the insights of shareholder value theory for the purpose of acquiring and divesting companies. The SHV approach, we believe, offers a superior basis for establishing what the medium-term impact of a merger or takeover will be. Essentially, it can establish whether any merger or acquisition will be in the interests of the acquiring firm's shareholders – a group that has not been particularly well rewarded to date.

MERGERS AND ECONOMIC CYCLES

Massive merger and acquisition activity has continued into the new millennium, easily surpassing the peak of the cycle in the 1980s – see Fig. 8.1. Cash-rich companies have been looking for other profitable outlets in the belief that, either by diversifying into new areas or by increasing their market share in their existing markets, they will prosper further. Cheap finance and buoyant expectations about the future also contribute to these merger waves, as does the willingness of the market to absorb all paper deals.

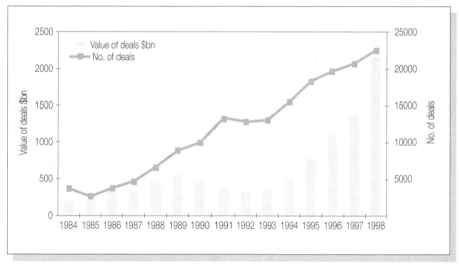

FIG 8.1 ● Worldwide M&A activity 1984–98

Source: Securities Data Corporation

The boom of the 1980s has both similarities and differences with that of the 1990s. In both, the background has been one of booming stock markets and high levels of bank lending available to oil the wheels for the required financing. But the underlying trends tell a different story. In the 1980s the fashionable conglomerates of the 1970s were broken up and an often hostile search took place to capture value from under-performing assets. The economics of such transactions were mostly based on driving out costs in the companies that were acquired.

M&A activity in the 1990s, on the other hand, has been more to do with the strategic development of core activities, the holy grail of global size and the drive for top-line income growth. This in turn has been sparked off by a shift to a low-inflation environment which has made it much more difficult for hard-pressed companies to pass on high costs as higher prices to their customers. The aim to drive out costs remains but these are not the costs of excess – which most companies had necessarily to deal with in the leaner years of the late 1980s and early 1990s – but rather the benefits available through combining similar business activities.

THE PROS AND CONS OF TAKEOVERS

Before looking at what can and should happen in the field of mergers and acquisitions, let us consider how effective such operations have been in the past. Shareholder value theory suggests that M&A activity is an important mechanism to keep capital flowing to the areas that need it the most. Capital, it can be said, will seek out the areas of highest return and provide investors with handsome rewards for the risks taken. The question is whether this has happened. At the moment the weight of evidence shows that it hasn't.

Table 8.1 summarizes the excess return made by the acquiring firm in various decades as established in a number of academic studies. It did not matter whether the transaction was a merger or a tender offer (bid). In all the cases surveyed the same trend is evident. Acquiring firms had a small excess positive return in the 1960s that had generally turned negative in the 1980s.

TABLE 8.1 ● **Excess returns following mergers and tenders: recent studies**[1]

Study	Transaction type	Excess return compared with the market during the ...		
		1960s	1970s	1980s
Loderer and Martin (1990)	Tender and merger	1.7%	0.6%	−0.07%
Jarrell, Brickley and Netter (1988)	Tender	4.4	1.2	−1.1
Bradley, Desai and Kim (1988)	Tender	4.1	1.3	−2.93
Asquith, Bruner and Mullins (1983)	Mergers	4.6	1.7	n/a

A McKinsey study[2] of the 1980s also concluded that a mere 37 percent of US acquirers outperformed their peers in terms of total shareholder returns. A slightly happier picture emerges in a 1996 survey, carried out in the USA by Mercer Management Consulting,[3] which found that of 300 transactions in the 1990s above $500 million, 53 percent outperformed their peers over the ensuing three-year period – implying that the other 47 percent either under-performed, or at best were just on a level with, their peers. More recent work, though, shows that, in 56 percent of takeovers, the acquirer's share price falls when a deal is announced. More depressingly, in more than two-thirds of takeovers, the acquirer's share price has underperformed the market a year after the event.

This leaves a large question mark over the economic rationale for many of these large transactions. If the market is generally fair in its valuation of companies on a stand-alone basis, how does that square with the economics of acquisition, where a 25 to 40 percent premium is a normal requirement for gaining control? Clearly, in shareholder value terms, it often means that the acquirer is passing over the value of the first chunk of available gains to the vendor shareholders. For the acquirer's shareholders to obtain any benefit, the income growth and cost savings have to be considerable.

This is illustrated by one well-known hostile transaction in the late 1980s, when a large US corporate paid a premium of 69 percent over the pre-bid rumor price for a pharmaceutical company. You did not have to be a genius to predict that the winners would be the target company's shareholders. Certainly the market saw it that way immediately and slashed the acquiring company's share price following the announcement. Although this might be an extreme case, the fact remains that shareholders of acquiring companies have not generally prospered, while the shareholders of the acquired companies have.

Shareholders of companies that have fended off unwelcome bids from outsiders have not prospered either. A 1996 study by Scottish Amicable,[4] which looked at 15 UK companies that had successfully fought off a hostile bid approach in the past ten years, showed that these companies subsequently under-performed the stock market by up to 25 percent.

These figures suggest that a lot of M&A activity pays insufficient attention to the question of whether any new combinations will in fact help increase SHV for the acquiring firms – which is the aim of the exercise. Indeed, while the act of taking over or merging with another company ought to raise shareholder value for the acquirer, the apparent inability of companies to ensure this suggests that M&A is sometimes an obstacle to achieving this goal.

This aspect can be more clearly seen in Table 8.2. Here we compare the premium paid in a merger, in this case measured by the premium in the market-to-book ratio, with the rate of return required to pay for it. The rate of return varies with the investment horizon, but the table clearly shows how high takeover premia require a large and sustained improvement in performance if the purchase price is ever to be fully justified.

TABLE 8.2 ● **Excess returns needed to justify premium over and above the "normal" rate of return (after Sirower[5])**

Bid premium	Rate of return required over 1 year	Rate of return required over 2 years	Rate of return required over 3 years	Rate of return required over 4 years	Rate of return required over 5 years	Rate of return required over 10 years
0%	15	15	15	15	15	15
25%	44	29	24	21	20	17
50%	73	41	32	27	24	19
75%	101	52	39	32	29	22

It must never be forgotten how much additional performance is required to justify a purchase price premium, particularly if the acquirer has to show some material benefits over a shorter, rather than longer, time period. As we said earlier, bid premia of between 25 percent and 40 percent are by no means unknown, and they require between 17 percent and nearly 30 percent extra annual performance from the target over a whole decade if they are to show value to their own shareholders.

But if bid premia require a large and sustained increase in performance from the target firm (and to a degree from the acquiring firm as well), why do these premia exist at all? We think the answer may lie in considering the market for corporate control, which helps explain why acquirers are often predisposed to pay over the odds for a company.

THE MARKET FOR CONTROL

It's a common story: a savvy predator spies a weaker rival and thinks that it can control and make more money out of its assets than the current incumbents can. The acquiring company's normally sane and careful managers are then driven systematically to over-pay for the companies they buy. As a result, a widespread destruction of shareholder value takes place, leaving observers to doubt the efficacy of capital markets. Can anything justify this apparently irrational behavior, or are we to ascribe it to *hubris* or to some other factor?

We think we can identify some reasons, and these can be found in the market for corporate control. The special feature of equities as opposed to debt is that equity holders actually own the company in a way that debt-holders do not. Just as we can talk about geared or "leveraged" companies on the debt side,

a rather similar phenomenon exists on the equity side too. Mergers and acquisitions, particularly acquisitions, offer the possibility for the equity holders of
one firm to massively increase their control of assets of another firm for a
sometimes surprisingly small amount of extra money. Irrespective of any
synergies achieved (see below), this alone can provide a tempting reason to go
on the acquisition trail.

Looking at acquisitions from a control perspective offers other insights too.
It can help explain why acquiring firms are prepared to offer premia to gain
"control," and also why "backward" acquisitions, when smaller companies
successfully take over larger rivals, occur. In this section, we outline a situation
in terms of the motives for a transaction; it is, however, the effects of the transaction that are just as important as the motives for its taking place – which may
be other than we describe. (It should be borne in mind that the underlying
reason for a transaction will be to gain access to superior financial performance.)

One important aspect to consider is the difference between the economic
value and the shareholder value of a company. The two are not the same, even
though they are closely related. We define the economic value of a company as
the total sum of resources it uses – including the sum of cash, debt and equity
used in the business. This differs from its shareholder value, which consists of
the sum of equity and cash used in the business minus the debt, and considers
the claims exercisable by shareholders on the total property and resources
owned by the enterprise. This is generally less than the economic value.

The control ratio

Let us now introduce the idea of a "control ratio," which is a type of leverage
ratio describing how many more assets are controlled from the equity base. We
define this as the inverse of the proportion of equity involved in the total of
equity, debt and cash. Thus if equity forms say 25 percent of this total lump of
"value," then we talk of a control ratio being 4.0 – you can control four times
as many assets on the basis of your equity stake. Broadly speaking, buying a
majority shareholding in another company is an effective way of increasing the
amount of control of assets per share. In the absence of any premia the effects
can be quite significant – indeed, they can almost be described as a bargain for
the acquiring firm's shareholders, regardless of any changes effected within the
"victim" firm by the acquirer.

TABLE 8.3 ● Two stand-alone firms – starting positions

	Cash	Debt	Equity	Economic value	Control ratio	Shareholder value
Firm A	10	50	150	210	1.4	160
Firm B	5	20	75	100	1.33	80
Total				310		240

Consider the hypothetical example outlined in Table 8.3. Here the equity position in firm A has a greater "leverage" than in firm B, since firm A has more debt and more cash. So firm A's equity holders control more resources than those in firm B. Now, one of the reasons for mergers and acquisitions is that, for a relatively small increment in the equity stake, the acquiring firm can control a much broader asset base. So let us suppose firm A takes a majority stake (51 percent) in firm B, by issuing additional equity, at existing prices and without any premia; what does the situation look like then?

The situation is described in Table 8.4. There is an increase in the equity of firm A, but despite this, A's equity holders now control more assets (all of company B); so the "control ratio" has risen to 1.65. A's equity has become more high-powered since it now controls both A and B, and there has also been an increase in SHV for firm A.

TABLE 8.4 ● Firm A acquires 50 percent of firm B by raising more equity

	Cash	Debt	Equity	Total value	Control ratio	Shareholder value
Firm A	10	50	150+37.5	247.5	1.65	240
Firm B	5	20	37.5	62.5		
Total				310		

Now, suppose A was to take over B, not by issuing extra shares, but by increasing its debt. The effect can be seen in Table 8.5: the takeover will effectively increase the shareholders "leverage" over the combined firm even more: the control ratio rises to 2.06. On the assumption that both firms are profitable, the benefits from increased control are considerable, allowing the acquiring firm's shareholders to gain access to the acquired firm's cash and earnings stream both now and in the future.

The additional debt does, however, reduce the shareholders' specific claims on the company. Using debt, then, has a slightly paradoxical effect: the equity holders control more assets, but in a narrower sense they own rather less than if the deal had been equity-financed.

For reasons we will come on to in the next chapter, this is more sensible than it seems. A company that is relatively certain of the future would rather not involve additional shareholders and so dilute their stake in what looks like a sure thing. On the other hand, if shareholders are not so certain about the future, then it makes a lot more sense to share the risk and bring more people into the firm, even if this means diluting existing equity positions.

TABLE 8.5 ● **Firm A acquires 50 percent of firm B by increasing its debt**

	Cash	Debt	Equity	Total value	Control ratio	Shareholder value
Firm A	10	50+37.5	150	247.5	2.06	202.5
Firm B	5	20	37.5	62.5		
Total				310		

Explaining high premia

Does this help explain why large premia are offered in acquisitions? We think it does. If the control ratio rises in both the equity- and the debt-financed acquisitions of Tables 8.4 and 8.5, we can say that bid premia reflect a willingness by an acquiring firm's shareholders to pay a "bribe" so that at the limit their control ratio will not go down (in Table 8.3, below 1.4, firm A's starting position). On this basis, in the equity-financed deal, the acquirers are willing to pay, at the most,

$$\frac{\text{economic value}}{\text{control ratio pre-acquisition}} - \frac{\text{economic value}}{\text{control ratio post-acquisition}}$$

or 310/1.4 − 310/1.65, which comes to 33.6. If you add this figure to the sum paid for the 50 percent equity share, you arrive at a maximum potential premium of just under 90 percent. This means that, in control terms, A's shareholders are willing to pay up to 90 percent more for the control of these assets.

For a debt-financed transaction, the premia get even larger. The reason for this is that the leverage exercised by the equity block rises more dramatically. In our example, the maximum potential premium the acquirer would be willing to pay would be 310/1.4 − 310/2.04, which comes to 69.5. In other words the acquirer is prepared to pay up to nearly 70 units more on a debt-financed transaction, and still not be worse off in control terms than in the pre-merger situation. This represents a premium of 185 percent over the increase in debt of 37.5 units.

Although these calculations may seem rather theoretical, they do describe what happens during and after a takeover. The reasons for doing the deal will lie elsewhere, as we shall see below, but the mechanics of what happens will be similar to what we have just described.

The "dog in the manger" syndrome

If the above analysis provides a justification for bid premia, arguments for them are not always couched in such terms. Very often bid premia exist for more fanciful reasons.

While many takeovers are characterized by a desire for greater expansion and power, a fair number of mergers and acquisitions are driven by strategic and defensive considerations. Left to their own devices, many firms would be happy to leave their competitors in peace, or to reject activities in "non-core" areas as being too risky. But often a management will be provoked into action to forestall the threat, real or imagined, of a close competitor acquiring, or making a deal with, another rival.

This "dog in the manger" attitude is founded on the belief that to steal a march on rivals by blocking off their access to a new market, or by boxing them into their existing market, will ultimately benefit the acquirer's shareholders. Where the aims of the acquirer are mainly of this defensive type, it seems to us that the new (larger) group's performance expectations will necessarily be more diffuse. Greater volume and "critical mass" may be thought just as important as raising margins or increasing efficiency. Friendly deals may be struck with the management of the acquired firm, allowing existing business practices to continue. With such an agenda, it is not entirely surprising that the acquirer's subsequent share performance is less than good.

KNOWLEDGE AND TIMING IN M&A

Why do acquirers behave in what seems, particularly to their own shareholders, an irrational manner? In addition to the factors mentioned above, we have often observed an information asymmetry between buyer and seller. The seller will almost always know more clearly what is being sold, and may have a restricted set of opportunities looking ahead into the future. The purchaser, on the other hand, has to make guesses about how the acquired company will fit into its plans, and what changes will be necessary in the acquired firm (and possibly in its own firm, too). The difficulties of pushing through changes if the merger or acquisition is to succeed will tend to be underestimated. Of course the acquirer has one option that the target does not have. If the estimated benefits over a given investment horizon don't "add up," then reasons can often be found for extending the investment horizon. There will always be some time period over which the acquisition will make sense in SHV terms.

The extent of knowledge the acquiring firm has of its target will depend greatly on the nature of the deal, as Fig. 8.2 shows. Generally least is known about a target when a hostile bid is being made, and the most is known in the case of a negotiated deal. Note too that the riskiness of the transaction is also at its greatest with a hostile bid.

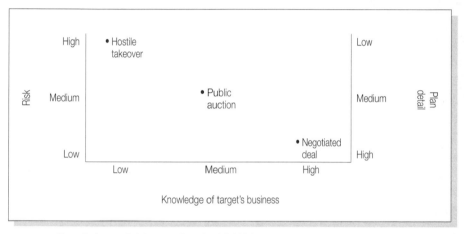

FIG 8.2 ● **Knowledge and risk associated with M&A transactions**

On top of the problems of information gathering, there are also time pressures. Establishing the finance and working out the details of a takeover are expensive. It often involves sharing a lot of highly confidential information with advisers, and leads to perturbations on the stock market. In situations like these, the interests of the acquired company's shareholders are relatively straightforward – they simply want to obtain the best deal now. They are rarely in the position of being able to delay; it is quite simply now or never.

The acquiring company, though, can afford to take a longer view. At the margin it is probably prepared to concede more to the seller, once the decision to go ahead with the deal is made. It can sometimes pay for the acquiring company to be seen to be fair, since this will add to its reputation in the future.[6] These factors, together with the "control ratio" mentioned above, largely account for the substantial bid premia paid for target companies, and takes the underlying valuation of the target some distance from a more soundly based view derived from a hard-nosed SHV framework. As the investment horizon lengthens so the question of performance improvement changes. As Table 8.2 showed, the annual increase in performance required to justify a merger lessens for each year, but you have to maintain this increase over a longer period of time.

Applying a SHV-oriented approach can, we believe, increase the proportion of M&A successes in the future even if it does so by reducing the flow of deals. It could also be applied as a corrective to the sometimes large egos of CEOs, and to the emotion of "getting the deal done."[7] We would like, then, to outline a shareholder value "charter" for acquiring firms' shareholders, which we hope will be useful in clearly specifying what a deal has to deliver in order to benefit the new owners of the combined larger business.

A FRAMEWORK FOR BEST PRACTICE

The link to SHV

Here, we will focus on the likely impact a merger or acquisition might have on the interests of an acquiring company's shareholders, and consider what steps are necessary to make a success of the transaction. We think the approach is logical and should provide a useful guide for any actual negotiations. Any potential purchaser should, we believe, be encouraged to follow this sort of procedure, if only to avoid having to pay fanciful prices for acquisitions of dubious quality.

We suggest a transaction value map along the lines of Figs. 8.3 and 8.4 (see later) as a means of assessing the effects of alternative acquisitions. (Much of what we will go through is drawn from an actual case.) The maps are intended to show how the market evaluates the situation at the time of the transaction. The attainment of the synergies will occur later, and may ultimately differ from the market's estimates; markets are quite good, however, at assessing the value of things on a one-year horizon. Let us look at the elements of this one by one.

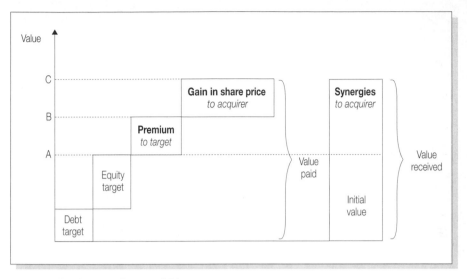

FIG 8.3 ● **A value-creating acquisition**

Initial values and resources used

Acquirer's pre-acquisition value (not shown in the diagram)

Throughout this discussion our point of view will be that of the acquirer's shareholders, and how the acquisition (or merger) might look to them. To this end, you must try to establish as clearly as possible the current stand-alone value of your own company – a process that also should include discussion of the economic value idea mentioned earlier. Remember that we have already seen why acquirers are willing to pay sometimes substantial premia for their acquisitions, based around the improved leverage their equity obtains in relation to the resources it controls. Now we need to know the total value of the resources of the enterprise, including debt. The difference between the book and the market value of the equity should be equal to the market value added, or the profits your company is expected to make over a given investment horizon in the future. If there are serious discrepancies between the internal corporate view and what the market currently thinks, now is the time to fix them. In any event, going into a merger or takeover situation, you must ensure the market is convinced that the proposed deal is a good thing.

The target: gathering data

You also need to build up an estimate of the stand-alone economic value of the target on the same discounted free cash flow basis as outlined above for your own company as the acquirer. Again, this is calculated by looking first at the cash flows and then at the cost of capital. There may be more uncertainties here about cash flow projections, particularly in the early assessment stage of the project when information is limited, and even more so if the target is a private company. The objective should be to arrive at an approximation of the cash flows which can be gradually refined as better information becomes available. This value is shown as the sum of the debt and equity in the diagram, and is marked at "A" in Fig. 8.3.

The purchase

For the reasons we have outlined above, it is unlikely that a bidder will simply pay the going market price for the equity and other assets. The acquirer is seeking to get more control cheaply, while the target is interested in maximizing its shareholder value immediately. So in many cases a premium will be paid, the size very possibly determined along the lines suggested above. This is sometimes called the "anticipated takeout value," and is the price that a bidder anticipates having to pay to be accepted by the target firm's shareholders. This is marked by "B" in the diagram.

The market's reaction

The premium paid does not mark the end of the matter. During the transaction, especially if it is a contested bid, there will be price movements in the acquiring firm's share price. History is replete with examples where the news of an impending deal is greeted with great enthusiasm by the market, while in other cases informed opinion looks very coolly on the proposal and marks the acquiring firm's shares down.

These contrasting reactions are illustrated in Figs. 8.3 and 8.4. In Fig. 8.3 the market reaction is positive, and the acquiring firm's shares are marked up to point C. This gain reflects an *ex ante* payment to the incumbent shareholders of the acquiring firm, who are receiving an increase in the value of their shares in expectation of great things to come in the future. Hence, the total "value" that is now at stake in the transaction has risen, and this is of great importance since it will greatly influence what has to happen later in the merged firm to justify the transaction.

Synergies

Synergy literally means "combined action," and in the context of M&A it is the advantage of combining operations in two or more units that is generally sought. By bringing units more closely together, an acquiring company will be looking to avoid duplication and to pursue economies of scope; a new combined entity should be able to take advantage of having assets in different locations to carry out existing business strategies more effectively.

Synergies can be seen in what is called the "value received" side of the deal. The acquirers have not only paid a fair price for the assets, but they have effectively entered into a commitment to produce sufficient value (additional cash flow) to justify the sums paid out. In Fig. 8.3 this extra amount that has to be produced is described as the synergies that will have to be produced from the transaction over the expected investment horizon.

It is not the purpose of this chapter to enter into a discussion about the wide variety of synergies, but it might be helpful to bear in mind that at a global, "consolidated" level synergies can be thought of as projects that will yield a positive return – or following Sirower,[8] their value should equal the difference between the net present value (NPV) of the synergy and the NPV of the premium paid to get it. Figure 8.3 is drawn so that this appears to be the case globally. It may be difficult, however, to really establish just what the premium paid was for any particular synergy.

The nature and scope of synergies often tend to be exaggerated, and companies can be too optimistic about when they will be achieved. Our analysis concentrates on cash flows, and it is useful to try and relate all expected synergies to this one measure, since this is going to be the most important way in which they will impact on shareholder value. Usually four basic sorts of synergies can be identified: cost savings, income generation, tax benefits and financial engineering.

Cost savings

Typically, acquirers are best at estimating areas for combined cost savings. These can be thought of as the "hard synergies" whose achievement one can be pretty sure of. For instance at Granada Forte (see below), head office costs were reduced from £75 million to £50 million, and an anticipated £20 million saving in purchasing economies turned into a £30 million saving. This meant that half the forecast savings were reached within the first six months of the merger. Something similar happened with the Lloyds TSB-Cheltenham and Gloucester merger. A 40 percent savings in headquarters costs in one year resulted in a £220 million saving by 1998, well on track to reach a £400 million saving target by the following year.

Synergies are often at their greatest when one company acquires another in the same industry. Some key points need to be made:

● The process needs to look at both the net present value of synergies available within the target, calculated at the target's WACC, and where relevant within the acquirer, at the acquirer's WACC. They will have to be compared to the cost of any incremental resources needed, along the lines of the VROI calculation shown in Chapter 6.

● It is fundamentally important for the acquiring company to involve operational management in its own relevant division or divisions in arriving at any estimates of likely synergies. This will help sort out problems arising from the use of different cost categories in the two companies, and from the differing distribution of work within them. Some plans to reduce headcount at different levels of an organization assume that things happen in the same place in the target firm as in the acquirer's. This is very often not the case, and the net saving in jobs may turn out to be rather smaller than expected.

● The estimated timing of the available synergies needs special attention. Here a preliminary assessment of the "softer" areas of possible integration becomes critical. Culture and organizational match and compatibility of systems and processes will all make a difference to the time in which synergies can be realistically achieved: in other words, you need to consider how soon synergy is possible – and how much. This can have a material bearing on gearing levels and on when a group may be expected to hit a pre-determined profitability target.

Income generation

Then comes the more difficult task of assessing the effect of an acquisition on income growth. The easier part will be to estimate the opportunities arising from such aspects as technology transfer and access to the target's distribution channels for the acquirer's products or services and vice versa. There are several examples of this. When Lloyds-TSB acquired the Cheltenham and Gloucester Building Society and Abbey Life they were able to sell those financial products to a much larger retail customer base. The revenue subsequently generated was much higher than the individual parts of the organization could have achieved on their own.

In the specific case of the Cheltenham and Gloucester, Lloyds-TSB transferred its mortgage product to the acquired company, and was immediately able to reduce its mortgage rate by 25 basis points. This helped raise the combined share of the mortgage market in the UK from 11 to 20 percent.

More intangible potential effects will need to be estimated, too. These may include:

● Loss of income in the target or acquirer from customer overlap (e.g. customers who currently dual-source from the acquirer and target – the "cannibalization" effect);

● Competitor reaction to the acquisition negating some of the assumed synergies;

● Intervention by regulatory or competition agencies.

The effect of these, in the assumptions made both in cost and income synergies, will mean that a variety of sensitivity analyses will need to be run at this stage, in order to arrive at a "most likely" scenario for preliminary evaluation purposes.

By assessing both the cost savings and the likely income generation effects of a merger on the acquiring and the target firm, you can reach an overall estimate of what sort of value the combined group should be able to achieve, after allowing for the costs of getting there. This needs to be carefully compared with the "synergies" already estimated in Fig. 8.3, and it goes without saying that it is important for the management of the combined enterprise to quickly establish whether the likely achievable synergies are consistent with what the market thinks is going to happen. In the words of Warren Buffett:

> The market, like the Lord, helps those who help themselves. But unlike the Lord, the market does not forgive those who know not what they do. … A too high purchase price for the stock of an excellent company can undo the effects of a subsequent decade of favorable business development.[9]

Financial engineering

You can now make a preliminary assessment of financing alternatives, bearing in mind that the form of finance has a strong bearing on any outcome. There is a considerable body of evidence that suggests that debt- and cash-financed transactions subsequently perform much better than those financed by equity alone. In an extensive empirical analysis Sirower[10] established that this is one of the major determinants of success.

Some acquirers may have little flexibility in the alternatives available – for example, a high level of existing debt may make financing through equity the only possible strategy. But let us assume here that, as an acquirer, you have full flexibility between equity and debt. The main constraint might be that debt will become marginally more expensive if it causes your overall debt rating to move into a lower category, and that the risks associated with equity will rise when debt exceeds what the market regards as a sensible level. We also need to consider that additional debt will effectively dilute the claims of the existing shareholders. Obviously, the main aim will be to finance the acquisition at the lowest appropriate cost of capital, sometimes with the secondary objective of creating a more effective finance structure.

In a recent transaction between Credit Suisse and Winterthur, financial engineering provided up to 10 percent of the forecast synergies. This was to be achieved by reducing funding costs through optimized capital management. Financial engineering can also allow an acquiring company to re-finance the target's debt at a more favorable borrowing rate without affecting the acquirer's credit rating.

Tax benefits

These can be divided into two types: tax "structuring" that enables the transaction to take place; and tax planning, which ensures that the new tax rate for the merged group is lower than the blended tax rates of the two stand-alone companies. Tax structuring is designed to avoid as many one-off tax charges, related to the deal, as possible. In particular, care is needed to keep any transferable tax losses that might arise through a change in ownership, and to ensure the minimization of any exposure to capital gains taxes.

Tax planning is designed to minimize ongoing tax liabilities, and mergers and acquisitions may provide a good backdrop against which to do this. Areas with the greatest scope for achieving tax reductions include transferring brands and other intellectual property to lower tax jurisdictions. The re-positioning of central purchasing and shared service centers in tax-advantaged locations can help as well. As you get into the exercise in more detail, so there may be additional chances to reduce tax burdens by pooling tax burdens of previously separate national subsidiaries, and pushing debt into high-tax subsidiaries. In this way the merged company can obtain benefits that were simply not available to its previously independent units.

Useful as these benefits are, a transaction needs to have a greater underlying logic to it than just tax savings. By their nature the tax savings are limited in time, and are rarely sufficient on their own to justify a complex merger or acquisition.

ACQUISITIONS THAT DESTROY VALUE

So far, all our discussion has been about an acquisition that is likely to increase shareholder value, or at least starts out with that happy set of assumptions. But as we have seen, many deals do not in fact deliver the goods. In contrast to the value acquisition of Fig. 8.3, the situation described in Fig. 8.4 is of a negative market reaction where the acquirer's shares are marked sharply downwards. Rather than having an immediate value gain "on account" and in expectation of better things to come, the dominant opinion is that the planned deal is never going to work, and the smart money looks for another home.

The gulf that has opened up is described in the shift from point D in Fig. 8.4, which describes what has been paid for the acquisition, to point E, which shows the expected outcome. Point E is lower than D by the amount the market decided to wipe off the value of the acquiring company's shares, represents an up-front capital loss and means that the deal starts off on the wrong foot immediately. The acquiring firm's shareholders will want to see a rapid improvement, so that their positions are at least no worse than they were before the deal was mooted.

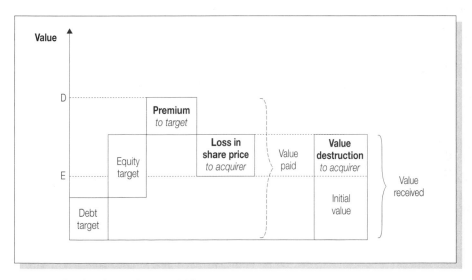

FIG 8.4 ● **A value-destroying acquisition**

In one sense, though, the task has suddenly become easier. The market's judgement of what is possible means that less is expected of the deal, and less additional cash flow has to be found. This mildly good news has to be compared to the cost, though, which in this case is an immediate reduction in SHV among the incumbent firm's shareholders. Pressure from this direction may take a sufficiently strong form to force management to subsequently "unscramble" the deal, or to encourage it to take other unwise decisions as a way of trying to fend off criticism.

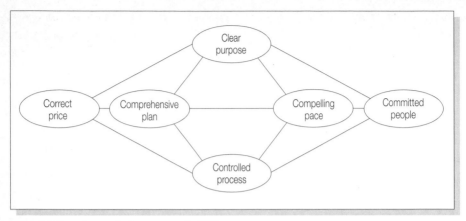

FIG 8.5 ● Requirements for success in M&A

A PRACTICAL IMPLEMENTATION FRAMEWORK

Deals are exciting; often in the heat of the moment an unrealistic bid is made for an acquisition, and a canny negotiator on the other side of the table then seizes it with both hands. At this point the "winners' curse" is born. In order to avoid this kind of situation, we feel that it is very useful to remain disciplined. The acquirer has to be ready to walk away from the deal if it does not stack up, and we believe that using the SHV-oriented approach outlined here is one way of achieving this.

Armed with the SHV approach outlined above, this section looks at some of the practical issues that have to be considered if a transaction is to succeed. Sticking fairly closely to this outline – as illustrated in Fig. 8.5 – should help you see the process as a whole, rather than thinking about the situation pre and post acquisition.

Clear purpose

It is important to assess deal opportunities within the context of a clearly articulated corporate strategy. It is useful to verify that the capabilities and competencies exist to do the intended deal, and there should be good coordination between strategic planning and business development functions at the corporate and business unit levels in the acquiring firm. The challenge here is to be clear and straightforward about what is going to happen early on. In the case of Lloyds-TSB, deals were rejected if it was felt management did not know enough about the target and the sector it was in. The deals that went ahead had to show good potential for integration into the existing businesses and be culturally compatible. This meant turning down a lot of good deals offered by investment banks. As the chairman and CEO of the Northern American subsidiary of a major European bank said:

> The most important value I've added to this company is the deals I didn't do. Being able to walk away from a deal is also very important. People will say "We'll never have another deal in this market." There's always another deal, and there are moments when it is better that your competitor rather than you completes it.

Controlled process

This is all about identifying and screening potential targets, and then moving on to price and carry out the deal. This then has to be integrated with the post-merger transition and integration process. At the end of it all, there should be a review to establish whether the transaction actually achieved what it was supposed to. The major challenge here is to achieve some balance between the inputs at one end with the probability of success at the other. As one manager put it, "If we go off track early on, the chances of recovering are very small."[11]

'Correct' price

A lot comes under this heading, and we have already looked at some of the issues earlier. At the end of the day, the right price will be one that allows the acquiring firm to earn a satisfactory return on its capital and to generate a positive SVA spread within the planned horizon. As we have seen above, a wide range of factors need to enter into the pricing equation, including such things as costs, revenue enhancements, process improvements and synergies.

The main difficulty is to maintain the analytical discipline needed to walk away from the deal if it starts to get too expensive. We would like to illustrate these points with a couple of cases.

Granada spent two years researching Forte and was "amazed" that the City of London had not spotted that Forte was loosely managed and therefore represented a good takeover target. There was some complementarity between Granada, which operated in public and contract catering, and Forte, which owned hotels and the Little Chef restaurant chain. After a lot of careful preparation, Granada went on to pay a 35 percent premium based on £100 million that had to be justified to the Takeover Panel. At the end of the day, the hotel market boomed and the cost savings were achieved very quickly. The deal has been a great success.

Vodafone-Airtouch-Bell Atlantic is a more complicated situation, since there were two rival bids for Airtouch. One came from Vodafone and the other from Bell Atlantic. The initial market reaction to the bids was interesting. Bell Atlantic's share price fell by 5 percent when the deal was announced, even though it was offering a small premium for Airtouch. As the contest developed, Vodafone's share price increased by 14 percent, even though it was offering a much larger premium for Airtouch. The market was more impressed by the general strategic fit the two companies had.

But, at the end of the day, when Vodafone was successful, it was left with the need to generate synergies of $20 billion just to break even on the deal. A tall order? Consider the following: the deal with Vodafone was going to lead to a much stronger position in Europe. The two firms, Vodafone and Airtouch, complemented each other here, and each was strong in areas where the other was weak. In addition, both companies used the same GSM hand sets produced by Nokia, Ericsson and Motorola. This, together with the roll-out of the universal mobile telecommunications system (UMTS) is creating the possibility of a seamless global service. There would be substantial cost synergies, and lower procurement costs for UMTS. There was also scope to consolidate customer care and billing functions. The combined group could also negotiate lower inter-connect fees with fixed line operators.

This was not all; the newly merged Vodafone-Airtouch company would have the third largest market capitalization in the UK, which would create additional demand for its shares among index trackers. Vodafone had confidence in the deal, and prided itself on having always paid a dividend since its listing on the London Stock Exchange. Even though the goodwill write-off was going to create accounting losses for the next few years, the growth story was impressive. The market saw this as a grand buying opportunity.

How did this compare with the Bell Atlantic offering? In the eyes of international investors, the deal was driven primarily by the US situation and market – where it was not all that clear what was going to be gained. Airtouch appeared to complement Bell Atlantic, since its business was everywhere except in north-eastern USA, where Bell Atlantic was strong. So far, so good. But a recent, earlier deal with GTE was going to create immediate regulatory hurdles, since there was a substantial overlap between GTE and Airtouch. It was expected that the FCC would insist on some asset disposals. The combination of difficulties in the USA and no obvious gain in Europe meant that the deal simply did not look particularly attractive, despite the initial modest, and hence "sensible" premium offered for Airtouch.

The rest is history. The market was willing to back Vodafone's more generous offer, since it could more clearly see that Airtouch was worth more to Vodafone than to anyone else. The price was right under these circumstances.

The plan and the pace

There is a close interaction between these two, since the clearer the plan, the easier it is to proceed at a good pace – and this can be crucial if the merger or takeover is to be a success. As detailed a plan as possible should be created: what must be done and when; who is responsible for each task; and what the intended benefits are – all should be specified. There has to be a balance between getting it done quickly – which means a smaller team – and involvement and "buy-in," which requires more people and slows things down. As a general rule of thumb, though, the better the plan, the faster the pace. Pace is important, since it is easier to make substantial changes early on. People expect change and they want to know what is going to happen. As one senior manager put it, "You want to do as much as you can on Day One."[12]

Committed people

Here is arguably one of the most important factors of all in determining whether or not a transaction is ultimately a success. It is terribly important to obtain "buy-in" from as many relevant groups as possible. A lot depends on an early identification of the winners and losers. The winners need guidance and motivation, while the losers have to be treated fairly. You may need to communicate with a wide circle of stakeholders, including those in the general community, especially if the deal is a complicated one. And of course, everyday business has to go on.

SUMMARY

Takeovers, as has often been noted, do not always succeed: much M&A activity is driven by non-financial considerations, it seems, and potential acquirers can appear to behave in an irrational manner. There is a tendency among M&A transactions to be carried away by the moment and over-bid for targets; for which existing methodologies generally fail to establish "fair" shareholder values. Given this, we have proposed in this chapter a more sensible value-based approach that carefully weighs up the costs and the benefits. We have outlined a way of looking at the market for corporate control which lies at the root of the willingness to pay takeover premia.

We have then tracked through how we might apply a SHV approach, concentrating in particular on the valuation and achievability of the synergies that make the deal worth doing. We then looked at what synergies can be expected in the form of cost savings, income generation, financial engineering and tax benefits. We ended by providing some practical hints for M&A transactions.

Notes

1. Loderer, C. and Martin, K. (1990) "Corporate Acquisitions by NYSE and AMEX firms: The experience of a Comprehensive Sample," *Financial Management* Winter, 17–33; Jarrel, G.A., Brickley, J.A. and Netter, J.M. (1988) "The Market for Corporate Control: The Empirical Evidence Since 1980," *Journal of Economic Perspectives*, 2, 21–48; Bradley, M., Desai, A. and Kim, E.H. (1988) "Synergistic Gains from Corporate Acquisitions and their Division between Stockholders of Target and Acquiring Firms," *Journal of Financial Economics*, 21, 3–40; Asquith, P., Bruner, R.F. and Mullins Jr, D. "The Gains for Bidding Firms from Merger," *Journal of Financial Economics*, 11, 121–39.

2. In Copeland, Koller and Murrin (1994) *Valuation*, 2nd edition. New York: John Wiley.

3. "Why too many mergers miss the mark," *The Economist*, 4 January 1997.

4. "Backing hostile bids is wise," *Independent on Sunday*, 11 February 1997.

5. Sirower, Mark (1997) *The Synergy Trap* (New York: Free Press), p.56.

6. "I believe that you should see benefits for both sets of shareholders. If you can price the deal so that the shares of both companies go up, then it's a good deal for everybody." Sir Brian Pitman, chairman of Lloyds-TSB.

7. "You have to be willing not to let the thrill of the chase get your testosterone flowing." Chairman and CEO of the US subsidiary of a European bank. Here and elsewhere in this chapter, quotations not attributed are from a survey where anonymity was promised.

8. See note 5.

9. Warren Buffet, Berkshire Hathaway 1982 Annual Report.

10. Sirower (see note 5). Details on the superiority of cash/debt financed deals as compared with equity financed deals can be found in Datta, Narayanan and Pinches (1992) "Factors Influencing Wealth Creation from Mergers," *Strategic Management Journal*, 13, 67–84; Travlos, N.G. "Corporate Takeover Bids, Methods of Payment, and Bidding Firm's Stock Returns," *Journal of Finance*, 42, 943–6; Myers, S. and Kajluf, N.S. "Corporate Financing and Investment Decisions When Firms Have Information that Investors Do Not Have," *Journal of Financial Economics*, 13, 187–221.

11. Chief Planner of a major UK industrial company.

12. Head of M&A of a large UK manufacturer.

RISING FROM THE ASHES: VALUE RE-CREATION AND SHV

Our economic system requires there to be both winners and losers. When everybody is competing against everybody else, someone is going to come in ahead, and equally someone is going to pull up at the rear of the race. Both are the natural consequences of a system in which risks are taken.

If consistent winners are – as we saw in the previous chapter – in the position of being able to expand their activities, consistent losers may have to consider whether they want to enter the next race at all. This chapter is primarily about the consistent losers, and what might happen to them. We will argue that a shareholder value approach can be successfully applied in value re-creation situations too – even though in such situations you will have to consider the interests of more parties than simply your shareholders.

All of which means that we will be talking about stakeholders again, and revisiting one of the themes of Chapter 1. This is because, when a company is in trouble, it needs to pay close attention to those stakeholders – suppliers, employees and, in particular, debt-holders – who no longer have any incentive to listen to those who nominally represent the shareholders. Frustrated and worried by poor performance, these stakeholders may very well "take back their marbles" and go off and play with someone else. To avoid such a situation, we will suggest an approach that might succeed in unlocking hitherto untapped sources of value. Let us see how this can be achieved.

STAKES AND SHARES REVISITED

Early in Part 1 of this book we showed that the longer-term interests of all a company's major stakeholders are similar. All are looking for above average returns – *shareholders* in the form of a good total shareholder return (made up of dividends and capital appreciation); *debt-holders* in the form of prompt repayment of principal and interest, so that at the end of the day they make a profit on their loans; *employees* in the form of higher than average wages and salaries, a decent level of job satisfaction and job security; and *customers* and *suppliers* in the form of a steady stream of goods and services either received or sent, at prices and conditions that ensure that they receive good value for the money they have spent. Putting the interests of shareholders center stage, we have argued, is ultimately the quickest and surest way of satisfying all these constituencies.

But let us look further at these parties, since the more detailed the view, the more disparate the groups will appear. Six distinct interests can be identified: shareholders, debt-holders, company management, employees, customers/suppliers, and the community at large. We will consider them in that order.

The shareholders

A company is owned by its shareholders, who provide it with its starting capital. Almost everything a company does is done formally in their name. Their liability is limited to the money put up and converted into shares, and this limits their downside risk, too. The worst that can happen is for them to lose their money. On the other hand, their upside opportunity is virtually unlimited: they participate in gains in asset prices and increases in the intrinsic or shareholder value that we have calculated earlier. Although their preferences for receiving their rewards may vary between income and capital gains, their main interest will be in the total shareholder return, a combination of capital appreciation and dividends. As we have said throughout this book shareholders desire a return at least as great as that obtainable on an investment of similar risk elsewhere in the market.

In the narrow terms of what shareholders are actually entitled to, however, the picture can look a little different. They have a "right" to a dividend as an income from their shares, subject to management approval. They can ask for their money back when the business is wound up, and they have the power to vote on a board of directors. Their approval for new capital issues is also required. But these powers are really rather remote from a firm's day-to-day operations, and are even more remote from influencing those decisions needed to create SHV.

Indeed, the actual experience of "traditional" shareholders suggests that their role is frequently even more restricted. As John Plender argues:

> While the property in a company consists of a whole bundle of rights which are spread around the various stakeholders in the business, with the shareholders nominally pre-eminent among them, the reality is the board of directors retains most of the powers of control … usually associated with ownership, up to the point of hostile take-over.[1]

This means that shareholders mostly delegate their authority and powers to the management team, who make all the operational decisions.

The split between owners and operators has led particularly in the UK and the USA, to a "hands-off" attitude on the part of many institutional shareholders, who typically do not become involved in day-to-day company decision-making. What institutional investors always consider is how any one investment is performing relative to others in their portfolio. Poor investment performance will cause many institutions to "vote with their feet" – to sell their shares in your company and buy those of other better performing companies, perhaps those of your competitors!

Admittedly, this approach is changing very gradually: as we shall see in Chapter 11, investors such as CalPERS in the USA and Mercury Asset Management in the UK are prepared to become more actively involved in management decisions. But this is still relatively unusual. So, although formally shareholders have a lot of power invested in them, in general they are poorly placed to exercise it. Indeed, shareholders' claims on company assets are generally last in line in a recovery situation; so before the unmentionable happens, an individual shareholder has every reason to want to be first out through the door.

It is investor mobility, therefore, that acts as an important check on management power. Managements react to this by ensuring their investors are rewarded – action that sometimes leads to the charge of "short-termism." In order to appease investors, and particularly those working from an actuarial background, companies are prepared to authorize substantial dividend payments, possibly in excess of what they can realistically afford. In 1994, dividends were over 30 percent of after-tax profits among quoted British non-financial companies, and this pay out rate was even higher in the USA.[2] Companies in Japan and Germany paid out a much lower proportion of after-tax profits as dividends. During the 1990s recession in the UK, 60 percent of companies maintained or increased dividends in the face of falling profits. By contrast, 28 percent cut dividends, while only 12 percent of companies passed their dividend payment. Most evidence suggests that companies have a target pay-out ratio for dividends, and aim to maintain this even when business conditions are poor. This can be value destroying.

Such behavior may be a case of over-emphasizing shareholder value, or rather giving it a far too short-term bias. It has given rise to the charge that such generous pay-out ratios, aided and abetted by a tax system that effectively penalizes retained earnings, have sacrificed long-term corporate (shareholder) value creation at the altar of short-term investment portfolio performance. While we would not entirely support this view, there is enough substance to it to suggest that tax reforms in the UK, for instance, might even up the balance between distributed and retained earnings.

There is another factor to bear in mind when we consider the shareholders, and before we look at the other stakeholders. This is the simple definition introduced in Chapter 1, where we stated that shareholder value was corporate value after deducting net debt. It might appear to follow from this definition that the interests of shareholders are inversely related to those of debt-holders; *ceteris paribus*, shareholders will appropriate more gains when the debt-holder stake is reduced to a minimum. Nevertheless there are occasions when shareholders will prefer additional debt finance to underwrite their expansion plans – as we shall see in the next section.

The debt-holders

Debt-holders have lent a company money, either in the form of bonds, or as a loan. Lenders have a prior claim on the business's assets, and their main interest is in their lending margin. Able to borrow money themselves at a lower rate (if they are banks), their margin is the difference between the rate at which they lend out and their own refinancing costs. Their primary concern is with default risk, or the risk that they might lose their money. Lenders are quite risk averse, since the loss of just one loan can often wipe out the profits of many other loans.

Under normal circumstances, a company can satisfy the demands of both shareholders and debt-holders. All participants will be happy. But a closer examination will reveal that debt-holders have a substantially more limited "stake" in a firm. Shareholders invest because they are looking for substantial upward gains, and they set this against the possible loss of their original stake. Debt-holders are much more limited on the upside. All they are ever going to make is the interest margin and their money back. If all goes well, they may then repeat the process, possibly stepping up the amounts involved and so making their profits in that way.

This is what makes debt so attractive for managements, and also for shareholders: it represents a source of finance that has voluntarily limited its participation in the upside. Managements, armed with reasonably good inside information as to their likely prospects, will see debt as a very useful source of finance. If there is a high probability that an enterprise is going to succeed, and its managers are privy to that information, then it will almost always make sense to raise additional debt, since this will leave more of the gains for shareholders. Furthermore, this same "information asymmetry" leads to another conclusion – that when a management is not all that sure of the future, it should aim to increase the amount of equity in the business to meet its additional financing needs.

It has long been noted that new equity issues normally form a small proportion of new funds for companies. In the USA rarely more than 10 percent of total external finance comes from equity, while the rest is made up of additional debt or is financed from retained earnings.[3] This emphasis on debt as a source of additional finance is entirely consistent with the differences between the amount of information available to managements and what is available to their investors.

Taking this argument further, we can observe that many firms prefer internal finance, and adopt targets for dividend payments that are related to their investment opportunities. These broad strategies at first sight appear to run against the grain of shareholder value. Dividend payments are necessarily "sticky" and don't move much year to year; target pay-out ratios only gradually change to reflect shifts in investment opportunities. The combination of sticky dividend payments and volatility in cash flows and investment means that there are periods when internal cash flows can exceed the dividend payments; in such circumstances the company will initially build up reserves and pay off debt, and then increase its pay-out ratio. When internal cash flows are inadequate to meet dividend payments, many companies will either manage the business for cash (for instance, by selling realizable assets) or raise additional borrowings before lowering its dividend pay-out ratio.

All of which suggests a hierarchy in a firm's attitude to finance – a sort of "pecking order" that puts debt as its first port of call, followed by hybrid or mezzanine debt, with equity as the least preferred part of the financing package. The reason is that managements are keen to protect the interests of existing shareholders, and that additional debt "ring-fences" the gains from any investment and ensures that they flow almost exclusively to shareholders. They share in the upside; debt-holders do not.

Recovery plans, therefore, have to take very seriously the interests of debt-holders, whose instincts will be to cut their losses and exit from their engagement in a firm as soon as they can. A key issue then may be to persuade debt-holders to swap their debt for equity, and so take a longer-term interest in the company.

Recent figures from the UK underline the issue for debt-holders. Broadly speaking only 23 percent of the value of loans was recovered through bankruptcy and insolvency proceedings once a business's difficulties had crystallized into insolvency procedures[4] – which means debt-holders have a material interest in trying to make sure none of their companies get into financial distress.

Management

A company should be run in the interests of its shareholders, who can appoint, or dismiss, its management. Management is an agent appointed to look after shareholder interests. That's the theory – but a considerable body of opinion suggests that in fact management looks after itself first, and the shareholders second. Where there are conflicts of interest, we cannot be sure that management will necessarily put shareholders first. Fragmented shareholdings, or the institutional "hands-off" policy referred to above, has resulted in considerable power being devolved to management, who can award themselves a substantial part of the value created by the company. To some extent, then, they compete with shareholders, and have to find an acceptable balance between their rewards, the cash the company retains for the future, and what is distributed to shareholders.

It is in recovery situations that the interests of management deviate most substantially from those of the other stakeholders. A company in difficulty is one that has been under-performing, with symptoms such as those in Fig. 9.1; it will already have made a series of poor decisions. In one recent survey (see Fig. 9.2), management failure was cited as not only the second most important primary cause of business failure but by far and away the most important secondary factor.

Any management team will probably look for ways to remain in place and participate in a recovery plan. But if the situation already requires the attention of business turnaround specialists, then it is highly likely that the first group to be sacrificed as new policies are introduced and implemented will be the management.

Employees

Employees represent the core of many businesses and collectively embody the know-how and human capital of the firm. Increasingly, it is a firm's ability to differentiate itself in this area that will create the conditions for successful longer-term survival. Employees can also have substantial financial interests in the firm. In some countries this can extend to having their pension fund assets invested in it. In others there may be forms of employee stock ownership, or

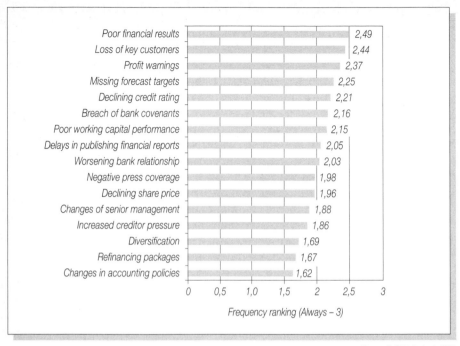

Source: PwC, Netherlands 1999

FIG 9.1 ● **Symptoms of under-performance**

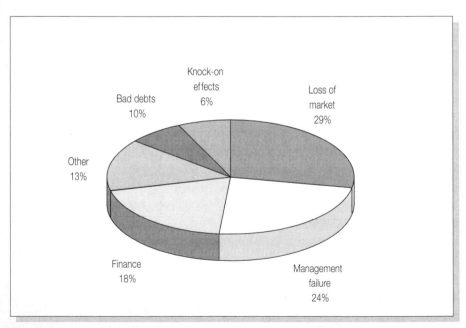

FIG 9.2 ● **Why do businesses fail?** Source: Company Insolvency in the UK: 1995/6, Society of Practitioners of Insolvency 1996

stock option plans. In some circumstances these resources can be used to assist in reconstruction.

In the short term, the interests of employees are to continue in full time employment and to receive payment for their services. In the longer term, though, there may be a parting of the ways. In turnaround situations in the UK, typically only 40 percent of employees remain with the firm once it enters a recovery program.[5] The issue for the employee will be to balance the probability of a successful future with the firm against an alternative offer elsewhere; meanwhile the management team has to ensure that crucial employees are retained, since their loss can jeopardize a recovery program.

Customers/suppliers

Customers and suppliers have a "stake" in a company that can sometimes be supplemented by an actual shareholding, as is often the case in Japan. The extent of this "stake" is difficult to judge – the depth of stakeholder commitment to the firm (especially customer commitment) will vary industry by industry – but we can identify two more extreme positions where the issues can be clarified. There are some industries where price is the primary determinant of getting business. Price elasticities of demand and switching costs are low, and neither customers nor suppliers have a significant stake in the company. On the other hand there are situations where switching costs and product differentiation are high, while price elasticities of demand are low. It is at times like these that customers and suppliers have significant stakes in the company, and would have a material interest in ensuring its continued survival.

These relationships can be cemented with long-term contracts, and possibly through cross-shareholdings. The "stake" can sometimes become so high that the customer or supplier buys the other out. When that happens a market transaction is replaced by an internal transaction and the company becomes more vertically integrated.

In recovery situations, it is important to convince both suppliers and customers that it is in their interest for the firm in difficulties to continue trading. This is easier to do where switching costs are high. A decision by either a supplier or a customer to desert and switch to a competitor can often be the last straw that breaks the camel's back.

When there is a switch or desertion this can lead to a spread in the financial difficulties, since the affected firm is now even worse off than before, and it may no longer be able to pay its remaining suppliers. Around 6 percent of company failures in the UK arise from this "knock-on" effect of other companies' trading difficulties.[6] Hence it is important for the reconstructing firm that suppliers and customers can be persuaded to hang on.

Local community/government

Finally we need to remember the government and the local community or communities in which a company operates. They have a stake, based largely on their role as recipients of tax revenue and providers of infrastructure. In the event of a business failure, they will have to bear the social costs involved in supporting laid-off employees, as well as possibly providing support for other companies in the area. Generally speaking, governments and local authorities have more interest in business preservation and continuation than some of the other stakeholders, particularly when the firm in question accounts for a high proportion of total tax revenue.

Even where the fiscal link is less pronounced, at least from the government's point of view, the company will still have legal and social obligations to the local and national community. These extend over a wide range, and include all contracts, support for local initiatives and combined undertakings, as well as compliance with laws on the environment, health and safety.

WHY DO BUSINESSES FAIL?

Clearly, different stakeholders in a company have differing interests, and in the later part of this chapter we will review how these can be integrated to find the best solution to what are difficult business situations. Before doing this, however, let us look more closely at some of the reasons why businesses fail.

One reason can be simply expressed as a *toleration of under-performance*. Research recently conducted by PricewaterhouseCoopers in the Netherlands found that 22 percent of the sales of the top 250 Dutch companies were derived from business units and subsidiaries that were destroying shareholder value. Yet only 12 percent of respondents admitted to having underperforming businesses at the time! On closer inspection it was also found that while many of the companies did have monitoring and controls systems in place, most of them concentrated on lagging rather than leading indicators, which is rather like trying to drive a car by looking through the rear view mirror.

Only a minority of the companies polled equated their lack of performance with measurements of their return on capital employed or by using SVA. Which means that many companies have developed a "blind spot," believing they are performing quite well when in reality they are already sliding down the "corporate demise curve" of Fig. 9.3.

Looked at another way, the causes of business failure can be broadly categorized as in Fig. 9.2 – which refers specifically to the UK, but we think can be considered reasonably representative of most industrialized economies. The most common reason given is that the company has experienced a *loss of market* – around 30 percent of all business failures are accounted for this way. This is a shorthand way of saying that the company's information about itself and the market in which it operates has been faulty. It has been caught out by developments, probably unanticipated, that have left it vulnerable to competitors. In more severe cases it could be that the market for this particular specialized good or service has simply dried up.

Although the onset of the crisis may come as a surprise, the underlying problems – weaknesses in strategic thinking, inefficient operations or poor marketing – may well have been affecting the enterprise for a long time before the collapse actually came. The first warning sign is the loss of competitive advantage; this is well on the downward curve before profits dive and/or costs rise.

These factors spill over into what is the second most frequently cited primary cause of business failure, that of *management failure*. As a 1996 report from the UK's Society of Practitioners in Insolvency (SPI) says: "It appears that … businesses still fail because managers lack skill, knowledge, energy or initiative."

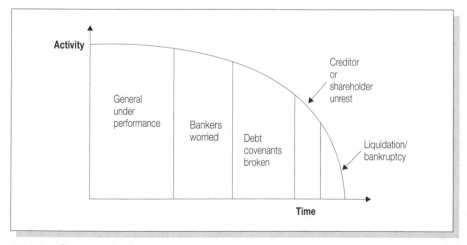

FIG 9.3 ● **Corporate demise curve**

The term "management failure" covers a multitude of errors, including the sins of over-optimism and imprudent accounting. But although there are occasions when management teams or CEOs seem almost willfully poor, few teams are entirely weak. They may lack effective leadership and some necessary skills, but in many cases their real failing is that they lack good information with which to manage. Many of these factors will be categorized as "poor management" but such a view could be too simplistic. A failing business also needs meaningful information just as much as any other: indeed, poor management information systems do more serious damage when companies face crisis and impending failure. In this position there is little time to take decisions – and good decisions need accurate data. Too often the available data are old, meaningless or both. A well-designed set of metrics focused on the important drivers of value (see Chapter 7) would have saved many a business.

A third factor is *unwise acquisitions*, or an *inappropriate expansion strategy*. This often comes down to a question of timing and finance. With the economy moving ahead, managers may decide to go for an expansion strategy that involves buying up another company. As we have indicated in the previous chapter, a deal might look good on paper but turn out less well when it comes to implementation: such issues can seriously stretch senior management time, and possibly involve taking on financial commitments in the debt area which leave the new larger company dangerously exposed to an adverse movement in interest rates, or to a slight downturn in the market.

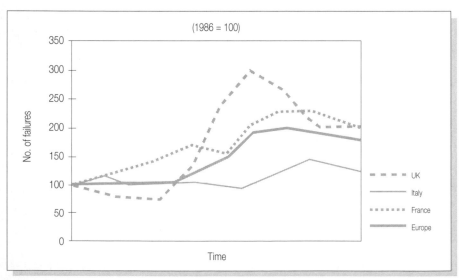

Source: Price Waterhouse

FIG 9.4 ● Rising number of business failures in the 1990s in larger European countries

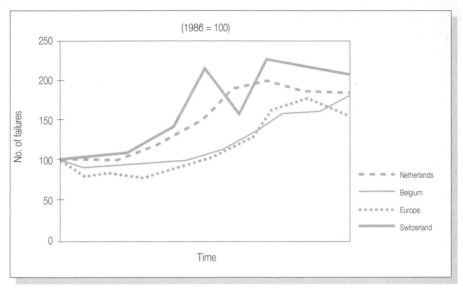

Source: Price Waterhouse

FIG 9.5 ● **Rising number of business failures 1986–96**

Over-aggressive financing at the end of a business cycle accounts for many company failures. Take a look at the last few leveraged acquisitions in the up phase of an economic cycle, and you will often find the next failures and restructurings as the economy turns down. It is a recurring feature of the business cycle that money chases deals more aggressively as the cycle wears on. A pattern emerges in which market participants will comment on the excessive prices being paid for businesses, while lenders will note that interest rate spreads have vanished. By the time the Indian summer of the economic boom is reached, industry buyers will often be outbidden by financial buyers, who will focus on growth prospects and efficiency gains to justify a price that seems to exceed the synergy gains that an industry merger might expect.

As the business cycle turns down, or the markets simply fail to deliver forecast growth, cash flow tightens. Business decisions become less than optimal as investment in operating plant or new product development is reined in, and the underlying value of the enterprise is traded in for short-term survival. If management and shareholders do not address such a situation, performance and value will erode; eventually the business will face a funding crisis and possible failure.

Business failure trends during the 1990s showed a delayed response to recession. In the UK a peak was reached about two years after the worst of the recession, followed by an improvement. In other mainland European countries insolvency rates rose more slowly, but seem to have persisted at higher levels for longer than in the UK.

UNLOCKING THE VALUE POTENTIAL
OF TROUBLED BUSINESSES

It is our view that many companies in distress still have the potential to become winning players again. Even those that do not have a long-term strategic position may have the capability for improved performance. There are some highly encouraging trends in the UK in this respect; recent figures suggest that nearly a quarter of all businesses that become "distressed" will be able to make a successful recovery.

Whatever the reason for the distress, to succeed in a recovery, you will need a process for re-creating value, and it is the application of this value process that we will look at in more detail. More extensive application of the value re-creating process will, we think, bring about a further improvement in the proportion of companies able to recover and prosper into the future.

Bearing in mind some of the facts and figures revealed in the previous section, we see considerable scope for developing a coherent approach to restoring, preserving and improving businesses that have fallen on hard times. Quite simply, the shareholder value approach can offer interesting and relevant insights into the way companies can be turned around. This section describes some aspects of this process.

The SHV approach to businesses or groups of businesses in serious financial difficulty can be very similar to the approach you would take to any operation that is destroying value. There are two important differences, however.

Firstly, there is usually little time available to effect change. More often than not it is a cash crisis that will have brought home to management and stake-holders alike the pressing need for change. The company may be in default of bank covenants, and its borrowing facilities fully drawn with insufficient to meet pending payments. A wave of unpaid trade creditors may be about to break and engulf the business. On the face of it, there will be little or no time to put in place the measures necessary to re-create value in the enterprise. Indeed, at this point the business's whole focus will need to be on survival.

On the other hand, this situation has one real merit. In a time of crisis people – managers, shareholders, employees – will accept the need for change and will probably countenance changes that they would previously have rejected. It is vital to recognize this and take the opportunity to achieve deep-rooted transformation in the business.

Secondly, the structure of stakeholder interests is always more complex than in a conventional value improvement exercise, because it is not management or shareholders alone who call the shots. Instead, as we have seen, a number of other interests such as bankers, bond holders, trade creditors, employees and even government all have a legitimate interest in the future of the business. They also have the power, in different degrees, to influence or control the process.

It is important, therefore, for management to be highly pro-active in communicating with these diverse groups. They will be impatient for information and progress; much more so than conventional shareholders. They will also be prepared to take unilateral action if they are not comfortable with the steps a company is taking to deal with the crisis. There may be a need for a different type of management, since some will not be able to cope with the situation.

Certainly this is a situation that can sometimes create conflicts of interest, as has been seen recently with Rover in the UK. There are occasions, too, when details of a restructuring plan have to be kept confidential, particularly when a deal is being set up.

FOUR OPTIONS FOR GETTING OUT OF TROUBLE

In any but the most hopeless situation, there will be a number of choices open to your business and its stakeholders. Figure 9.6 shows how to set about securing a better understanding of the business and its value potential – after which the four basic options are: to sell the enterprise as it is; to wind down or close it; to go for a short-term performance enhancement strategy which opens up an option to either keep the business or sell it; or to undertake a value recovery plan. There is one final, fifth, option – the regrettable but sometimes necessary insolvency route. There are times when this can provide a better basis for subsequent recovery than the other options.

For the purposes of this chapter, however, we shall concentrate on the first four. The table in Fig. 9.7 gives an assessment of the options, ranking them according to their potential for creating value – which, as you can see, corresponds to their risk.

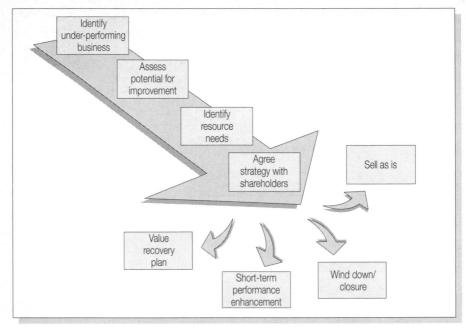

FIG 9.6 ● Value recovery: the diagnostic trail

The first three options

In the case of the *first option*, to sell the business as quickly as possible – or as quickly as is consistent with obtaining a reasonable value – the lenders may be happy to accept a highly discounted "fire-sale" price if it secures their position. Indeed, they may resist any delay or other course of action that offers them only additional risk.

The *second option*, a liquidation of the assets in the form of a wind-down or closure, may be appropriate where the assets have significant value to a purchaser – in effect, a greater value than they have to the business. Such a case might be a factory site with substantial redevelopment value and with an operation which it would be uneconomic to move elsewhere. But this course of action may also require funding – exits are rarely cheap. The company may also have to be careful not to surrender important ground to the competition, nor to damage unnecessarily other healthy parts of the business. Although liquidation is not a constructive possibility in terms of business preservation, or from the perspective of the employees, it may be the best strategy for maximizing value – as long as no political intervention is likely, or that legal requirements concerning employee protection are not too stringent.

Some stakeholders may be prepared to take the *third option*, of short-term performance enhancement. They will accept this if they are still not sure whether the business will be worth keeping or will eventually have to be sold. They will accept an element of risk but be unwilling to commit either enough time or money to see through a full turnaround, which they may also see as a high-risk choice compared to the relatively quick process of performance improvement leading to a sale. This third option would not involve any repositioning of the business. Rather it focuses only on improving the performance of the existing business, either by raising the effectiveness of business processes or by eliminating poorly performing operations, products or customers.

Allied to tighter controls on working capital and a selective program of capital expenditure to maintain fabric and competitiveness, such action would enhance performance as measured by the value drivers of operating cash flow and working capital. However, since it will do nothing for business growth prospects, its capacity to enhance value will be limited. It is also a short-term strategy: initial success should not dissuade stakeholders from pushing through a sale when the strategy delivers improved results. To delay may only reveal deeper strategic weaknesses that cannot be resolved in the short term and may undermine selling efforts.

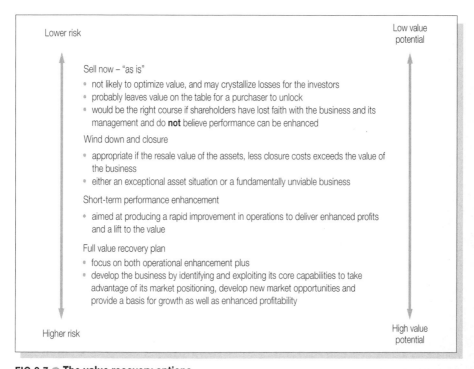

Lower risk — Low value potential

Sell now – "as is"
- not likely to optimize value, and may crystallize losses for the investors
- probably leaves value on the table for a purchaser to unlock
- would be the right course if shareholders have lost faith with the business and its management and do **not** believe performance can be enhanced

Wind down and closure
- appropriate if the resale value of the assets, less closure costs exceeds the value of the business
- either an exceptional asset situation or a fundamentally unviable business

Short-term performance enhancement
- aimed at producing a rapid improvement in operations to deliver enhanced profits and a lift to the value

Full value recovery plan
- focus on both operational enhancement plus
- develop the business by identifying and exploiting its core capabilities to take advantage of its market positioning, develop new market opportunities and provide a basis for growth as well as enhanced profitability

Higher risk — High value potential

FIG 9.7 ● The value recovery options

The fourth option

The option of pursuing a full turnaround is the most far-reaching approach, with inevitably the highest risk. It will be appropriate in circumstances where the business has a strong strategic position or is capable of achieving one. All phases of the value recovery process set out in Fig. 9.8, from *Stabilization* by way of *Analysis* to strategic *Repositioning* and *Strengthening* of the operations, will be involved. This approach carries with it the greatest upside of the four options, as well as requiring the greatest commitment in time, money and management. Needless to say, the techniques of value management set out in Chapter 7 are as appropriate here as they are in a successful company.

Let us then look in more detail at the four phases of value recovery that will be necessary if you or your management go for the option of a full business turnaround.

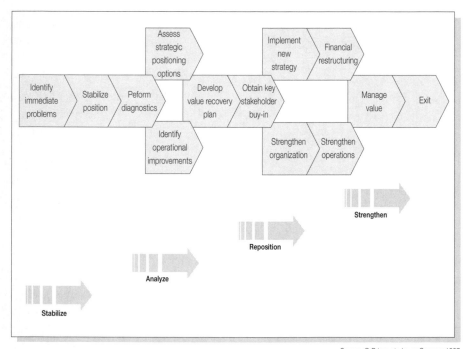

Source: © PricewaterhouseCoopers 1997

FIG 9.8 ● The value recovery process

Phase one: stabilize

Clearly, the first step in many troubled situations, before attention can be turned to value re-creation, is to *stabilize* the business. First and foremost, this stabilization phase requires management to become focused on urgency. There is no time for refined analysis: you may have to make some decisions that could damage long-term value. So be it – the alternative is probably failure and unplanned insolvency, which will destroy value much more. The focus in this phase is twofold:

● cash – not maintainable free cash flow, just cash;

● reducing the losses and cash demands of the business.

To this end, you must analyze the business quickly to assess how to reschedule payments, reduce working capital needs and re-negotiate future commitments. Non-core assets or businesses may have to be sold quickly to generate cash. The purpose of this apparently wild dash for liquidity is to finance the continuing cash demands from trading, and to buy time.

There is no point in regarding these measures as an end in themselves. Their purpose is to eliminate the urgent need for additional cash in the business and to convince skeptical lenders that the business is under control. Only by building credibility in this way can you, as management, buy time to put in place a proper strategy for re-creating value in the business in the medium to long term. One way of doing this is to consider the following approach, which can quickly identify the main options available to your stakeholders.

Phase two: analyze

If your business cash needs have been stabilized, and your important stakeholders have been persuaded to buy into a turnaround process, you will need to *analyze* the position and prospects of the business. Institute a thorough financial analysis: ask what results the business can achieve, what debt it can support, and what unknown contingencies threaten. There is no point in starting a turnaround only to discover part of the way through the process that additional liabilities are surfacing or resulting from business decisions, and that they cannot be met. Here we would recommend applying many of the techniques we have introduced earlier in this book.

However, your analysis must also focus on the strategic position of the business, and its operational effectiveness. What are its core competencies, and are they being properly exploited? Which products and which customers should be retained and which eliminated? The end product of this diagnostic phase should be a better understanding of the choices open to your business's stakeholders and management – choices that are focused around products or processes offering competitive advantage in selected markets. On this basis, and with the buy-in of key stakeholders, it will be possible to begin rebuilding value. As you will have gathered, such a process will follow the same lines as the ones we proposed in Chapter 7's "value transformation" program.

At this stage, you should have identified not only the business's value potential and the means of unlocking it, but also what resources you will need. These resources are in *time*, *capital* and *management*: any program for re-building value has to take all three elements into account. Time may run out, for example, when important contracts expire or losses use up all borrowing facilities. Equally, there is no point in promoting a turnaround plan that will require new capital if the stakeholders are unwilling to commit themselves to it.

The SHV approach, by making several aspects of the situation clearer and more transparent, provides a good informational basis on which to persuade some of the debt-holders of the value of holding on – either because they improve the chances of getting their funds back, or because they can convert their limited opportunity as regards the upside into something more concrete by swapping debt for equity. As we have implied earlier, this is not necessarily something the original shareholders will welcome with open arms (since it will dilute their share of any eventual gains). But all the participants will have to be helped to see how, by postponing some of their expected gain, they can nurse the company back to health.

Finally, your management team and its advisers have to be demonstrably capable of delivering the plan. This will often call for additional resources, since the existing management may have already been found wanting. It is unlikely to be able to convince anyone that it can pull off the difficult task of re-creating the value its earlier actions have destroyed. Often a business will be forced into an early sale – and a resulting loss in value – by a lack of realistic alternatives to the current management team. A quick sale may also be unavoidable if the stakeholders are uncomfortable about allowing the time, or putting in the necessary cash, for the business to continue.

Phases 3 and 4: Reposition and strengthen

After analysis, the next and most crucial stage will require you to produce a *value recovery plan* which all major stakeholders must buy in to. Details here will vary with each case, making generalizations difficult, but initially you will have to decide what can be done using existing resources, and what will require additional input from your stakeholders. Once you have acquired time and created a breathing space, it will be up to the new management team, probably aided and strengthened by some outside advisers, to try and produce the tangible new shoots of growth, which will be required if the patience of some of the stakeholders is not to be exhausted.

It is not just the company itself that will face meltdown if things go wrong; the other stakeholders too are facing the same disaster. But this is a great spur to innovation. Necessity, as they say, is the mother of invention.

A two-part plan

The value plan will need to have two distinct parts. The first will involve *financial re-structuring*, which means you must take a cool look at your operation from the financing point of view. Any new structure will have to deal with some of the questions of information asymmetry outlined earlier in this chapter. Normally, as we have said, a successful company management will try to bring in more debt when a good outcome is reasonably certain, enabling the upside to be distributed to the shareholders and not to the debt-holders. Debt spreads risks, but does not (hopefully) penalize the rewards.

By the same token, a financial re-structuring that involves raising more equity is sending out contradictory signals to the market. As arguably the most expensive form of finance in the longer term, equity is something a company will look for only when it knows the outcome of its plans is far from certain. This helps explain why stock prices often fall when a new equity issue is announced – and why existing shareholders are so reluctant to agree to restructuring plans that effectively water down their future returns.

Debt-holders too can be faced with unpalatable decisions, especially if they have to convert outstanding loans into equity. Debt-holders will do this mostly when they have given up virtually all hope of getting their debt repaid. In other words they will only swap debt for equity when they perceive that participating in an uncertain future income stream is better than no income at all![7]

Once a re-financing package has been agreed, it will be possible to work on the basis of a new target capital structure, and hence a new target weighted average cost of capital. This can then become the new criterion by which to judge whether your new plans are working out or not.

The second part of a value recovery plan will need equally radical measures for *organizational strengthening*. The options here could include a wholesale replacement of management, a new management structure, and the installation of a new executive remuneration program that very specifically links rewards to the achievement of several tightly defined targets in the recovery process. You will thus strengthen the operational side of the company and attain improved efficiency levels as a more focused approach replaces earlier and less successful strategies.

By combining a new financial structure with new organizational packages, you will be able to lay down a sound basis for the recovery and recreation of value – very much along the lines described in previous chapters. As the recovery process continues and consolidates, you may ultimately find it possible to find a new purchaser for the company, a purchaser who is willing to pay a good price. We are then taken back into the considerations mentioned in the previous chapter, where we found that it is often the sellers of companies that end up making the greatest profits.

The successful sale of a recovered and preserved company can ultimately make the trials and tribulations of the recovery process worthwhile – so long as the participants can afford to wait, and so long as the company really has a reasonable prospect of living up to its new promise.

THE VIRTUES OF VALUE RE-CREATION

In troubled business situations, the issues of value management are not different in kind from those facing any business keen to improve its value performance. The potential beneficiaries, however, may be a wider group of stakeholders – some of whom will have to be convinced of the need to work together to build up the value of the enterprise. Not all stakeholders, probably, will have the same appetite and patience for a thorough value recovery effort. In such a situation, you will need to make even more strenuous efforts than usual to communicate your strategy, plans and progress.

The SHV approach we have outlined here is part of a continuum, beginning in Chapter 7, that runs from highly successful groups by way of poor value performers and value destroyers to failing businesses. In all cases this approach is a sound basis for developing strategy and improving performance; indeed, our focus on long-term maintainable free cash flow fits well with the instincts of lenders.

One distinctive feature of troubled situations is the way that an impending failure can inspire change and overcome a management's innate conservatism. Radical change becomes practicable, while a more stable situation would have permitted inertia. This is the key to much of the improvement that can be wrought in a crisis situation.

A value-oriented approach such as that embodied in the recovery process of Fig. 9.8 is a useful tool for ensuring that all stakeholders – employees and creditors as well as shareholders – buy in to the appropriate recovery plan. It combines the pressing need for change and urgent action with a necessary focus on longer-term value generation. It does not prescribe one right way forward. Rather it encourages a proper exploration of the options and the risks that accompany each – providing a basis for taking decisions that optimize the value of a business.

SUMMARY

Our consideration of the uses of SHV analysis for the value recovery process began by going back to the division of interests between shareholders and other stakeholders. When a company is failing, the interests of these others, especially debt-holders, come to the fore, and equity is low down in the "pecking order." In this situation, a management must strive to communicate as much information as it can to all parties who can influence the outcome – employees, customers, suppliers, the community at large as well as to debt-holders and shareholders. After looking at the causes of business failure, we turned to a consideration of the ways that a company can be "turned around." There are four options for getting out of trouble: of these, only the fourth, a full recovery plan, will make substantial use of SHV analysis. Such a plan would have, again, four phases – stabilization, analysis, repositioning and strengthening – and ultimately this strength would be based on a combination of financial re-structuring and a new organizational package. But as we noted, crisis situations are also moments of opportunity, when doing nothing is not an option and innovation is more likely to be on the agenda.

Notes

1. Plender, John (1997) *A Stake in the Future* London: Nicholas Brealey.

2. Plender, op. cit.

3. See Bealey and Myers (1984) *Principles of Corporate Finance*, 2nd edition (McGraw-Hill) table 14.3, p. 291.

4. Society of Practitioners of Insolvency [SPI], Sixth Survey of Company Insolvency in the UK, 1995–6.

5. Ibid.

6. Ibid.

7. More recently there have been improvements in the secondary market for debt in the UK. This can sometimes be de-stabilizing, especially where there are demands for "asset-stripping" as part of the sale of the debt.

PART

SHV IN ACTION

SECTOR APPEAL

et us begin to narrow our focus. We have backed up our claim that the shareholder value approach has a wide application by showing, in the three chapters of Part 2, how it can be used not only in normal circumstances but also in mergers and acquisitions as well as business turnaround situations. Now we are going to move from a generic, global way of looking at companies to a more detailed examination of some of the variety of industries and sectors that make up a modern economy.

This chapter, then, reveals a few aspects of the thinking that has been going on at PricewaterhouseCoopers on the question of applying SHV to concrete cases. No two companies are the same, of course; but by developing models for particular sectors such as utilities or insurance, we can identify common factors and the relevant value drivers that must feature in any SHV analysis of a company in that sector.

Shareholder value is not, in our view, a one-size-fits-all solution to the question of performance management. Unlike some SHV advocates, we will argue that there are occasions when the basic approach requires substantial revisions and adaptations; your company may not be best advised to take just any off-the-shelf value-based management solution and apply it automatically. In areas such as telecommunications, pharmaceuticals, oil and high technology – areas that we will deal with below – we have to look carefully at whether and how the seven "value drivers" might need to be modified. There are also areas not normally associated with SHV, for instance finance, where we believe the approach can be fruitfully applied. These too we will deal with below.

CASH FLOW AND COST OF CAPITAL

Back to definitions

Before plunging into the details, it is worthwhile pausing to consider the areas where it might be necessary to adapt the basic SHV approach. In the "normal" model, three main areas have to be considered. These are:

- Cash flow forecasts – is it practical to define a free cash flow number?
- The cost of capital – will adjustments need to be made here?
- Residual value calculations – what assumptions lie behind them?

Typically we talk about free cash flow, defined as net operating profits after tax minus changes in fixed investment and in working capital. Depreciation can be either included in its entirety in the cash flow definition, or the replacement part of depreciation can be subtracted from the free cash flow, on the grounds that it is a necessary expense required to maintain the business. In most businesses this is not a big problem, but it does become more important in capital-intensive industries. Here depreciation charges – which are not cash flow items – can substantially boost the EBITDA figure and so make the cash flow larger than would be the case with other earnings-based measures.

Of course it may be reasonable to argue that the depreciation "charge" is not available for distribution, and therefore should not be counted as being part of the free cash flow. One sector where this is a particular issue is the utility industry, where large investment programs are required over many years. The size of depreciation allowances, which are tax deductible, can become important. Tax relief on depreciation will lower the effective rate of taxation, and so add to the pool of funds theoretically available to be distributed to share-holders. Which means that EBITDA figures are going to be a lot bigger than EPS-based figures, and the shareholder value approach will tend to flatter performance in this sector.

Equally, in the financial services sector it can be quite difficult to find a relevant cash flow measure. Large flows of funds occur, but a distinction has to be made between funds that belong to the customers – which for sake of argument can simply "walk out of the door" – and funds that truly belong to the shareholders. SHV analysis requires a clear understanding of the property rights embodied in your company; in the financial services sector it helps to be absolutely clear about what belongs to whom.

The situation can be further confused in this sector by the existence of flows between the profit and loss and balance sheet for all sorts of sensible precau-tionary reasons. A definition of a free cash flow has to ensure that there is no double counting; so it is important to "ring-fence" the enterprise and, like a customs and immigration officer, ensure that you only count what goes through this border, ignoring what goes on inside.

Intangible assets and the cost of capital

Even though we dealt with this topic in Chapter 3, there are other aspects that we as SHV practitioners may need to consider. Cost of capital calculations depend crucially on being able to determine accurately the amounts of capital involved in a business. Not only does this require a clear view on current equity and debt, but also how they are going to evolve over time. It is a far from straightforward matter to be able to forecast balance sheets – which is what is required here.

There are further difficulties, of which one of the most important is the value placed on a company's assets. Traditional accounting measures are concerned almost entirely with book values; shareholder value, however, requires a market value approach, or what can be called a mark to market system. In this approach, you may need to know what the economically useful life of assets are, a point we raised earlier in Chapter 6.

The value of assets also has to be adjusted for various intangible items. Here it is helpful to think of four basic types of intangible assets:

- innovation capital
- structural capital
- market capital
- goodwill.

The question of valuing these assets is starting to become a serious macro-economic issue. Intangible assets not only form a significant part of total invest-ment, but there is evidence that, as Fig. 10.1 shows, investment in intangible assets is growing faster than for fixed assets. (This point is a worry for govern-ment statisticians.)

How can intangible assets be measured? SHV analysis takes account of the variety of approaches to answering this question, and sets reasonably clear priorities. With *innovation capital*, for instance, current accounting practice is to expense these items. A SHV approach would ideally like to see R&D capital-ized, and so included in the company's asset base. Current accounting practice overlooks innovation capital entirely; as a result there are often considerable discrepancies between the book and market value of companies. Recent work by Lev and Sougiannis[1] shows statistically significant and economically meaningful relationships between R&D and subsequent cash flows, and suggests that stock markets take implicit account of R&D investments, regard-less of whether they are reported formally in financial statements.

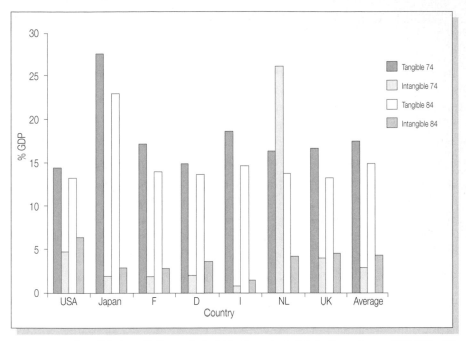

Source: *Technology and the Economy – the Key Relationships*, report on the Technology/Economy Programme (OECD, 1992), p. 113.

FIG 10.1 ● **Tangible and intangible investments**

It is important, then, to make adjustments in the balance sheet to reflect investments in R&D assets. Other adjustments need to be made, too, for *structural capital*: under this heading come items like intellectual capital and knowledge assets. Here, some credit should be given for organizational coherence and flexibility – the ability of an enterprise to adapt successfully to changes in circumstances. Elements such as workforce loyalty and skills (human capital) should have a value put on them, too.

Market capital, our third "intangible," consists of established brands, trademarks and other "mastheads" such as magazine titles in publishing. As useful assets contributing to the success of a company, these undoubtedly have an economic value: increasingly brands are bought, sold, licensed and managed in just the same way as other businesses. Just like their tangible counterparts, too, intangible assets need to show a satisfactory rate of return.

Although there are measurement difficulties, we think it is possible to identify brands that are sustainable business assets, often reinforced by high levels of advertising spending. Brand valuation is a controversial issue in mainstream accounting, but in the context of shareholder value we think it is a useful way of arriving at an improved estimate of an enterprise's assets involved in the business.

Taking account of these additional capital inputs will inevitably push the quantitative basis for SHV analysis away from standard accounting treatment. Since the definition of a firm's asset base is broader than that used by accountants, and includes all those items necessary to form an "economic" opinion about it, the results of such an analysis are going to differ, sometimes markedly, from more conventional accounting approaches.

Note, though, that one of the SHV approaches introduced in Chapter 6, SVA, is highly dependent on a running total of the economically defined asset based used in the business. This in turn will be a function of the new investment taking place and the rate of depreciation on the assets. In practice, it may not be easy to estimate this rate of depreciation – even if it needs to be done in order not to move back into the world of tax-driven depreciation rates.

Finally, *goodwill* needs to be accounted for properly. The tax and accounting treatment of goodwill varies considerably. The IAS (international accounting standards) period for depreciating goodwill is 20 years. This is likely to become more and more the accepted global standard for the required depreciation rates. Formally, the US GAAP allows a much more lenient 40-year depreciation period, but recent practice is pointing to an effective 20-year limit. The UK GAAP system is also comfortable with depreciation periods of up to 20 years. But exceptions are allowed ("rebuttals") and companies can seek other methods for valuing their intangible assets, some of which are getting closer to the economic definitions mentioned above.[2]

Note that, in the treatment of all these assets, we are striving to find what their "replacement" cost is – a technical but important matter. In our earlier discussions on CFROI and the SVA model (see Chapter 6), we looked at the role of a company's asset base and the distinctions that need to be made. Practitioners must carefully consider this aspect when using SHV models.

RESIDUAL VALUE

Calculations of residual value are normally carried out to give an indication of the continuing value of a business. They are based, as we said in Chapter 6, on the assumption that, at the end of the planning period, the business could be sold; a residual value calculation is basically a way of reaching an approximation of that value. As with any approximation, residual values work better in some circumstances than in others.

Under "normal" circumstances, taking a ten-year forecast period, the residual value will account for between 50 and 60 percent of the total value. As the forecast period diminishes, so the importance of an enterprise's residual value grows. However, with a start-up venture there is not only little historical information to go on; the future is also full of uncertainties. Unable to put very plausible forecasts together, we may have to rely for our valuation to a great extent on the residual value, which is itself dependent on an assumed cash flow or NOPAT in the final year, as well as the capital structure of the business and forecast interest rates.

Our experience of applying shareholder value includes several industries where special treatment of the residual value is needed. In resource industries, for instance, particularly oil and gas, we might specifically model a company's value on the expected lifetime of its oilfields, insofar as it is known. But where this remains too imprecise, we can simply make certain assumptions about the discovery of new resources and the depletion of existing ones to work out a life expectation for their given resources. Current behavior, possibly informed by the company's past record of discovering new resources (and being profligate with ones it has), will create an amended residual value, which could vary significantly between companies.

Similar concerns can arise in the financial sector, where for some enterprises income has an annuity type of profile. However, it will still be possible, on the basis of today's activities, and with the help of a few simplifying assumptions, to get an idea of the potential stored-up business within the firm. Life insurance, an important part of the insurance industry, falls into this category.

Special treatment will also be needed for new start-up companies, often in the high technology sector. Here, short product cycles mean that cash flow forecasts, which in any case are highly uncertain, are also very short – throwing the burden of any valuation heavily onto the residual value estimate. Later in this chapter, we will explore the "real options" methodology that offers a solution to this difficulty, and possibly points to one way in which SHV models might move in the future.

We will now turn to particulars. In this chapter's survey of the application of SHV to a selection of sectors we start with finance, where we will look at models that have already proved useful for the banking, insurance and fund management sectors. We will then move on to high technology and pharmaceuticals – industries characterized by fast technical change – before turning to the oil and gas sector. Finally we will examine two industries that share recent experience of privatization and deregulation: the telecommunications and utilities industries.

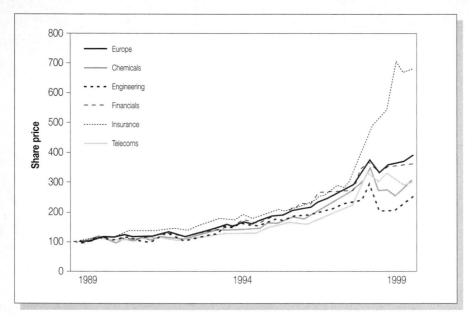

FIG 10.2 ● European TSR by selected sectors, 1989–99

FINANCIAL SERVICES

An under-performing area

One would have thought that the financial services sector would be more familiar with shareholder value issues than any other. Indeed, it is – but it is almost entirely with other people's shareholder value, and relatively rarely its own, that it concerns itself. The complications and special treatment that financial services require frequently lead managements to conclude that somehow their sector marches to a different drum from the rest of the world, and therefore it should not concern itself unduly with SHV analysis. We believe that both banks and insurance companies can be analyzed using the SHV approach just like other sectors – so long as certain adjustments are made in the model.

As we noted early in this book, the banks have provided an important part of the "glue" supporting the consensual, "stake-holding" view of the world that is particularly prevalent in mainland Europe and in Japan. Their recent performance, though, has left something to be desired, and except for one or two countries, banks have tended to under-perform in European stock markets. This is highly significant, since the banks are now less able to play their old role, and increasingly have to determine whether their investments and "strategic" holdings are aiding them in their own quest for shareholder value. Recent changes associated with the internet and online equity trading are giving a further emphasis to these trends and are highlighting the problems the sector is having in showing sustained SHV creation. As Figs. 10.2 and 10.3 show, both banking and insurance have significantly under-performed in Europe for several years. Indeed, they have been the worst performing sectors in the entire stock market. And, although the picture in the USA is better, that has only come about after several years of very poor performance during the last US recession at the beginning of the 1990s.

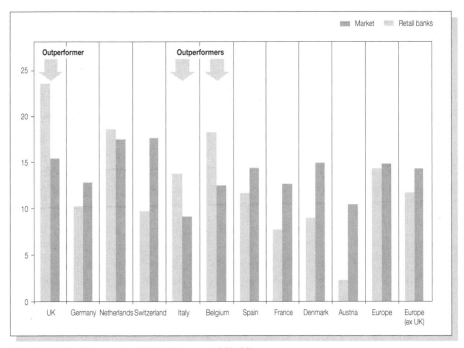

FIG 10.3 ● Banking sector TSR in Europe, 1988–98

Banking

You will recall that we have referred to one financial institution, Lloyds Bank, that has performed outstandingly in SHV terms, and has adopted a strategy that over several years has paid off handsomely. This is to some extent an exception in its field – one organization that has probably pioneered a process that others will have to follow, since it has clearly shown that it is possible to create shareholder value in the sector.

Our banking model is designed to value banks "externally" – that is, using publicly available information. It uses an equity approach and defines what we can call an "affordable dividend" similar to the free cash flow concept used in other models. By identifying those cash flows that accrue to shareholders and separating them out from the rest, we can "freeze" the debt position of the bank for the purposes of SHV analysis. Free cash flow in a financial institution can be thought of as the dividend-paying capacity of the business. This is not the same as cash flow in an accounting sense: banks have specific regulatory capital requirements and they cannot, except with special permission, issue dividends that reduce their share capital.

Like all SHV models, the banking model is forward-looking and relates forecast cash flows to current market capitalization, using publicly available information to arrive at free cash flow figures. Initially, it can be based on a relatively restricted amount of external information, but if internal information is available, we can develop the model in much greater detail – but still along the same lines as described here.[3] Just as with our other models we have the combination of benchmarking, valuation and sensitivity analysis – see Fig. 10.5, which is very helpful for understanding the competitive position of banks.

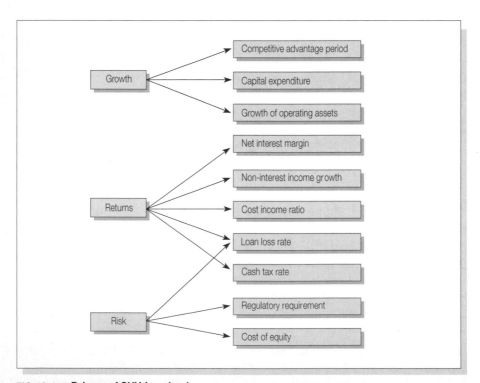

FIG 10.4 ● Drivers of SHV for a bank

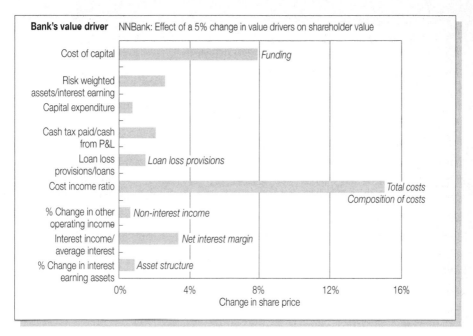

Bank's value driver   NNBank: Effect of a 5% change in value drivers on shareholder value

FIG 10.5 ● **Effect on SHV of changes in value drivers (example)**

As Fig. 10.4 shows, there are ten key value drivers of shareholder value for a bank proposed in this model, and these ten can be linked to the familiar three generic value drivers of growth, returns and risk. At the risk of going into technicalities, let us look at the ten drivers.

What the value drivers mean ...

Competitive advantage period

This is the period over which the bank is expected to earn an operating return (net operating profit less tax) in excess of the cost of equity (share capital employed times the cost of equity, using unlevered betas). This period is clearly difficult to estimate. The quantitative approach to estimating it could be to calculate the average duration of a bank's assets as a measure of "locked-in" value. A qualitative alternative would be to take a view of how sustainable the bank's competitive advantages are in the marketplace, and base a figure on that – we suggest three to five years, given that banking products are typically easy for competitors to duplicate. Free cash flows are then adjusted to mimic the end of the growth duration period; capital expenditure reverts to maintenance capital expenditure only (default of 75 percent) to reflect the cessation of new investment as no positive NPV projects exist. Furthermore, growth of operating assets and operating income reverts to a long-term inflation rate.

Capital expenditure

This is the amount spent in the year on new fixed assets, net of disposals. All capital expenditure is immediately charged to the equity holders. We therefore assume that there is an economic equivalence between funding capital expenditure completely from equity, and funding it from both equity and liabilities and then repaying the liabilities as the asset depreciates.

Growth in operating assets

Operating assets are made up of loans and other earning assets. Other earning assets include such items as short-term deposits, loans to banks, short-term investments, government securities, and long positions in securities. A forecast net interest margin on operating assets is used to calculate a forecast for net interest income. Changes of the overall level of operating assets are not considered an equity cash flow item since these are customer cash flows which are financed by depositors. This assumption is summarized by the maxim "every loan creates a deposit."[4]

Net interest margin

By this we mean net interest income as a percentage of operating assets. It is used as a proxy for the net interest cash flow margin from the operating asset portfolio. It is often pointed out that interest income includes a large accrued interest component and hence is not a cash flow measure. For our purposes it is reasonable to assume that for a large portfolio of loans with staggered maturities, accrued interest will be a good measure of interest cash flow. While we are aware of the importance of timing differences, we assume that the duration of both deposits and loans will remain roughly constant for the forecast period.[5]

Non-interest income growth

Non-interest income is made up of such items as fees, commissions and trading income. It is forecast using a growth projection. An alternative would be to use a proportion of total income.[6] We also separate out trading income from fee and commission income where we can.

Cost-income ratio

The cost-income ratio is a measure of the percentage of total income required to cover cash expenses. The cash expenses includes depreciation, since this is a commonly quoted and recognizable ratio. Depreciation is added back in the "affordable dividend" model.

Loan loss rate

Loan loss provisions are used as a proxy for the cash flow implications of non-performing assets. Once a default is incurred, the bank must repay the lenders, but receives less than the full amount of cash from the borrowers, and thus suffers a cash outflow. This effectively transfers the financing of the dud loan from liabilities to capital (reflected by a charge to the profit and loss account, which reduces shareholders' equity), and is effective as soon as the provision is made, not on the maturity of the loan.[7]

Cash tax rate

This is the actual cash tax paid in the accounting period and normally relates to the previous year of trading. When this figure is unavailable, accounting tax net of movements in deferred taxes can be taken as a proxy. If the cash tax figure is available, then the value driver should be expressed as a percentage of earnings before depreciation and amortization in the previous year.

Regulatory requirement

The regulatory capital requirement for banks and other financial institutions means that cash flows are withheld from shareholders in order to maintain capital adequacy. Our SHV banking model calculates the free cash flow implications of capital adequacy as a function of the risk-weighted assets and targets for tier one capital (equity capital and reserves) and total capital ratios.

Cost of equity

The cost of equity is calculated using the capital asset pricing model (CAPM) discussed in Part 1. We only look at the cost of equity, since the debt element is partly accounted for as a function of the regulatory reserves, and so we use unlevered betas.

How the banking model is different

Utilizing these ten drivers, we can put together an affordable dividend forecast model for a bank, as in the example – a simplified view – shown in Fig. 10.6. While it may look easy, it can be deceptively so: the derivation of some of the forecasts, and the links between some of the figures, can be more complex than represented here. You will need a good understanding of banks and their finances, aided by the interpretation of sector experts well informed about current and future developments.

What makes the banking model different from other sector models? The most significant difference is in the treatment of fixed assets and in the capital adequacy adjustment. A fixed asset account is maintained throughout the forecast horizon based on capital expenditure levels and the rate of depreciation of fixed assets. As Fig. 10.5 shows, the depreciation charge is added back to the free cash flow[8] and capital expenditures are deducted (based on a

Value drivers

	2001E	2002E	2003E	etc.
Total operating assets	642,858	680,236	716,610	
→ *Growth in operating assets*	*23.77%*	*5.81%*	*5.35%*	
Net interest income	11,189	11,783	12,390	
→ *Net interest margin*	*1.74%*	*1.73%*	*1.73%*	
Other operating income	7,056	7,154	7,799	
→ *Non-interest income growth*	*22.27%*	*1.39%*	*9.02%*	
Total operating income	18,245	18,936	20,189	
Operating expenses	(12,344)	(12,953)	(13,610)	
→ *Cost income ratio*	*67.66%*	*68.40%*	*67.41%*	
Add back: dep'n & amort	876	915	972	
Loans loss adjustment	(1,400)	(1,075)	(1,133)	
→ *Loan loss rate*	*0.22%*	*0.16%*	*0.16%*	
Total cash inflow from P&L	5,377	5,824	6,420	
Tax paid	(1,427)	1,546)	(1,704)	
→ *Cash tax rate*	*26.54%*	*26.54%*	*26.54%*	
Capital expenditure	(1,536)	(1,625)	(1,712)	
→ *Capital expenditure*	*0.23%*	*0.23%*	*0.23%*	
→ *Capital adequacy adjustment*	*(4,691)*	*(1,420)*	*(1,382)*	
Affordable dividend post pref	(2,449)	1,061	1,449	etc.
→ NPV at *cost of equity* 10.2%				

Competitive advantage period

Shareholder value

FIG 10.6 ● **Banking model**

percentage of operating assets). After the competitive advantage period, the level of capital expenditure is adjusted to maintenance capital expenditure.

The capital adequacy adjustment is also a special feature of our model, and underlines the point (often neglected by the banks themselves) that there is no such thing as a free lunch. Growing the balance sheet involves ensuring that there are adequate reserves to meet regulatory requirements.

These are not easy to calculate *ex ante* using external information, but let us assume the bank has target tier one and total capital ratios, and that these targets will be achieved. The bank is then assumed to move, as if in a straight line, from its current capital levels to its targets over the periods specified. Using forecasts for the future risk weighting of assets, we can then infer the amount of tier one and tier two[9] capital from the target ratios and the level of risk-weighted assets. In our view, "excess reserving" can be treated as a potential reduction of funds available to shareholders for distribution.

However, it is worth noting that many banks view "excess" reserves as being necessary not only for prudential reasons, but also as a way of bringing down their own re-financing costs on the tier two capital. Our own analyses suggest that too high a level of reserves on balances destroys more shareholder value than it creates.

In arriving at forecasts, and in understanding the inter-relationship between the variables in the banking model, some points need to be carefully considered:

● Bank profits from inter-mediation are affected by the structure of assets and liabilities and the underlying volatility of interest rates.

● Funding long-term assets with short-term liabilities will earn a greater spread in the forward part of the loan when mismatch risk is greatest (known as "riding the yield curve"). Further, the "endowment effect" of retail deposits enables banks to widen net interest margins during periods of high interest rates. These factors make it difficult to forecast future income from historic performance.

● Using the cost of equity to discount post-interest free cash flows heightens the sensitivity of this key value driver. This "equity" approach is necessary to reflect the fact that value can be created on the liabilities side of the balance sheet.

● The stringency with which BIS capital adequacy guidelines are enforced varies between countries. The actual risk weighting mix can also vary sharply from year to year. Complex and changing regulations affect shareholder value.

● Off-balance-sheet activity affects shareholder value and is difficult to forecast.

Even though a model of this kind is surrounded by many simplifying assumptions, we have found it helpful in examining many of the underlying problems of banks and identifying weaknesses. More importantly, when this SHV analysis is combined with a more detailed look at items like value at risk, and risk-adjusted performance measures, we have been able to put together a multi-dimensional diagnostic tool that provides very useful insights into the banking business.

Insurance

The insurance sector too is facing major challenges, not the least because recent stock market performance has been less than impressive. Competition for business is increasing as a result of the deregulation and the crossover into the insurance market of non-traditional providers such as bancassurers, who often have a captive customer base. There is also some convergence taking place, with long-term savings plans operated outside the industry competing with conventional life assurance schemes. The increasing sophistication of customers has sharpened the focus on value creation. Evidence of these changes and challenges comes in the form of a wave of mergers among UK insurance companies, and the decision by some to enter into new business areas, such as Prudential launching Egg, an online bank.

Financial reporting in the insurance industry is based on the historical development of regulation, financial reporting standards, generally accepted accounting principles (GAAP), and classical business management and control. Actuarial influences play their part, too. None of this sits easily with shareholder value.

The operational side of the business has timing complications which are amplified by the need for an effective investment strategy, which requires a long-term perspective. It also makes a difference what type of insurance company is being analyzed. In a "vertically integrated" composite insurer that controls its own distribution network, additional life policies result in an inflow of front-loaded fees and commissions which are retained within the company. There is thus an incentive to write new business in the short term, even if its profitability later on is questionable.

On the other hand, in a more decentralized insurance group that does not have its own distribution system, the bottom line on writing new business might look rather different. The profitability of newly acquired life business might be negative initially, since commissions to the distributor or sales force are often higher than the premium, and hence the incentive to write new business is rather low, even though its longer-term profitability might be quite high.

Internal management information, then, will not always be sufficient to strike a balance over time that will result in decisions aligned with SHV creation. From outside a company, it is even more difficult to extract meaningful information on its product mix and therefore the cash flow implications. With such information rarely in the public domain, it is no surprise that the sector is so poorly understood by financial analysts, who are often reduced to recommending insurance stocks entirely on their dividend-creating properties, with little thought to longer-term capital gains.

Cash flow basics

Although they are complex, at the end of the day insurance companies are still businesses operating under the same set of conditions as everyone else. They too have to show gains to their investors, and they too will come under the scrutiny of the markets. The model we have developed for the insurance industry therefore follows the banking pattern, where shareholder value is calculated on an equity basis, and the "affordable dividend" is the business value plus net book value of investments minus debt, where:

$$\text{Business value} = \frac{\text{Insurance cash flows}}{\text{Cost of equity}} + \text{Residual value}$$

Insurance companies perform three basic functions, each of which generates its own distinctive kind of cash flows. *Risk cash flows* result from their core business and relate to the evaluation, acceptance and spread of risks. *Investment cash flows* are generated when they act as financial intermediaries or investment managers. And *service cash flows* occur when they deliver administrative and other services, including for instance risk and investment-related services, for captives. It is also useful to distinguish between the two branches of insurance, general and life.

General insurance

By this is meant insurance for property, theft, fire and other such events. It is generally taken out by a customer for several years. In looking at general insurance, we need first to define an operating cash flow. Investment income belongs entirely to the shareholders in the general insurance industry, and hence should be added to the cash flows. The official solvency requirements are not particularly exacting, even under EU requirements, and most companies hold much larger reserves. As with the banking sector, we can make good estimates of future solvency requirements in the industry.

Investment assets only enter the picture in our model as part of the cash and other financial assets the insurance company has on its books, at market values, and at the start of the forecast period. Since, by definition, these assets will only grow by whatever the equity market risk premium is, they cannot add to shareholder value. Some adjustments may have to be made where new business is gained, resulting in more money to invest. As for the cost of equity, in general insurance it is treated in the same way as for other companies, following standard CAPM practice.

There are other value drivers over and above the usual ones that are peculiar to insurance. These include the volume of new business, the ratio of the business retained by the company (related to the importance of re-insurance), as well as factors contributing to claims and losses. They are all to be seen in Fig. 10.7, while Fig. 10.8 which shows an example of sensitivity analysis in the usual manner (compare Fig. 5.11 in Part 1) applied to insurance.

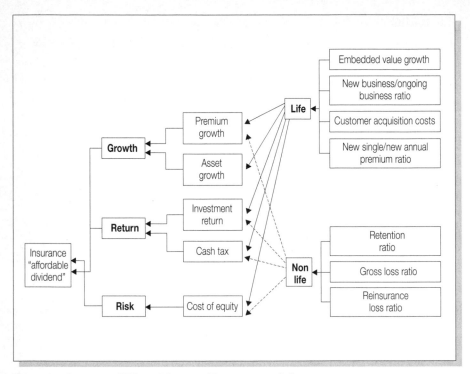

FIG 10.7 ● **Insurance SHV model: general insurance cash flow**

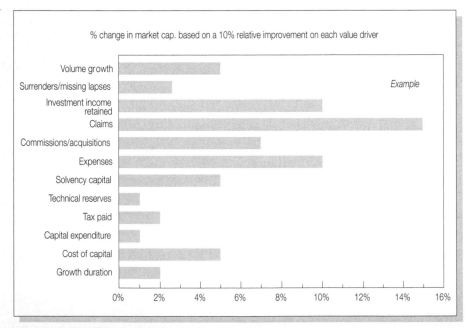

FIG 10.8 ● **Sensitivity analysis for insurance companies**

Life insurance

The subject of life insurance is a complex one, but a simplified view can be seen in Fig. 10.9. It all comes down to "property rights" – or who at the end of the day owns any surpluses earned on investments but not contractually promised to the client. In our view, life insurance is unlikely to generate much in the way of additional returns to shareholders. In cases where the policy holder obtains what he or she was promised, then there is nothing left over to shareholders – this is the central line in the diagram. The situation is more interesting when achieved investment performance differs from the promised sum. Where it is less, then the company and its shareholders have a contractual obligation to meet the promised payment, probably out of reserves, marked by the upper line. This situation can occur where erroneous forecasts about annuity income are made combined with too generous promises to policy holders. Where the sum promised is less than the investment performance achieved, then the difference will accrue to the shareholders, marked by the lower line. Here the shareholders stand to gain additional value. This simple principle highlights the crucial role that the question of property rights plays in understanding how to raise shareholder value performance in the insurance industry.

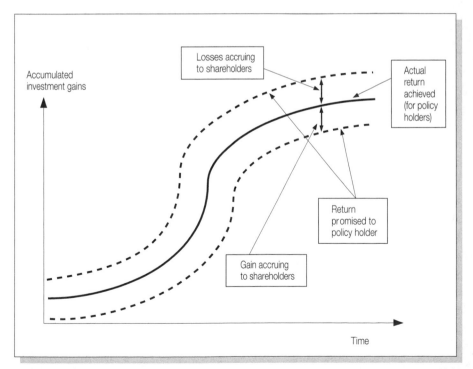

FIG 10.9 ● **SHV and life insurance**

Fund management

The final area in the financial services sector we want to feature is the investment management industry. Curiously, it seems that one of the last things on the minds of fund managers is looking after their own shareholder value, rather than that of their customers. Where else do you find the strange situation in which a sector's SHV rises faster than the value of a client's money; where a company's own SHV appears disconnected from what it actually does?

Shares in fund management companies prosper in bull markets and underperform in bear markets. Like the tides, managers think there is little they can do to affect this "natural" state of affairs – a state all the more alarming when you realize that many banks and insurance companies see expansion into the fund management business as being very desirable in its own right. It will, they think, provide a stable earnings base, just as other parts of their businesses become more volatile.

Publicly quoted fund managers in the UK show strikingly different total shareholder returns. As Fig. 10.10 shows, insurance companies having internal asset management groups performed significantly worse than the rest. Figures like these show very clearly that while some managements have very much had their eye on the ball, others' attention seems to have been wandering.

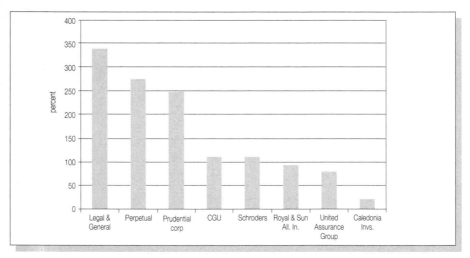

FIG 10.10 ● **Fund managers' TSR**

At PricewaterhouseCoopers we have looked more closely at how fund managers actually manage their businesses, once again applying the insights of SHV theory to the industry. There are, we have concluded, seven drivers that greatly influence shareholder value and which have been combined in a "Fundbuilder" model. The seven are:

● commission income/average funds under management (FUM)
● funds under management growth (average)
● EBITDA margins
● cash tax rate
● capital expenditure to sales
● cost of capital
● competitive advantage period.

Let us take these one at a time.

Income/average funds under management (FUM)

This gives an indication of how successful a business is in concentrating on activities with reasonable returns. More detailed analysis can show how this differs across asset classes, type of customer and sometimes by geography and market. Although there are different legal compliance costs, the fact remains that there are significant variations in the overall "gross" margins earned in the industry. While, for example, retail and wholesale fund management may appear to be different types of business, managements must understand that the one may be inherently more profitable than the other. In the interests of SHV, choices may very well need to be made.

FUM growth

This is a key driver for the business, since it largely defines the gross income created. Distinctions have to be made between the change in value of the existing funds and the value of new funds and mandates won. FUM growth will also be a function of the firm's perceived success in managing customers' money relative to the competition. These various effects need to be carefully separated out, since better performance resulting from good macro market conditions should be distinguished from better performance resulting from direct management action. SHV performance is improved when both the macro and the micro environments are performing well.

EBITDA margins

This refers to the margin earned by the firm after deducting all its costs and expenses, but before interest tax, depreciation and amortization. It gives a broad indication of a company's efficiency. Figure 10.11 shows that while the investment management companies surveyed have been successful in pushing up revenues, their staff costs have been rising more rapidly, suggesting that EBITDA margins are under pressure. Managing the EBITDA margin is something that companies in the sector find rather hard to do, necessary though it is.

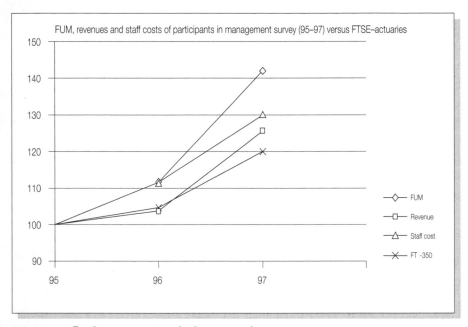

FIG 10.11 ● **Fund management and other companies**

Cash tax rates

These represent a deduction from free cash flow, and vary from company to company in the sector.

Capital expenditure

Often thought of as small beer, since the numbers are so often dwarfed by others, such as the funds under management. But capex can be a surprisingly large drain on company resources; there are very real questions relating to the efficiency with which it is spent. Fund management groups spend large sums on items such as information technology, back-office systems and the like, not all of which feeds through to the bottom line in terms of improved performance.

Cost of capital

Most fund managers are effectively debt-free, so that this reduces to the cost of equity. This is a more demanding hurdle rate than some realize, especially if returns are being earned in the fixed income markets.

Competitive advantage period

The period over which a fund management company is expected to create SHV by having a return on capital greater than the cost of capital can in this industry be relatively short, and it is difficult for companies to maintain a sustained competitive advantage for more than a few years.

Benchmarking and flexing

Equipped with information about these seven drivers, we can use our model to use benchmarking and sensitivity analysis to provide a valuation of the company in question and thus see how the company should manage its scarce resources to enhance SHV. As we have said earlier in this book, the objective of benchmarking and flexing is to analyze the financial drivers of the company and so reinforce the message of shareholder value throughout the company.

Managing companies in this industry is as often based on intuition and "feel" as it is on cool appraisal. Often there may be a lack of information about client profitability, which can lead to investment managers trying to retain a client relationship even though it is not a profitable one and so destroying SHV.

Another issue is that of staff costs. "Star" fund managers can be lured away from competitors in the belief that they will improve fund performance and so bring some of their clients to their new company. The SHV model allows a cooler assessment of whether the additional costs caused by employing the star will ever generate sufficient new business to add to existing SHV. Finally, the model enables management to see more clearly where their profits are coming from, and so "steer" the business to focus more on higher margin products and clients.

Financial services back on track?

This brief overview of SHV models in the financial services sector has, we hope, shown that even in this difficult area it is possible to apply SHV analysis successfully. What we have described here is a methodology that enables financial institutions to be analyzed in a similar way to firms in other industries, suggesting that their problems are very similar.

Some banks in the UK have made a start in the right SHV direction, and they have been joined by others in mainland Europe. UBS is one bank that found itself challenged by an advocate of a more SHV-oriented approach. Recent takeover battles such as SocGen–Paribas in France, and for Natwest in the UK, are also motivated in large part by efforts to improve shareholder performance. Still, a large number of big financial institutions in the rest of Europe and Japan are very unclear about how they are going to increase their shareholder value in the future. It is never too late to try!

PHARMACEUTICALS, TECHNOLOGY, THE INTERNET, AND KNOW-HOW-INTENSIVE INDUSTRIES

Areas of uncertainty

There is certainly something different about technology-intensive industries when it comes to SHV analysis. The uncertainties and risks involved are very high, and since the pace of technological change is so fast, effective growth duration periods can be very short indeed. Here we will look at two SHV applications. One is the pharmaceuticals industry, where there are quite specific competitive conditions, often limited by current patent law, and by the ease or difficulty with which companies can actually patent new drugs; the other is the more generic high-technology area, covering such industries as biotechnology, semiconductors and computer software.

Our look at high-technology industries will involve trying to put a value on the options facing a company once a project has reached a certain stage in its life. Since companies in this area are frequently small and in start-up situations there is a close identity between the project and the company.

But for both areas our models will aim to bring a detailed industry understanding to bear on the question of SHV determination. Given the high rate of failure, particularly in the start-up area, we feel it is important that managements are given the opportunity to align their policies with shareholder value.

Pharmaceuticals

Recent trends

The whole issue of SHV is becoming ever more relevant to this sector, and a survey of recent trends helps to explain why. The pharmaceutical industry experienced double-digit sales growth rates in the 1970s and 1980s, and significant year-on-year profit increases, supported by price flexibility and strong sales from "blockbuster" drugs (commonly defined as those drugs having annual sales exceeding $1 billion).

The industry remained highly fragmented over this period, with no one company having more than 10 percent of the market. Indeed, if looked at more closely, many of the leading players in the industry are dependent on the continued success of a rather small number of products. Figure 10.12 shows the example of Warner Lambert, which has been strikingly dependent on one product, Lipitor, and it is by no means the only company in this position.

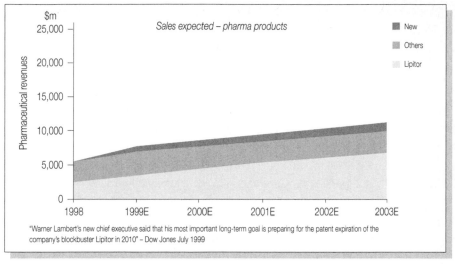

Source: PwC; Morgan Stanley Dean Witter February 1999

FIG 10.12 ● **A pharmaceutical company dependent on one product**

The common strategy of major pharmaceutical companies in the past has been simply to allocate significant resources to R&D with the aim of generating blockbuster drugs. These compensate for under-performance elsewhere in the product portfolio as well as mitigating the effects of manufacturing and other operational inefficiencies – the average rate of asset utilization in the industry is only 20 percent.

There have been increasing signs that these strategies are no longer working their old magic; the industry's previously buoyant sales growth has now fallen to just 6 percent a year. Among the contributory factors are:

● Longer and stricter product development processes. Formal phases of development were introduced as a result of the Thalidomide scandal in the 1960s. The length of the development process has now increased to an average of 10 to 12 years, costing $400 million to $500 million.

● Slower rate of discovery of new chemical entities (NCEs), which are the basic fuel for the development pipeline. Changes arising from the new combinatory chemistry have yet to feed through.

● Fewer blockbusters.

● Pharmacoeconomics, which has introduced a need to demonstrate cost-efficiency, in addition to efficacy and safety. Public sector health providers are becoming increasingly cost conscious and skeptical about the apparent benefits from new drugs.

● Generic competition encouraged by US laws, which allow competitor companies to prepare for commercialization of "me-too" drugs even before patents expire. This can have dramatic effects on the cash flows earned by aging products.

The consequence is increasing pressure to manage R&D funds for value and assess alternative sources of revenue with an understanding of the specific drivers of value within the pharmaceutical industry. These pressures are also behind the recent mergers in the industry as it has become aware of the problems caused by too little attention to SHV. There has been very varied shareholder value performance of the main players in the industry over the last few years. They range from highly impressive TSRs of over 90 percent in a year (Hoechst in 1996) to a negative TSR of minus 6 percent in the same period (Roche, who did nevertheless achieve a much more respectable 30.5 percent return over the five years from January 1992). Shareholder value also varies greatly when compared to the company's local stock market, with little general pattern emerging.

The SHV model

In line with our practice in other sectors, our model includes several features specific to the pharmaceutical industry. One of the most important of these is the skewed pattern of sales by product, which can tail off quite quickly after patents expire. A typical product life cycle is shown in Fig. 10.13.

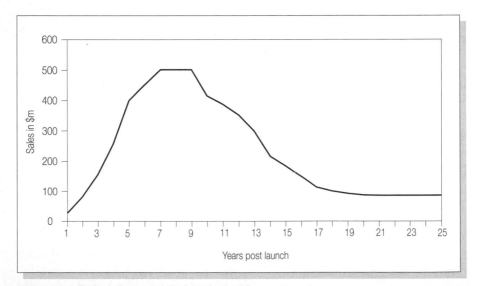

FIG 10.13 ● **Typical pharmaceutical product cycle**

Under favorable conditions, such a pattern can produce a strong positive cash flow, with marketing expenses falling as the product matures. However, the strength of this flow depends greatly on an ability to maintain sales even after patents have expired, and on customer loyalty strong enough to resist the temptation of cheaper "me-too" products made by competitors. Neither of these two factors are anything like as powerful as they once were in the industry. The profit-generation capabilities of a "good" drug are described in Fig. 10.14.

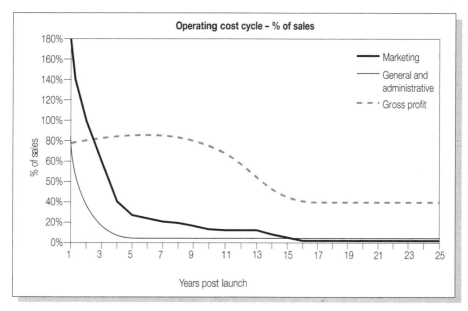

FIG 10.14 ● **Profit generation capabilities of a "good" drug**

One SHV model for this industry derives aggregate cash flow projections for the existing portfolio of products on the market from:

● the typical pattern of cash flows for an average drug within the operation;

● the mix of stages within the existing portfolio of products.

In Fig. 10.15 we identify three areas that are of particular importance for SHV in pharmaceuticals. Firstly we have the whole area of the efficiency with which R&D expenditures are made, bearing in mind that they are also adding to the total capital of the company. The second is the advantages obtained in speeding up the launch of a new product, which can have a dramatic effect on

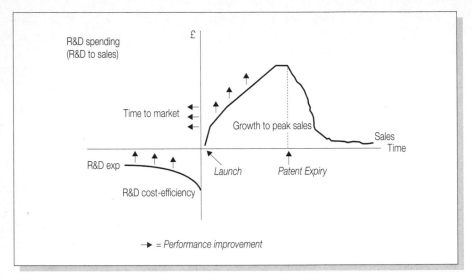

FIG 10.15 ● **Stages of production in the pharmaceutical industry**

the subsequent profitability of the operation, extending as it can the effective life of the product. Thirdly we have the speed with which sales can be grown. Here it is very important to try and obtain a "first mover" advantage. Note though, having the product first in the marketplace is not necessarily sufficient to guarantee subsequent success, and there have been occasions when later entrants have been able to take the jackpot owing to their better therapeutic performance and more favorable pricing.

Figure 10.16 shows the connections between the generic drivers of shareholder value and the industry-specific value drivers. Among the listed drivers to consider for each drug are key parameters like the level of peak sales, the speed of sales decline following the appearance of competition from generic products, and whether the product was developed in-house with a higher gross margin. Additional factors such as the time to market and costs of development also have to be included.

Applications

We see our model as being particularly helpful in addressing the question of the shareholder value implications of important changes taking place in the industry. These can include establishing answers to "make-or-buy" questions and "disintegrating" the value chain, outsourcing parts of the production and distribution process. Considerations can range from examining the usefulness of using contract research organizations who can handle parts of the clinical

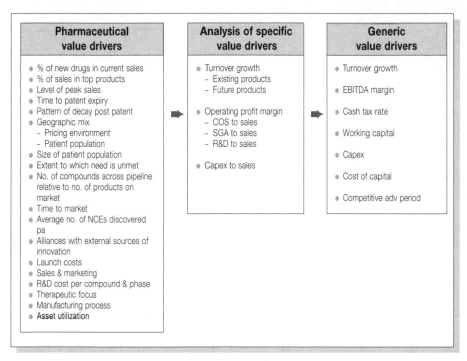

FIG 10.16 ● **Industry-specific and generic drivers of SHV in pharmaceuticals**

trial process, through to asking whether it makes sense to have an internal sales force if its functions can be better handled by an outsourcing arrangement.

High technology, internet and start-ups

Under this heading we subsume technology-intensive industries where innovation is the driving force. They are often emerging industries created through the development of new technology, e.g., the internet, biotechnology, or pollution control. Or they can be more or less mature industries which continue to show technology intensity, such as parts of the IT industry: semiconductors, computer hardware, and computer software or consumer electronics.

Innovation is at the centre of this sector, as are highly optimistic expectations about the future. Recently, this has led to what some see as "fanciful" valuations of companies that trade at extremely high multiples of anything you care to name. Applying to such companies the sort of SHV models so far outlined can be difficult, simply because of an acute lack of reliable information. Indeed, a lot of the information that is available shows negative cash flows, and thus cannot be easily used to justify the existing high values assigned to such stocks by investors.

There have been several reactions to this. One group of investors has been content to run with the tide and proclaim that the time has come to throw away the old valuation methods and adopt entirely new ones. For the time being this may only be relevant for the new hi-tech and internet sectors. One such approach increasingly mentioned in this context is that of using "real options," which we will look at in more detail below. Another, more skeptical, view is to say that the market is greatly overheated, and that the basic SHV models can reflect the true reality of the companies concerned, namely that the market is expecting sustained growth of close to 100 percent a year for several years, accompanied by very high margins. The term "scaleability" is used here to suggest that there are strongly increasing returns to investors as the volume of business grows. Internet companies don't need anything like the same commitment of resources to support a given volume of business – or so the explanation goes. The view adopted here is that existing approaches should be heeded and not thrown away, while some measure of the reward for flexibility can be seen by taking a "real options" approach to valuation. R&D and the technology life cycle can be linked within the framework of an SHV model. Under the name "TechnologyBuilder," our model aims to put the valuation of technology companies on a more objective basis and incorporate much of that "gut feeling" into quantitative valuation.

The two components of high-tech value

In dealing with high-technology companies we must distinguish between two sorts of value. Firstly that arising from the value of existing assets, and secondly that from the company's future growth opportunities, over and above those captured in the normal cash flow forecast. This can be defined as:

$$MV = VEA + VGO$$

where MV is market valuation, VEA is value from existing assets, and VGO is the value of the company's growth opportunities.

The first component of company value, that from existing assets, is the value of the capitalized free cash flows (FCF) that are being generated from the firm's current endowment, i.e. a perpetuity of the FCF anticipated for the current year. To calculate the anticipated FCF, we follow our standard ValueBuilder procedure. This is shown graphically in Fig. 10.17.

The stock market's current view on the value of a company's future growth opportunities (VGO) can be determined as the difference between the market valuation of the company (i.e. the current market capitalization plus debt) and the value from existing assets. In order to get a feel for the market's perception

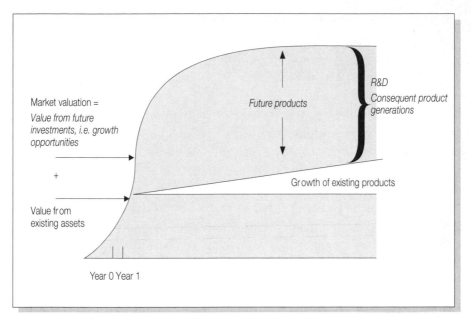

FIG 10.17 ● **Evolution of FCF, VEA and VGO over time, illustrating a product life cycle**

of the VGO of a number of technology firms, we made the calculations shown in Table 10.1: first, we worked out the value of existing assets (in column 4) as a perpetuity of the anticipated FCF (in column 2), using the company's weighted cost of capital (WACC, in column 3). We then subtracted the value of existing assets (in column 4) from the market valuation of the company (in the first column) to arrive at the market's perception of the VGO (in column 5). In the last column we express the VGO as a percentage of the market value of the company.

All of this goes to show that, in the technology industry, growth opportunities account for a large proportion of a company's total value, in most cases more than 70 percent. Or to put it another way, a naïve SHV/DCF approach will tend to radically undershoot the valuations currently available in the marketplace. Note that the stock market valuation of companies that have never been cash-positive works on exactly the same expectation.

What are the micro drivers?

Using a standard SHV model allows us to perform a familiar sensitivity analysis to find how a company's value might be affected by changes in the seven drivers. And, as we have seen earlier, the level of detail can be increased by "drilling down" from macro drivers to micro drivers. In the high-technology

TABLE 10.1 ● **Market valuations of companies' future growth opportunities (VGO)**

Companies	US$ (million)	Market value (2/2/2000)	Anticipated FCF 1999	WACC	Perpetuity value of FCF	Perceived value of growth opportunities	% of market value
Hardware							
Dell Computer		32,459	800.4	11.9%	6,226	25,733	79.3%
Hewlett-Packard		75,596.0	2,864	11.1%	15,598.1	49,320.7	65.2%
IBM		217,934	5,177.5	10.2%	50,759.8	13,611.9	76.7%
Semiconductors							
Motorola		36,648	1,184.0	11.0%	10,736.6	25,884.3	70.6%
Intel		208,874	4,237.5	11.2%	38,638.8	169,735.0	81.5%
Consumer electronics							
Thomson		6,136.9	552.0	9.4%	5,872.3	3,807.4	77.0%
Philips		38,552.0	345.6	10.1%	3,421	33,137	86.0%

sector, these driving forces vary from area to area, so individual micro drivers have to be used.

Take the computer hardware industry, where cost pressures and scale economies are dominant. Since semiconductors now account for 40 percent of the cost of a PC, chip content is becoming a pervasive shareholder value driver in this industry. In the semiconductor industry the drivers are related to Moore's Law (which predicts a doubling of processing capability every 18 months) and by book-to-bill ratios. In the internet industry we have drivers like churn rate, views per page and so on.

A matter of options

As SHV practitioners we can also look at a company's future growth opportunities (VGO) from a bottom-up company view, based on internal management information, where it is available. The VGO will be based upon the company's internal know-how, which offers a number of options on different future strategies. For instance know-how could have been gained through previous investments in products with multiple product generations or through research and development efforts.

These options are very similar to the options on stocks in financial markets: both are concerned with the right, as distinct from an obligation, to do something. In the financial markets it is the option to buy an underlying asset, and in our SHV view it is the option to invest in a project at an anticipated investment cost once the know-how is available. Our model can provide a valuation of these future growth options, and hence verify the top-down approach followed by so many financial analysts. (Share prices in high-technology stocks are very sensitive to news flows, and thus to the reappraisal of the value of various options.)

As we have seen, our model splits company value into two components: value from existing assets and value of future growth opportunities (VGO). The VGO is the sum of all future innovations. We look at each of these innovations via the four phases of the technology life cycle which follow basic research: invention, innovation, diffusion and maturity, using option pricing.

The key insight behind this approach is that each phase can be considered a "real" call option on the next phase of the life cycle. Registration of a new patent (invention) offers an option to develop a marketable product, whose market introduction (innovation) in turn offers an option to set the standard in the market (diffusion), which contains an option to become the market leader and reach a certain level of peak sales (maturity). Exercising these "call options" at any one stage depends on a management's assessment of how profitable the technology concerned will be.

Alternatively, each phase can be looked at as offering a "put" option – an option to abandon the development process and recoup some or all of the cost by obtaining a liquidation value if conditions turn out unfavorably. Figure 10.18

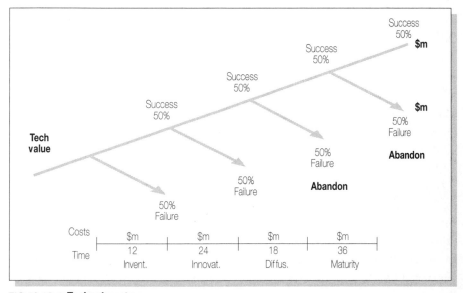

FIG 10.18 ● Technology tree

maps the "engine" of the VGO of technology companies, the "technology tree," against the four phases of a technology life cycle.

Valuing innovation

The crucial parameters for valuing the technology tree, the so-called option drivers, are:

- the probabilities of reaching the respective next stage;
- the time horizons of the individual stages;
- cash in- and outflows, namely the expected cash flow in case the target for the maturity phase is reached;
- costs (which are saved if the process is abandoned); and
- liquidation values.

Although industry averages exist for probabilities, timings, and, to a certain degree, for cash flows, the model allows for individual companies to use their own figures if they differ from these averages.

Sensitivity analysis can show the influence of these option drivers on the value of the relevant technology or project and on company value. Through it, you can for example answer questions such as "What happens to our company value if we manage to improve the success probabilities of our R&D process for a certain product, or for all products, by X percent?" Our model also helps put a value on "internal flexibility" – a firm's ability to appraise a project quickly, to decide whether to proceed with it and possibly speed up (or delay) the next step in the process.

Our model assumes that after a company's competitive advantage period (CAP) is over, the return on new investment just equals the cost of capital so that no additional company value is created from new investment. In many cases, the length of the technology life cycle determines the length of the competitive advantage period. The residual value, i.e. the component of the company value that arises after the CAP, is the perpetuity of a percentage of FCF at peak sales. It enters the technology tree together with the FCF that arises during the CAP.

Once they have established a track record of innovation – and a commensurate ability to generate sufficient demand for their products – most technology companies are faced with two choices when it comes to new projects. They can either decide to shoulder all the risks involved by making a full investment and trying as hard as possible to ensure it pays off. Or they can evade the risks by doing nothing and waiting for market trends to become clearer – by which time a bolder competitor might have taken the lead. But there is a third possibility: to manage the risks by acquiring growth options. A growth option offers a company the internal or external flexibility to participate in future growth at very limited risk to shareholder value.

They can, for example, invest in potentially cash-negative joint ventures and strategic networks, i.e. alliances with suppliers and competitors undertaken for the sake of "being in business" with the right partners rather than for immediate profits. Academic studies have shown that managers intuitively attach a much higher value to such investment opportunities than would be justified on the basis of a discounted cash flow valuation.[10] Again, option pricing theory offers ways of valuing this often neglected, highly intangible but nevertheless often significant source of the VGO.

Real options drivers

The two-component approach of our "TechnologyBuilder" SHV model enables valuation to be done using the most powerful information both from the present (cash flows from existing assets) and for the future (success probabilities, timings, cash flows). We now want to suggest a way in which the real options approach can be usefully combined with some of the SHV models that we have been explaining earlier. We can continue to operate in a DCF framework, but use this to incorporate some of the insights about options. The combination can be very helpful in establishing a wider range of feasible values for an enterprise and can enhance our understanding of the value of flexibility.

Let us return to our earlier example, in Chapter 6, of a VROI calculation for judging whether a project should proceed or not. We will use Table 6.1 in Chapter 6 and amend the figures to take into account a new "lumpy" investment in Year 3 – see Table 10.2. Since we are talking about an expensive project for this year, the VROI ratio is now under 1, and according to this "decision rule" the project should be rejected. But supposing we break the project down into two phases, Phase A and Phase B. Phase A is the same as for the first three years of projects, but after that assumes that the business continues more or less as before, with no great changes to either investment or achieved cash flows. This is shown below as Table 10.3, where we have taken all the annual investments and lumped them together and treated them as a single outflow in Year 1 (£31 million). This gives an NPV sum of £58.8 million.

TABLE 10.2 ● VROI calculation for a technology company

At a WACC of 15%	Year 0	Year 1	Year 2	Year 3	Year 4	Year 5	Year 6
Profit after tax (PAT)	16.0						
Assets employed (nominal)	80.0						
Incremental cash flow		12.0	14.0	12.0	15.0	21.0	30.0
Discount factor		0.9	0.8	0.7	0.6	0.5	0.4
Present value		10.8	11.2	8.4	9.0	10.5	12.0
Residual value							300.0
Present value of residual							120.0
Present value of cash flows							61.9
Total present value pre-strategy	106.7						
Total present value post-strategy							181.9
Total assets employed inflation adjusted. (3% inflation assumed)							95.5
Incremental net investment		5.0	8.0	100.0	7.0	8.0	5.0
Present value of incremental investment		4.5	6.4	70.0	4.2	4.0	2.0
Total present value of incremental investment							91.1
VROI calculation							
(Post-pre) strategy value							75.2
VROI = (post-pre) strategy/ PV incremental investment							0.8
Q ratio = (post-pre) strategy value/total assets (inflation adjusted)							1.9

What happens when we look at Phase B? This is shown in Table 10.4, where there are a couple of things to note – first, that the NPV value is now at £82.9 million and, second, that we have reduced the discount rate. The reason for this is that, having embarked on Phase A, the risks involved in Phase B will generally be lower. It will also have the effect of adding greater weight to the later cash flows that the project creates.[11]

TABLE 10.3 ● **Real option calculation, Phase A: all investment made in the initial year**

	Year 0	Year 1	Year 2	Year 3	Year 4	Year 5	Year 6
Incremental cash flow		12.0	14.0	12.0	10	11	12
Investment		5.0	8.0	6.0	5.0	4.0	3.0
Sum of investment		−31.0					
Residual value							100
Discount factor @ 15%		0.9	0.8	0.7	0.6	0.5	0.4
Present value per year		−17.1	11.2	8.4	6.0	5.5	44.8
NV (sum of years)		58.8					

TABLE 10.4 ● **Real option calculation, Phase B: additional investment in Year 3**

	Year 0	Year 1	Year 2	Year 3	Year 4	Year 5	Year 6
Incremental cash flow				0.0	5.0	10.0	18.0
Investment				94.0	2.0	4.0	2.0
Sum of investment				−102.0			200.0
Discount factor @ 5.5%				0.85	0.81	0.77	0.73
Present value per year				−86.9	4.0	7.7	158.1036
NPV (sum of years)		82.9					

Now, having got this far we need to think how to cast this problem in a way that can be analyzed in an options framework. Figure 10.19 describes what we need in order to do this.

Option valuations can be reduced to five variables. These are the stock or share price, the exercise price, the time to expiration, the risk-free rate of return and the variance of the stock returns, otherwise known as the volatility. If you have information on these variables, it is then possible to calculate an option value using the formula on the right of the figure. If we can obtain values for NPV_q (see below) and for the time-adjusted volatility factor T, then we can use these to establish what the option value is. This option value can then be added to the initial value of Phase A to establish the overall value for Phase A. Figure 10.19 shows the mapping of the categories used for forecasting a project's various stages onto the categories needed to calculate the underlying option value.

So the present value of the incremental assets used, or the cash flows created by the project, can be interpreted as being similar to the stock price needed for

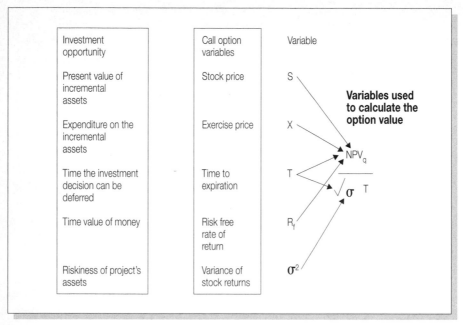

FIG 10.19 ● **From investment strategy to real option value**

(after Tim Luehrman)

an options price calculation. The investment spending for the project can be thought of as the exercise price. The time the decision can be deferred, or the time when the project is expected to start, can be thought of as the time to expiration. The time value of money (the discount rate) is the same as the risk-free rate of return used for option price calculations, and finally the riskiness of the project's assets is equivalent to the variance in the stock returns, or the volatility of the stock.

All these items are the same as those needed to calculate the value of an option, and this is exactly what we can do here. We calculate the adjusted NPV number, NPV_q, which is the present value of the created cash flows divided by the present value of the expenditure needed for the investment. Similarly, on the risk side we need to know the volatility, here assumed to be 0.4, and the time factor, which is three years. We bring this together as in Table 10.5.

The two figures to bear in mind here are the values for NPV_q and the "risk" factor, the volatility multiplied by the square root of the deferral time (here, three years). With the help of the ValueBuilder™ model, for a NPV_q value of .955 and risk term of .693, we obtain a value of .255.

Now, where does the real option value enter into the picture? We interpret the .255 as being equivalent to the additional value an investor would be willing to pay for Phase A of the project in the light of the developments expected in

TABLE 10.5 ● **Real option analysis**

	S = PV of the Phase 2 assets	X = investment spending to obtain Phase 2 assets	Risk free rate	Time	Discount factor	NPV$_q$	Impact on Black Scholes value	Implied volatility	Time	Sigma square root of time
New base case	82.9	102.0	1.055	3	1.174	0.955	0.255	0.4	3	0.693

Phase B. In other words, an investor will be willing to pay an additional 25 percent (expressed as a decimal) over and above the price of Phase A to purchase the option of proceeding to Phase B. In this case we take the NPV of Phase A, which is 58.8, and add to that the Black-Scholes adjusted value of Phase B (82.9 × .255, or 21.15). Or in other words, the real option value of Phase A is

NPV Phase A	58.8
Call option value, Phase B assets	21.15
Total	79.95

What we have done here is to use a very simple example to try and show how much the "flexibility" of creating an option on Phase B is worth. Other cases exist where the NPV values can be very small, and most of the value is embedded in the option to proceed to later stages. This is a situation that is often met in newly launched high-tech and internet stocks. This approach may assist in establishing a different context within which to value a project where there is little available information, and helps to focus management attention on the relatively most important phases. Indeed, it offers a fresh perspective by suggesting that technology companies essentially are managers of a portfolio of options. Its technology life-cycle-based approach might well represent the missing piece in the technology valuation jigsaw.

Finally, a brief note on some of the sensitivities involved. Just as we can see what happens with the other models when one of the underlying value drivers is flexed, so we can do the same with the real options model. The results can be seen in Fig. 10.20.

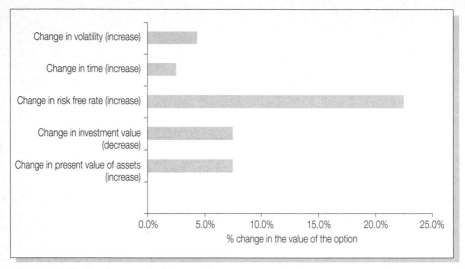

FIG 10.20 ● **Real option sensitivity analysis**

OTHER SECTORS

Oil and gas

The important oil and gas sector is often associated with large integrated companies that control all stages of production from exploration through to retailing. In recent years the emergence of effective secondary markets between each of the various stages of production means that it is no longer essential for an oil company to be present in all aspects of the oil business. As a result, the question of which parts of the oil business create shareholder value has been given greater urgency.

Our approach to the oil and gas industry is not only to look at the different stages of production, shown in the simplified value chain at Fig. 10.21, but also to give some thought to the connections between them.

Oil and gas companies once used to be led exclusively by professionals from technological backgrounds who, although competent in technical aspects of petroleum engineering, were not always as sensitive to the issues surrounding valuation and finance as they could have been. The wave of restructuring in the form of corporate mergers and takeovers that overtook the industry in the 1980s was to some extent a response to this, as falling oil prices focused attention on the process of value creation.

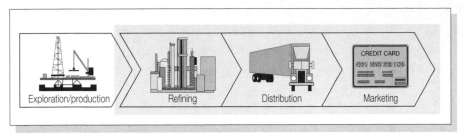

FIG 10.21 ● Simplified value chain for oil and gas industry

With the oil companies of the 1990s and beyond increasingly being steered by professionals with finance backgrounds, due attention is now being paid to shareholder rights and to communicating to the market about issues that impact on company value. For example, at its triennial investor relations briefing in December 1996, Royal Dutch/Shell outlined its mission as the creation of shareholder value based upon the themes of profitability and portfolio management, focus on growth and the containment of costs.[12] It has subsequently come under much criticism for having failed to deliver on these promises.

Another oil major that adopted and incorporated the SHV focus in its strategy is British Petroleum (BP). By proactively identifying value creation opportunities and value-destroying business lines, it has been able to deliver improved performance and provide shareholders with real dividend and capital growth. At its 1996 AGM, Sir David Simon, chairman of BP said: "Shareholder return is our key performance measure."[13] Clearly, oil companies that fail to deliver value are becoming vulnerable to corporate raids in the next phase of restructuring. BP has been able to use its superior performance in SHV terms to create a platform on which it was subsequently able to take over Amoco and become the third largest oil company in the world.

Special features of the oil and gas model

Upstream: exploration and production

The features most difficult to include in a shareholder value model are concentrated in the upstream end of the business. Here, great uncertainties with respect to the size and quality of reserves, as well as the expected life of oilfields, can affect subsequent valuations. The growth duration period, therefore, should be treated as being that of the average life of the oil fields currently owned and operated by the company.

But this is only part of the story. There is also the question of valuing the continuing operations of the company after the end of the forecast period. In our view they can be approximated by referring to the discovery/depletion ratios of the companies. Companies with good discovery rates and relatively slow rates of depletion are going to be "oil rich" in the years to come; equally, a company that is profligate with its existing reserves, and is not good at discovering new oil sources, will not be.

Other features in the oil industry include a long investment horizon between the pre-license phase and commercial production that can involve significant capital expenditure – for instance exploration costs, development costs and production costs. There is often little correlation between exploration expenditure and the value of reserves. The major economic value of a field lies in the underlying oil/gas reserves and is a function of estimated reservoir life and US dollar oil price.

The US dollar price of crude oil is one of the key exogenous drivers of value – if not the key one – for the upstream industry: it has a major influence, together with production volume, on turnover. Crude oil price is in turn a function of the supply/demand relationship. On the supply side, the OPEC producers, with their huge oil reserves, play a major role in influencing crude prices. On the demand side, oil prices are influenced by several factors such as the individual refined product demand, economic growth, seasonal weather and so on. Furthermore, a company might be producing, in different quantities, several qualities of oil, each with a different price in the market. In overcoming these seemingly complex problems, we need to differentiate between long-term underlying trends and the short-term "noise" that impacts upon prices. It is the long term that is more relevant in a valuation exercise, although it helps to understand the short-term issues. All of this complicates the forecasting of oil prices into the future.

The main drivers in the model are shown in Fig. 10.22 below. On the E&P (exploration and production) side, oil companies have very minimal inventory, as crude is transported from well-head to refinery as soon as it is produced and so working capital is not a key driver of value.

Downstream: manufacturing to marketing

The oil and gas industry is an interesting combination of unusual and "usual" factors. While the upstream part of the business requires some rather specialized drivers, this is not the case with the downstream part of the business. Indeed, we find that the generic SHV model can cope quite well with the downstream end: an oil company's valuation can be based on the familiar seven value drivers. Although the processes involved are extremely complex, externally the refining business is a manufacturing business. The raw material – crude oil – is physically separated and chemically treated to yield a range of

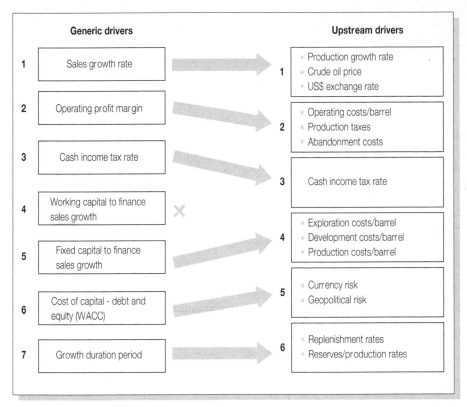

FIG 10.22 ● **Generic and upstream drivers in oil and gas**

salable products such as gasoline and kerosene. In this respect the refining industry can be compared to the chemicals manufacturing sector which can also be analyzed using the generic models.

Obviously account has to be taken of issues such as environmental regulation and over-capacity (which impact hugely upon the refining industry's margins). Furthermore, there are differences in product demand in different geographic regions; hence the need for geographic and/or market-based segregation of the value drivers.

The transportation and distribution sides of the oil business entail the movement of hydrocarbons from production source to manufacture and from manufacture to end user. We can easily identify the value drivers by examining what impacts upon value of companies operating in the transportation sector. Again, a cash flow valuation can be performed based on the seven key drivers. This is also true for marketing and retailing. Activity here covers the selling of many different refined petroleum products to different groups of consumers –

for automotive and marine transport, for aviation, and for manufacturing industry and utilities. Oil and gas marketing have value drivers comparable to businesses such as supermarkets and high street retail chains.

The variety of factors impacting on cash flows in the petroleum industry make it one of the riskiest around, with commensurately high returns expected by investors. Uncertainties to which the industry is particularly exposed include the scale of investment required; the uncertainties in timing and pattern of cash flows; state participation and government influence; the political and economic risks; high taxation and stringent regulation on matters such as environmental compliance.

For the downstream part of the oil and gas industry, then, the generic approach enables us to make a cash flow valuation and identify the macro and micro drivers that are creating or destroying value. The upstream part of the industry, on the other hand, is driven by a unique set of micro drivers; for this the SHV approach can be tailored by conceptualizing the specific drivers of value.

Telecommunications

Under the bright glare of SHV

In the past few years there has been a marked increase in interest in shareholder value in telecommunications. This has accompanied a global trend away from state-owned monopoly suppliers of a "plain old telephone service" (POTS) to sleeker, and more profitable, suppliers of a whole range of telecommunications services, many of which simply did not exist a few years ago. In particular, technical changes have meant that there is now a whole new world of mobile phone users and suppliers that simply wasn't there until recently. The expansion of the internet has also helped changed the landscape for all phone operators.

An industry previously dominated by state owned "natural" fixed line monopolies has woken up to the fact that privately owned new entrants are much fleeter of foot, and have rapidly moved to increase the supply of telephone services for a public hungry for them. The new entrants have been doing so at higher levels of efficiency and at lower consumer prices than state-owned enterprises thought possible.

Previously tied to the apron-strings of government for their investment needs, fixed line telecommunications companies now have to raise capital in the financial markets, and reward their shareholders in the same way as other companies. Their great interest in SHV is therefore understandable, even though their record in meeting shareholder expectations has sometimes been variable.

Over the past 15 years an average of US$9 billion per annum has been raised by telecommunications companies across 40 countries. More than two-thirds of this amount has been absorbed by the privatization of NTT (National Telephone and Telegraph) in Japan and BT (British Telecom) in the UK. Deutsche Telekom's IPO and the privatizations of France Telecom, STET (1998), Telstra (1997), MATAV and Turk Telecom have boosted the amount of equity raised to over $35 billion in 1997 alone.

The pace of change has been extraordinarily rapid. Fixed line, predominantly nationally based companies have had to review their positions in the light of global developments. In so doing they have struggled to form alliances and joint ventures that might allow them to create global channels for voice and data transmissions and to reach a far wider range of consumers than those in their "back yard."

By the same token, the newly emergent mobile phone operators are also seeing advantages in being able to serve their client base more globally. In so doing they can capture more revenues, reduce their own roaming charges, and probably increase the sums obtained from other users of their system. The last few years has seen a marked shift in M&A activity towards the mobile companies, as they seek to become larger players on the telecoms stage.

Changes in the regulatory environment have also been a catalyst for increased competition. Telecoms operators need to stimulate top-line growth and enhance operating efficiency to retain market share. Over the coming years, the global liberalization process in telecommunications will be shaped by a number of factors – among them EU legislation that *de facto* has opened most European markets to competition in basic telecommunications services; the passing of the US Telecom Bill in 1996; the Japanese government's decision to break-up NTT; and successful WTO negotiations in 1997.

At the time of writing these processes are in full swing, and it is interesting to note that SHV is a concept used by all participants to justify their actions. The recent hostile takeover of Mannesmann by Vodafone-Airtouch was as good an example as any in showing how far the SHV tide has risen. Mannesmann was an archetypal multi-divisional German company sitting astride two entirely different divisions: old-style heavy engineering and tube manufacture, and new-style digital mobile phone systems. Mannesmann's expansion into mobile phones had been partly financed by international institutional investors, interested in buying into a growth area in the German economy. This helped create the conditions for the eventual takeover. Although not well known in

Germany, Vodafone was able to offer a more convincing SHV case to the institutional investors (including those based in Germany) and so add Mannesmann's successful D-2 mobile phone network to its own, laying the foundation for a global mobile phone company. A breathtaking development however you look at it.

So far, fierce competition and price deregulation has led to decreased revenues for incumbent fixed line operators through market share losses and price erosion. As a result, operators have been seeking to find replacement revenue streams at home from value-added services such as mobile, internet and virtual private networks (VPNs) while investing in opportunities outside their domestic markets with perceived higher growth potential. Meanwhile, with some US$30 billion of new equity finance required in Europe alone in the next few years, competition for capital is fierce.

Within this environment, we have found it very helpful to have a SHV model more specifically built up around the concerns of the telecommunications industry. It looks in some detail at both the macro, top-down end of the business, as well as being able to link these broader-brush changes to industry-specific micro drivers. This model can support analysis and measurement of shareholder value at both the strategic and at the operational level. Whether the business unit uses a fixed PSTN (public switched telephone network), a mobile network, cable TV or data network infrastructure, such a tool can be used to determine projections of each business unit's financial status.

Some examples of initiatives undertaken by telecoms operators to generate shareholder value are given below in Fig. 10.23, under the headings of each relevant value driver. (See also Chapter 7 for more general initiatives.) Of course, any new venture may have an impact on more than one driver; and each operator will have different key drivers of value depending on its competitive and regulatory environment.

Under the heading of revenue or turnover growth, it is also worth noting the importance of new IN (intelligent network) services such as premium rate services, chargecards, voice mail, freephone, VPNs, personal numbers and the internet, and of the "bundling" of services. Margins can be affected by such actions as the introduction of shared services (or alternatively, outsourcing), the centralization and consolidation of back office operations, such as some finance functions; and systems initiatives in network configuration and network management. The capital expenditure/fixed capital driver can cover matters such as asset financing – leasing and sale-and-lease-back arrangements – and, for companies expanding abroad, hedging and risk management. And under "competitive advantage period" can come factors such as the role of new

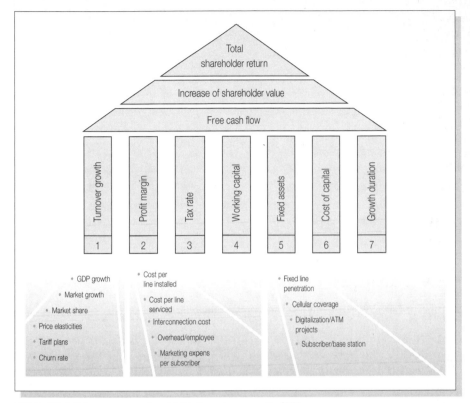

FIG 10.23 ● **Telecoms operators' initiatives to generate SHV**

entrants versus incumbent advantages; the nature of the regulatory regime; and access to infrastructure.

Measuring SHV in telecoms

Many operators have, or will soon have, decentralized their organization through the creation of profit-responsible customer-facing business units. This has been done in order to improve responsiveness and attain closer under-standing of customer needs as well as to reduce costs and improve efficiency. Line managers have thereby gained greater responsibility and accountability.

In addition, compliance with regulatory requirements for cost-based charging for interconnection with other operators has created the need for a financial separation between the network and service provider units. This "line of business" organizational structure brings with it new challenges and issues. In Fig. 10.24 you can see that growth in the numbers of mobile subscribers, access payments and receipts, as well as the overall EBITDA margins are the most influential drivers of share value in this example.

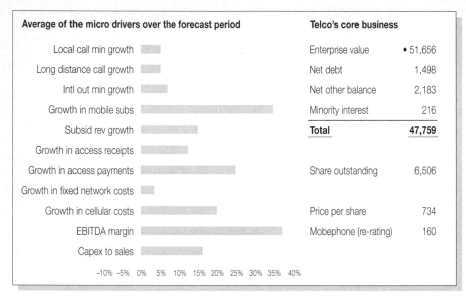

Average of the micro drivers over the forecast period		Telco's core business	
Local call min growth		Enterprise value	• 51,656
Long distance call growth		Net debt	1,498
Intl out min growth		Net other balance	2,183
Growth in mobile subs		Minority interest	216
Subsid rev growth		**Total**	**47,759**
Growth in access receipts			
Growth in access payments		Share outstanding	6,506
Growth in fixed network costs			
Growth in cellular costs		Price per share	734
EBITDA margin		Mobephone (re-rating)	160
Capex to sales			

–10% –5% 0% 5% 10% 15% 20% 25% 30% 35% 40%

Source: PwC analysis

FIG 10.24 ● **Telecoms micro drivers over a forecast period**

To ensure that management for shareholder value creation is implemented at every level, virtual business units or value centers can be set up to address this issue. These value centers can be organizational business units, product or customer groupings, or can be project based. An example is the creation of an internet value center that serves residential and business customers and uses different access infrastructures.

Transfer pricing and negotiations

Our experience with network operators moving to a line of business structure has shown that the transfer pricing process is one of the most difficult to get right. It is important that this mechanism is well designed and agreed beforehand. Many operators either institute a cost-plus-50-percent mark-up on network services – which provides little incentive for service providers to enhance value – or spend an inordinate amount of time arguing about the level of transfer pricing and how it has been calculated. Some of the issues that arise are:

● difficulties in allocating costs of shared network infrastructure;

● lack of a framework or "rules" for commitments and pricing between internal providers and purchasers of shared services;

● inability to define internal service-level agreements in terms of the required functionality, quality, cycle time, volumes and cost;

- little incentive for internal providers of support services to be more efficient than third-party provider;

- customer-facing business units unable to forecast future demand and deliver the volume of commitments made;

- the question of whether transfer prices are based on actual costs or are related to market prices – and of what sort of transition plan if starting with the former.

Revenue growth and margins are two of the most important value drivers for telecommunications operators. Indeed the two are connected. Most operators need to drive improvements in staff productivity (and other costs) in order to find new resources that can be dedicated to revenue growth or revenue retention activities. So how can a telecoms company make rapid employee productivity gains that will free resources for reinvestment? We give one example focused on a telecoms field force and/or customer service operation.

Performance management

One example where our SHV model has been used is in looking at how to achieve a substantial – 15 percent – reduction in customer-facing staff costs. (This could also apply to the field/maintenance force.) By carefully measuring and managing their activity, it is possible to install initially what is effectively a self-financing pilot study. When successful, this can then be rolled out into the rest of the organization.

Applied to a substantive part of an organization's resources, this could lead to a significant improvement in margins. For instance, taking a telecoms organization – which has around 10,000 people in field operations, maintenance and customer support – a 15 percent saving would deliver some 1,500 headcount savings which in turn (using an average $40,000 per annum cost of employment) would deliver approximately $60 million annual savings. (Note that the underpinning framework that is needed to help implement the suggested improvements in margins and growth is based on an activity-based cost management exercise – see the following section for more about ABCM.)

Utilities

A new world

Utilities, like telecommunications companies, have been dragged into the world of shareholder value and competition by governments keen both to realize cash, in order to ease their deficits, and to encourage greater competition and efficiency – leading to lower prices to consumers (most of whom also vote). Even in the USA, privately owned utility companies, hitherto cosseted by reasonably generous rate of return regulations, are experiencing fresh challenges that may well result in more deregulation, and a stiffer wind of competition.

The issues facing most utilities can be summarized under eight headings:

- *Regulatory environment:* introduction of open access to utility systems, stricter environmental guidelines.

- *Competitive pressures:* rapidly intensifying competition – survival of only the fittest. This includes not only competition between suppliers for wholesale consumers, but now for retail customers too.

- *Speed driven and customer driven markets:* customers' ever-rising expectations must be met more rapidly.

- *Industry structure:* mergers are concentrating and reconfiguring markets.

- *Technological innovation:* new product and market opportunities are created, requiring more skills.

- *Market globalization:* more diverse customers/suppliers/employees; more complex relationships among them.

- *Information availability:* information superhighway gives customers/competitors instant access.

- *Ruthless capital markets:* private financing and ownership of utility systems; investors demanding focus on SHV.

All over the industrialized world, then, there are moves afoot to introduce shareholder value concepts into utilities. Once assumed to be unexciting "pipes, wires and poles" businesses, they are now waking up to the growing influence of investors. The challenges of privatization, market liberalization, the introduction of competition in areas such as electricity generation and power supply, and dynamic changes in generation technology have combined with a tightening regulatory environment and growing investor influence to place huge pressure on utilities looking to increase shareholder value.

The effect of these changes has been loss of revenues by incumbents as new entrants have won market share by lowering prices; competition and price regulation has not allowed increases in profits pro-rata to increases in volume. In the face of nearly static revenue growth, utilities have been trying to substitute revenue streams at home with value added services (such as energy management schemes and customer demand profiling) while investing in opportunities outside their domestic markets with perceived higher revenue growth potential. At the same time, accessing the capital markets for equity and debt financing subjects a utility to the scrutiny of institutional investors. Management decisions on joint-ventures, foreign participation, negotiations with the regulator and performance in the domestic market are reflected almost instantly in share prices.

As a result, there has been a high level of consolidation, takeovers and mergers in the utility sector, particularly in the competitive energy markets of Australia, Scandinavia, the UK and the USA. Many utilities in these markets have had to decide whether to acquire and become a global player or to be acquired. For a number of US utilities, the introduction of competition into the electricity and gas sectors in the UK has provided useful experience, but the rush to acquire Britain's RECs (regional electricity companies) has been based more on a desire to take advantage of a window of opportunity than anything else. The EU directives on the right of access of third parties to grid systems owned by others is further evidence that the comfortable conditions for many incumbents in the European energy and utility market are unlikely to persist in the future. The recent merger between Veba and Viag in Germany is one indicator of this.

Takeover activity has certainly benefitted the shareholders of acquired companies. The average gain for shareholders in the UK's acquired RECs since they were privatized in 1990 has been some 300 percent. This has put pressure on the utilities that wish to remain independent. The recent trend for many of the UK independents to return cash to shareholders through special dividends and buy-backs suggests both a shortage in new earnings enhancing opportunities and a strategy aimed at returning surplus cash to shareholders.

It does not, however, guarantee shareholder loyalty. In 1995, Northern Electric successfully defended a takeover attempt by Trafalgar House with a shareholder package of some £300 million. In 1996, they faced a second takeover attempt from Cal-Energy and, despite offering further payouts to shareholders, were narrowly defeated by the bidder's cash offer. As for the acquirers, only time will tell. The share prices of the US utilities that acquired electricity distribution companies in Australia and the UK in 1995 and 1996 did not outperform in 1996 (they fell by an average of 4 percent against the average utility index).

Utility sector value drivers

Our model has been built up with the electricity generation and distribution industry very much in mind. It basically follows the standard seven-driver approach, but contains greater detail within the main drivers. The main drivers are shown in Fig. 10.25.

In our work with utilities, we have found that to get to the operational decision level requires shareholder analysis at the business unit level. This process has been assisted by the introduction of competition, which has required utilities to unbundle their activities into their principal businesses – for an electricity company these are generation, transmission, distribution and supply.

The next level of analysis is that of the operational value drivers, which in the generation unit of an electricity company would include, among other things:

- production costs measured in terms of p/kWh (kilowatt hour)
- non-production costs (p/kWh)
- load factor
- fuel mix (in megawatt-hours or MWh) accounted for by nuclear, coal, gas, hydro or other
- growth in total MWh sales
- average price, which can be linked to forecast pool prices or contract prices.

For an electricity or gas distribution business, the operational value drivers would include:

- operating cost per customer
- operating cost less depreciation per customer
- operating cost per units distributed
- electricity/gas distributed per employee
- distribution operating profit per customer.

For water companies, meanwhile, there is a different but related set of drivers.

Regulation and SHV analysis

Most businesses are in a position where incremental revenue creates an increase of shareholder value. This is not always the case in regulated network industries, where a price formula may or may not allow increased volume to be trans-

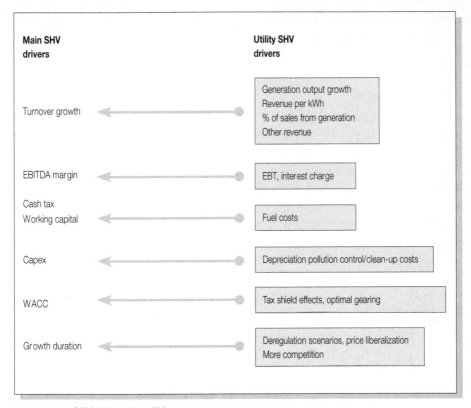

FIG 10.25 ● **SHV drivers in utilities**

lated into increased costs. In certain instances, increased volumes and revenues can destroy value because costs increase faster than revenue, with some customers served at below cost. This raises a number of issues:

● What is the SHV effect of lost revenues from competition and price regulation?

● Which of the current business units are contributing to shareholder value, and which are not?

● What is the contribution per customer category or from the major customers?

● What is the potential contribution to shareholder value from the portfolio of new initiatives?

● Should the same criteria be used to assess green-field investments, such as independent power plants – which may not improve shareholder value in the short term, but can provide long-term revenue and earnings growth – as existing operational assets or companies?

- What cost of capital should be used to assess initiatives?

Transfer pricing

As with telecommunications, this is not an easy issue to get right. The transfer prices between businesses are the same prices that allow other companies to use the networks. In the UK, the transfer price is being tested in detail as even the smallest domestic customers are now able to choose their electricity supplier. Our experience is that many companies either institute a mark-up on network services, which provides little incentive for service providers to enhance value, or spend an inordinate amount of time arguing about the level of transfer price and how it has been calculated. The underpinning framework that is needed to support effective transfer pricing is activity-based cost management (ABCM).

What this means is that leading utilities around the world are moving from spreadsheet-based cost allocation systems to establishing sophisticated ABCM frameworks and systems that are capable of supporting multi-dimensional profitability analysis. In addition to activity-based transfer pricing, which is focussed on the product or service dimension, ABCM can be used for profitability analysis in customer or market segments and geographic market area. Typical uses include transfer pricing, market segment decision-making, pricing strategy, regulatory compliance, network investment, business re-engineering initiatives, and financial planning. This can then be linked through value-based management to ensure that the changes and strategies being planned are consistent with the goal of raising SHV.

Experience with utilities

In the first benchmarking and valuation phase, we have found that, in most cases, the discounted value of analysts' projections of future cash flows has closely correlated with the market capitalization. In the one instance where the market capitalization was significantly below the DCF valuation, the cause was identified as an investor relations issue: the share price of the company rose rapidly soon after this was brought to management's attention by PricewaterhouseCoopers.

The most sensitive of the seven value drivers have generally proved to be operating margins and the WACC. As we have observed, revenue growth in a highly regulated utility may not lead to increase in shareholder value; however, an improvement in margins and a lowering of the cost of capital will. Also, in the case of water utilities in the UK, fixed capital is an important value driver an importance that reflects the high levels of capital expenditure required to replace, what is in most cases, an aging infrastructure.

Where operating margins are the most sensitive of the value drivers, a number of utilities we have worked with have carried out a value mapping exercise with their principal business units. We have also developed an electricity-specific spreadsheet model that can value-map its generation, distribution, supply and non-regulated businesses.

As for the WACC, most utility companies accept that the cost of debt is cheaper than the cost of equity – even though after privatization many of the UK utilities were reluctant to take on significant amounts of debt. This is in contrast to the US utilities, which, although investor-owned for many decades, have traditionally had gearing levels in excess of 100 percent. The start of takeover activity in the UK electricity sector in 1995 went some way to changing all this – witness the case of Northern Electric's successful defense against Trafalgar House referred to earlier, where the increased returns to shareholders were financed by taking on increased debt. Most of the other RECs followed suit, and the average gearing level of UK RECs rose from approximately 20 percent in March 1994 to over 80 percent two years later.

A word of caution, however. The software packages and sector models for SHV analysis that we have referred to here and in earlier sections of this chapter are, it has to be said, just analytical tools. They do not change culture or behavior and are, therefore, only a partial solution. More fundamental changes are required within a company if the enhancement of shareholder value is to become enshrined as the company's principal objective. Value-based management – the process that we outlined in Chapter 7 – is crucial.

SUMMARY

In this chapter we first looked at some of the problem areas that the application of shareholder value theory might focus on – areas such as the definition of cash flow; intangible assets; the cost of capital; and residual value. All or some of these topics have a bearing on the sectors examined here. In addition, we have examined how the "real options" approach to valuation can be applied in the high technology firms and elsewhere in the "new economy." We saw how our SHV models varied from the "basic" standard when applied to a number of sectors: banking, insurance and fund management; high technology and pharmaceuticals; oil and gas, telecommunications and utilities. This has meant identifying value drivers specific to each situation.

Notes

1. Lev, B.L. and Sougiannis, T. (1996) "The capitalization, amortization and value of R&D," *Journal of Accounting and Economics,* 21, 107–38.

2. Companies do have the option to "rebut" these depreciation rates, and to provide other means of valuing their goodwill and intangibles. However, if they do so, they can then open themselves to impairment charges in the event of a subsequent downturn in their activity. Prudent managers tend to opt for the more predictable depreciation charge. See *International Accounting Standards: Similarities and Differences*, PricewaterhouseCoopers 1998 and 2000.

3. The current version of the model is designed to operate based on the standard format published by IBCA for over 8,000 banks worldwide. Previous versions were based on Bloomberg data.

4. Consider a simple example of a customer taking a loan for £100 on the same day that another two customers deposit £25 each. The £50 in total new deposits goes towards funding the loan, with the shortfall made up by a wholesale deposit.

5. See Copeland, T., Killer, T. and Murrin, J. (1996), *Valuation*, 2nd edition (New York: John Wiley), pp.505–7 for a slightly different way of treating this issue.

6. Miller, W.D. (1995) *Commercial Bank Valuation*, John Wiley & Sons.

7. Madden, C. (1996) *Managing Bank Capital*, Wiley.

8. Depreciation is treated explicitly in this manner to illustrate its non-cash nature, but also to provide a common definition for the cost income ratio.

9. Tier two capital mainly consists of subordinated debt, preferred stock and long-term loan capital.

10. Howell, S.D. and Jägle, A.J. (1997) "Evidence on How Managers Intuitively Manage Growth Options," *Journal of Business Finance and Accounting*, Spring.

11. See Luehrmann, T. "Investment Opportunities as Real Options," *Harvard Business Review* July/August 1998, p.12 for more details on this.

12. Shell triennial investor relations briefing, 16 December 1996.

13. "BP sharpening focus on improved SHV efficiency," *Oil and Gas Journal*, July 1996.

SHV AROUND
THE WORLD:
THE EMERGING
CONSENSUS

Having looked at how shareholder value theories can be applied to particular industrial or trade sectors, let us now return to the wider global context that makes SHV such an urgent subject. As we argued in Chapter 1 and elsewhere, the globalization of markets has increased the pressure on publicly quoted companies for economic returns on the money that investors have entrusted to them. What effect, then, has this pressure had in individual countries? How do the particular conditions of a country – its history, its culture, its traditional ways of doing business – affect the adoption (or rejection) of shareholder value as a concept?

This chapter aims to put SHV in its international context, grouping together countries that are in similar situations with regard to SHV. We will not be providing comprehensive guides to these countries' markets – for which we recommend the PricewaterhouseCoopers information guides *Doing Business in...* (available from local PricewaterhouseCoopers offices). Our aim is simply to home in on those features of individual markets that we think have a bearing on SHV analysis and value-based management issues.

Since the first edition of this book came out, at the end of 1997, the global march of SHV has proceeded apace. Increasingly, in the global competition for capital, companies and countries that wish to prosper have to deliver the best returns. Figure 11.1 indicates that, in terms of total shareholder returns delivered over the last ten years, the US economy is the model to follow. This chapter aims to show how SHV is proving to be an effective guide to creating and sustaining wealth, and how a range of different countries are rising to meet this challenge.

STAKES AND SHARES REVISITED

Before we look at individual countries in more detail, let us return to one of the themes of Chapter 1 – the differences between a shareholder and a stakeholder view of the world.

To start with, let us consider two dimensions of SHV within an individual firm: the distribution of the shares, and distribution of the voting power of the shares. Taking the distribution of shares first, you can have a dispersed share-

Accumulation Indices – five years to June 1999	Annual equivalent TSR
Australia	9.3%
Canada	16.0%
USA	29.0%
Germany	17.2%
France	18.2%
United Kingdom	19.8%

Source: ASX – Monthly Index Analysis

FIG 11.1 ● **Total shareholder returns – five years to June 1999**

holding structure, where the majority of shares are held in small volumes by a wide variety of investors. This is typical of a SHV-oriented system that is open and transparent for all participants. In contrast is the situation where a company's shares are closely held by a small number of shareholders, each of whom has a large individual bloc of shares. This is more typical in a "stake-holder" economy. Secondly, there are differences in voting structures. At one end of the scale there can be a highly democratic one-share-one-vote system, while at the other are a range of different kinds of shares, some of which are more valuable, and have more voting power, than others. Here too we can have dispersed or concentrated voting power for shares.

The various combinations of ownership and control outlined in Fig. 11.2 can be associated with differences in behavior, which we have allocated to the quadrants marked there from A to D.

Even at this level of generality we can think of differences in behavior that are likely according to whether ownership and control are either dispersed or concentrated. In quadrant A, where both ownership and control of the company are dispersed among a large number of shareholders, there is a high level of liquidity, in that there is a viable secondary market for the shares. This makes it easy for investors to diversify out of the stock should they so desire. There is a relatively high degree of transparency, which can help lower the cost of capital, since holding these stocks is less risky for investors – they can switch out of the position fairly easily, and so demand a lower risk premium.

On the negative side, there is a lack of direct control or monitoring of management, and a degree of "free riding" – investors can hitch a ride without becoming involved in the details of what management do. This lack of direct monitoring, though, is alleviated by the overall disciplining mechanisms of the

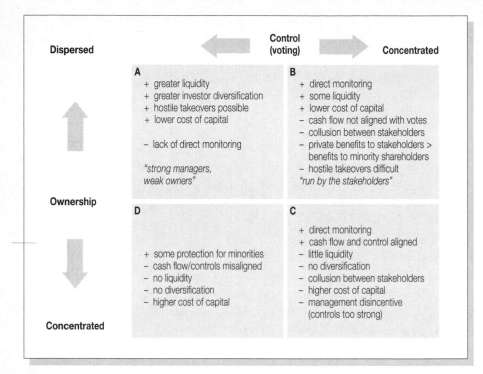

Control (voting)

Dispersed ← Control (voting) → Concentrated

A
+ greater liquidity
+ greater investor diversification
+ hostile takeovers possible
+ lower cost of capital

– lack of direct monitoring

"strong managers, weak owners"

B
+ direct monitoring
+ some liquidity
+ lower cost of capital
– cash flow not aligned with votes
– collusion between stakeholders
– private benefits to stakeholders > benefits to minority shareholders
– hostile takeovers difficult
"run by the stakeholders"

Ownership

D
+ some protection for minorities
– cash flow/controls misaligned
– no liquidity
– no diversification
– higher cost of capital

C
+ direct monitoring
+ cash flow and control aligned
– little liquidity
– no diversification
– collusion between stakeholders
– higher cost of capital
– management disincentive (controls too strong)

Concentrated

FIG 11.2 ● **Ownership and control patterns**[1]

marketplace. Hostile takeovers are possible; ultimately, sub-standard management performance can be punished by shareholders who can be swayed by superior offers from other potential owners.

Quadrant A, then, requires an efficiently operating capital market; in its absence, or where the shareholders fail to keep their eye on the ball, you can create a situation described as "strong management, weak ownership." Managements can largely set the agenda and seek to maximize their gains while paying too little attention to the shareholders, dispersed and disorganized as they are. (This separation of ownership and control was first noted in 1932 by Berle and Means[2] as characteristic of modern economic life.) The markets in the USA and the UK approximate to the Quadrant A model, as to a perhaps lesser extent do Canada, Australia and the Netherlands.

Quadrant B describes a rather different situation. Here there is still a relatively dispersed ownership structure, with shares widely held in small lots; but the voting structures have been arranged to give a particular group or groups a privileged position. Since there may now be different classes of shares, there is still some liquidity (free float) in the market, and investors can still diversify their holdings and invest elsewhere if they choose. The existence of a strong voting bloc makes it easier for a management to be monitored, and the cost of capital can remain reasonably low.

But Quadrant B has distinct downsides too. The dominant stakeholders could collude to determine a management course that is not consistent with meeting the expectations of all shareholders. The stakeholders might force contractual arrangements on the company, either as a supplier or as a customer, that do not in fact best serve its broader interest. The private interests of the stakeholders therefore gain at the expense of general shareholder value. The dominant stakeholders can also block any takeover attempts. Quadrant B describes a situation of "stakeholder power," where both general management and general SHV interests are weakly represented. We think that Japan, and several mainland European countries such as France and Germany, fit this model quite well.

In Quadrant C, a more extreme version of quadrant B, we have highly concentrated forms of both shareholding and voting structures. All the issues raised by Quadrant B are evident here to a more exaggerated degree. There is significantly less liquidity as the shares are now almost entirely divided up among the stakeholders. Liquidity is low, and investors can no longer easily diversify their holdings. The cost of capital in this view will be higher than in A and B, as investors will require a risk premium for investing in illiquid stock. Since the stakeholders are in complete control and can monitor management quite easily, there may be little managerial incentive: trying to propose a plausible longer-term management strategy that runs counter to the stakeholder interest is unlikely to be fruitful, and management might not bother trying. We think that there are several smaller markets in the world where this type of behavior can be seen. It is typical of many emerging markets, and Quadrant C characteristics can be seen too in countries like Italy and Austria, where liquidity in shares is often very low.

The Quadrant D situation is the least likely to occur. It requires a stratification of shares so that the voting stock is closely held. Non-voting stock could then be widely dispersed, but is of little importance in influencing decisions. It is possible for managements to be quite strong in this environment, especially if the voting stock is held by a relatively passive foundation that keeps an arm's-length distance between itself and a company's management.

Stakeholding loses ground

Do these differences in shareholding patterns have any wider impact on corporate behavior and on the economy? Our contention is that wider, more transparent and democratic arrangements are superior to those characterized by close control on the part of stakeholders. Is there any evidence for this?

Figure 11.3 is based on material provided as part of a European survey on corporate governance. It shows the size of the average stake of the largest stakeholder in a publicly quoted company. For instance, in Germany the average size of the stake owned by the dominant stakeholder in a German listed company was almost 50 percent of the total equity – a characteristic that is also associated with a low level of stock market capitalization. Mapping the stakeholder information onto estimates of the size of the respective countries' stock market capitalization as a proportion of GDP shows an association between smaller stock markets and stakeholders with large blocs of shares. As the size of the dominant stake comes down, so the stock market gets larger as a proportion of GDP.

A glance at Fig. 11.3 will indicate an apparent trade-off between levels of stock market development and the willingness of important stakeholders to surrender control over "their" companies. We think this is part of a rather lopsided convergence process where the more stakeholder-oriented parts of the world are increasingly adopting the habits of, and becoming like, the shareholder-oriented "Anglo-Saxon" markets of the USA and the UK.

Why is this occurring? The stakeholder approach is characterized by a tripartite arrangement between private "stakeholders." These might consist of the founding family behind the company; long-term finance (either as equity, or more frequently as debt) supplied by banks or insurance companies; and the government, who own some of the shares either directly, or indirectly through another state-owned enterprise. Such an arrangement was often set up in the aftermath of the Second World War as a way of encouraging long-term growth

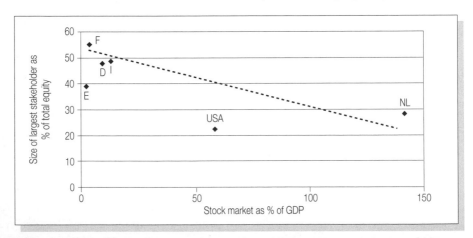

FIG 11.3 ● **Trade-off between size of dominant stakeholding and stock market size, 1995–6**

and development: free from the tyranny of short-term stock market performance, enterprises could plan for the future.

The stakeholder approach worked well in industries that were largely
protected from international trade. They may have been either nationalized, or
partially nationalized, with the government holding a "strategic" interest.
Alternatively, there could have been interlocking shareholdings among the
main producers, allowing them to collude at the expense of consumers and
smaller shareholders.

In such a protected environment, the wider circle of stakeholders could be
relatively well served. The suppliers obtained "protected" prices, often aided
and abetted by rules stipulating that only local suppliers could bid for business.
Employees were well looked after, as some of the "monopoly" gains were
handed out to them as higher wages and salaries. Employees increasingly
thought of customers as a nuisance; engineering and "security of supply" issues
took priority. Customers, on the other hand, had little choice, since the
producers were effectively a monopoly. And even where there was more than
one producer, price controls might ensure that there was little true competition.

This secure and comfortable world might have continued indefinitely but
for a couple of factors. Firstly, the internationalization of both the financial and
goods markets meant that more efficient foreign competitors, often from a
more transparent SHV-oriented system, could compete on more or less equal
terms. Interlocking shareholdings and controlling interests become less useful
when your entire competitive base is threatened. These new entrants were also
capable of tapping into much larger and deeper international capital markets,
and in so doing could escape the thrall of the banks.

Secondly, the coalition of interests sustaining the stakeholder arrangement
was itself under pressure and was starting to break down. This became particularly apparent when an enterprise needed more capital to finance its future
expansion. The banks, heretofore the major providers of finance, were finding
that, with the decline in inflation and "disintermediation," it was harder to
satisfy the demands of their own investors. They started to review their long-
term "strategic" holdings in a variety of stakeholder industrial companies –
holdings that had frequently under-performed the stock markets, and therefore
contributed to the banks' own problems. As a result, strategic investment
networks in countries like Germany have gradually been dismembered; in
Japan, too, the *Keiretsu* (mutually interlocking shareholdings of groups of
companies affiliated to a house bank) are in a process of decline.

Governments' willingness to provide further investment has also wilted.
The realization that perhaps a government is less good at the manufacturing

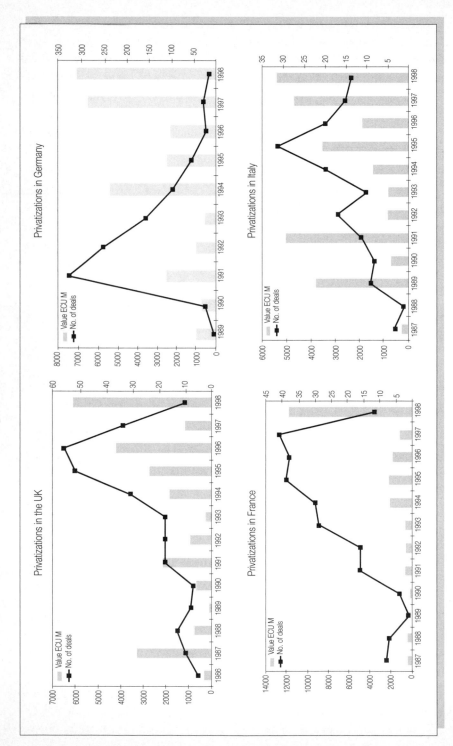

FIG 11.4 ● Privatizations in the four largest European economies

and allocating of goods and services than it thought has coincided with increased budgetary pressure. Maastricht and the Euro have kept government deficits and borrowing under strict control within the EU, and this example has been followed elsewhere. Under pressure, governments have realized that they cannot continue to finance equity risk investment and are privatizing. Instead, they are concentrating more on the regulation of market behavior and on introducing public finance in partnership with private in cases where there is an identifiable market failure.

Finally, the original stakeholder or family investment group might be less than enthusiastic about putting more money into an area of declining profitability; perhaps they too might sell out to a leaner and more efficient competitor, and use the money for something more lucrative.

This, of course, is where the absence of a well-developed capital market starts to hurt. As stakeholder arrangements break down, so it becomes increasingly necessary to replace them with something that ensures an equivalent or superior supply of capital. It is here that countries with better-developed stock markets have gained an advantage. The broader, deeper and more liquid the market, the easier it is to channel capital into the areas where it can earn the highest return. Stakeholder arrangements become increasingly difficult as incumbent groups become larger and less coordinated and in the main less able to compete and earn a satisfactory return on their capital.

The importance of flexible and liquid markets is very clear at present with the huge shift of capital taking place into the "new" economy – a shift that is hindered where capital is locked up and facilitated in shareholder economies where surplus capital is returned to shareholders and recycled to where returns are highest.

Faced with these pressures, stakeholding companies are beginning to realize that their future lies in taking a more independent view on pricing and volumes and in better rewarding investors for the capital that they have contributed. When a government is no longer prepared to add funds to an enterprise, but actually wants to end its commitment and receive something back for the investments it has made, change is necessary. Companies have to put "stakeholding" thoughts behind them and arrange their affairs so that they can compete. Newly privatized groups are starting to pay close attention to their cost base, and to the process of de-regulation.

Judging by the UK experience, it is no exaggeration to say that efficiency gains of between 25 and 50 percent are possible in a more competitive deregulated regime. The resources released can then be used more productively – which appears to be happening.

An emerging SHV consensus?

Some of the trends we have been referring to can also be seen at work in Fig. 11.5, where we have ranked countries by their market capitalization as a percentage of GDP in 1997. As we can see, countries such as the UK, the USA, the Netherlands, Sweden and Switzerland have made it into the 100-percent-plus club, and Hong Kong (to 1997) had also done very well. We think that these are the markets that broadly belong to our Quadrant A – markets characterized by dispersed ownership and liquid markets, and to a greater commitment to SHV.

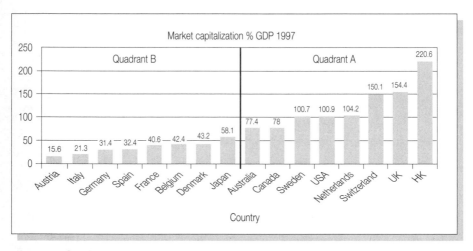

FIG 11.5 ● **Stock market capitalization and GDP 1997**[3]

Some of the smaller countries in our diagram, notably Sweden and the Netherlands, have recorded particularly impressive growth. Indeed, the countries that have shown the largest gains in the value of shares as a proportion of GDP – see Fig. 11.4 – are also among those that have shown superior economic performance over the last few years. This trend adds further weight to the view that access to efficient domestic capital markets is a benefit and not a hindrance towards better economic performance.

Since the capital market generally requires more transparency, more liquid markets and more even treatment for all shareholders, this trend suggests that the influence of the stakeholder model is waning, and that these countries are moving closer to the models provided by the USA and the UK. On this "Anglo-Saxon" side, however, there is no great room for complacency. The issues we

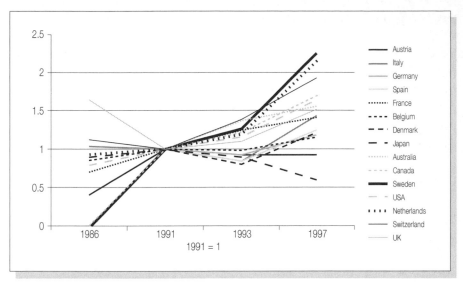

FIG 11.6 ● **Changes in market capitalization to GDP ratio in selected countries, 1986 to 1997**

identified earlier in this chapter concerning the separation of ownership and control can easily have the effect of bolstering the power of incumbent management at the expense of shareholders. It is therefore reassuring to report that there are indications of increasing SHV activism that will keep shareholders very much in the front row when it comes to assessing corporate performance. The recent upsurge in mergers and acquisitions, probably a sign of a maturing business cycle, shows that the disciplining mechanisms imposed by the market are alive and well.

COUNTRY VALUES

As national financial markets have continued to develop, so some of the differences and similarities between them have become clearer. Let us now look at the state of SHV across the globe, beginning with the "Anglo-Saxon" markets of North America and other shareholder-friendly countries. We will then work through other "developed" economies such as Japan and some of the more important Western Europe countries still operating along stakeholder lines but often in a process of transition. The chapter will end by considering a selection of "emerging" markets that seem to us to have the potential to set foot on the world stage in terms of value creation.

THE SHAREHOLDER-FRIENDLY COUNTRIES

We have established in Fig. 11.3 and elsewhere that "SHV-friendly countries" share certain characteristics. Stock market capitalization of their quoted companies has been equivalent to over 80 percent of GDP; 20 percent or more of their populations own shares – which is larger than for stakeholder economies. Around one-third of all shares are owned by private households, while the proportion of shares owned by insurance companies, investment trusts and foreign investors is around 20 percent, 12 percent and 20 percent respectively. In contrast to stakeholder countries, conspicuously few shares are owned by corporates, banks and governments in SHV-friendly economies, where the absolute size of investments by pension funds and insurance companies is larger. Perhaps most importantly, institutional investors tend to keep a far higher proportion of their investments as equities and not in bonds. The SHV-friendly group, then, has the much better developed and more liquid markets that are necessary to sustain an "equity culture."

In Europe, as we can see from Fig. 11.4, this group of countries generally has experienced better than average performance in terms of stock market performance over the last decade, with the UK and Switzerland showing the least dynamism. But pre-eminent in this group stands the USA, which has by far the largest financial markets in the world.

USA

Widely considered to be the world's most advanced free market economy, the USA has an established culture of share ownership. The Securities and Exchange Commission (SEC), set up in 1934 to protect shareholders from over-ambitious company promoters and to restrain the power of incumbent boards, presides over a sophisticated regulatory regime that determines the content and timing of financial reports filed by publicly traded companies. The result is that, more than in most other countries, investors are provided with timely business and financial information about the companies they put money into. With a corporate control structure directed towards maximizing value for investors; it is no surprise that it was in the USA that much of the early work on SHV analysis took place. Indeed, with the wealth of US practices and examples cited throughout this book, a special section on the country's economy is almost redundant.

With stock prices based on managements' ability to deliver expected returns, the USA's institutional investors are becoming increasingly sophisticated in their assessment of company values. Their focus, as we have noted elsewhere, is moving from an extrapolation of growth from accounting-based earnings to free cash flow-based economic models which more explicitly capture risk, growth and returns on investment.

In 1996, Price Waterhouse LLP commissioned a survey of 30 of the largest US equity investment managers to determine their approach to stock valuation. This confirmed that a cash flow-based economic model which explicitly reflects expectations of risk, growth and returns has become central to these investors' outlook. As one analyst put it, "Cash flow is typically a better and cleaner number ... [it] is ultimately the value of what the shareholder is buying." Earnings per share, on the other hand, while a "convenient shorthand," were seen as "fraught with subjectivity."

Equity research groups at US securities firms – the "sell side" – have been slower to develop the SHV approach. Heavy emphasis is still placed on accounting-based earnings, although they are beginning to recognize that EPS growth does not explain value growth in the long run.

As the investment community in the USA has become more sophisticated in its company analysis, so corporate managements have had to adjust – not only by ensuring that they assess investment, operating and financial decisions in terms of value creation for their shareholders, but also by improving their investor communications programs.

There may still be more to do, however; the survey referred to above also asked the investment managers to report whether they got enough information from companies relating to the seven drivers of shareholder value. More than 50 percent reported they did not get enough information on competitive advantage period, cost of capital, and working capital investment. In response to this, companies are being much more specific on the competitive positioning of each of their principal businesses, making sure investors are well informed on their competitive advantage periods.

Many companies are also setting explicit debt/equity capital structure targets to manage expectations on the cost of capital and the use of future cash flows. And, as far as communication is concerned, a good number of managements are making sure their shareholders know they are applying the same investment disciplines and performance standards throughout their business. To take just three recent annual reports: in 1996 Coca-Cola stated that "because economic profit is the most accurate measure of the value the company is creating, we now use it to drive decisions at every level of the business." RJR Nabisco declared its objective to be "a total of 20 percent or better after-tax cash return on common shareholder equity. ... All capital investment decisions will be evaluated in terms of the potential cash return on equity to the individual operating company and in comparison to potential returns from other RJR Nabisco business." Similarly, Monsanto committed itself to "a financial metric that would create new levels of share owner value" – one "that is economically based and tied to cash flows rather than one that is accounting based."

New economy pressures

The pressure for returns is ever present in the USA, further emphasized by the use of quarterly reporting. This reduces the time period between management decisions and the point at which their effects become evident and have to be conveyed to the market. Two recent trends are altering the dimensions of the debate.

The first is the upheaval caused by the so-called "new economy" companies based largely in technology, telecommunications and media. Within an astonishingly short period some of them have grown very large in SHV terms. As of April 2000, 13 of the top 25 US companies by stock market capitalization come from this group, displacing many older-established firms. This has created a serious challenge for longer-established companies, who have watched as their investors have diverted new funds into these faster growing entities. While there may be uncertainty about the more recent arrivals, there is rather less doubt that companies like Cisco, Intel, Sun and several others are likely to have a significant presence in the market for several years to come. Their existence, and the more recent rush into more fancifully valued internet stocks, is making senior management ponder how they can adapt their own companies to take advantage of this investor interest in high-tech and the internet. This has driven home still further many of the messages found elsewhere in this book.

The second trend is that US companies are now exposed to a much greater demand for information and disclosure than earlier. This too is aided and abetted by the internet. There is, for instance, a wider range of institutions interested in corporate reporting than ever before, and they require a wider range of information. Labor unions, non-governmental organizations, the news media, as well as some individual consumer and business customers, are starting to consider wider aspects of their purchase decisions. For some, these decisions can be influenced by environmental or ethical standards.

Many US companies are starting to respond by increasing their own levels of disclosure, mostly voluntarily. In its annual survey of S&P 500 companies, the Investor Responsibility Resource Center found that 61 percent of US companies in 1997 had published a public environmental report, with many more companies saying they expected to publish their first such report in the coming year. Fuller disclosure of activities may also be a defense against views circulated on the internet about particular companies, some of which may be ill-informed and biassed. It is becoming ever more important for company managements to get their message across.

Officially, too, several initiatives to encourage higher levels of disclosure and reporting are under way. The aim here is to bring a greater convergence between US and non-US reporting standards. For instance, the Global Reporting Initiative, an alliance of international organizations headed by the US-based organization CERES, was established in 1998 to "help bring together and harmonize the numerous initiatives on corporate environmental reporting that have developed independently around the world, shaping them into one set of coherent, consistent global standards." In addition, the US Financial Accounting Board proposed, in 1998, that companies include more non-financial information in their annual reports, including information on employee turnover, measures of customer loyalty, numbers of defective products and ethical issues related to the company – the sort of information that is included in our "Blueprint Inc." company in Appendix 1.

Shareholders as activists

The traditional view of the Anglo-American brand of capitalism is that its large and liquid markets encourage "short-termism" in investors. The only thing that shareholders are interested in, in this view, is the financial gains that accrue in the near future from their investments, giving rise to the earlier claim about the separation of ownership from control and to a regime characterized (see Quadrant A in Fig. 11.1) by "strong management and weak owners." There are, however, signs that shareholders are beginning to take a more active interest in the companies they invest in. We think that this is paving the way to a more transparent system where investors will find it easier to establish how well their investments are performing on a medium-term view. One good example of this trend towards greater shareholder activism is CalPERS, the California Public Employees' Retirement System.

US pension funds are, it has been claimed, the world's largest non-governmental pool of investment capital. They represent the savings of millions of ordinary workers, who have contributed a part of their pay each month in order to assure themselves of a decent income on retirement. The trustees of each fund are responsible by law to their "beneficiary members" for the prudent management of their savings; they must use the funds entrusted to them for the exclusive purpose of benefitting these members. Hence there is constant pressure on a fund's trustees to increase returns on investment, within the limits of prudence.

At the same time, a fund like CalPERS, with an investment portfolio of some $110 billion and almost a million pensioned or still working members, has such large holdings that even a phased sale of its shares in some individual companies can disrupt the market. Further, given the scale of its investments, it cannot easily switch capital back and forth among companies or sectors without affecting the price.

Such a situation has meant, for CalPERS, a more interventionist attitude to the companies it invests in. In particular, it is keen to create as level a playing field as possible for investors, and so seeks improvements in corporate govern- ance. In this way, the rights of minority investors are strengthened. Where it sees management under-performing it will initially ask for meetings with directors, and seek to get some changes in policy. If private meetings do not do the trick, then it is quite capable of going public with its concerns. Every year CalPERS publishes a list of poorly performing companies, benchmarking them against others in their field using an explicit SVA/EVA methodology (outlined in Chapter 6). If necessary, CalPERS is willing to become involved in some very public shareholder uprisings against incumbent management.

As Robert F. Carlson, a senior member of the CalPERS board, said in 1994: "Pension funds are now filling a void in which the management of public corpo- rations had become autonomous and, in extreme cases, unaccountable to the very share owners of the corporations paying their salaries."

This type of shareholder activism is increasingly becoming part of the investment landscape in the USA, where executives and other Wall Street investors have grown accustomed to this hands-on approach. An intervention by CalPERS is generally considered a sign that a company's results will improve. According to a study by Wilshire Associated, where companies had significantly under-performed the S&P 500 index in the five years before having their shares bought by CalPERS, they went on to out-perform the index over the next five years.

While we are primarily concerned here with shareholder activism as a means of increasing SHV, there are a number of other organizations and pressure-groups taking an activist stance who are pursuing other, but not neces- sarily unrelated, agendas. This may include encouraging companies to adopt more environmentally or socially aware policies.

Crossing the oceans

In pursuit of value, and in order to achieve the optimum relationship between risk and reward, many US funds have adopted a long-term policy of increasing the international component of their shareholding portfolios. According to analysts, the percentage of their assets held abroad will have to more than double, from 8 to nearly 20 percent. There is also mounting evidence that many of the domestic concerns of US investors are becoming the concerns of foreign investors too. Certain aspects of the US experience are now spreading to other regions of the world.

Initially hesitant, US funds are increasingly bringing pressure to bear for more information and transparency from the companies they invest in. Here again, CalPERS appears to be in the forefront.[4] As William Crist, president of its board of trustees, told European businessmen, "Outside the US, the traditions, laws, habits, practices and markets are quite different and changing rapidly. We're speaking to directors to seek companies with good internal structures to ask them how they work." Not only are they finding out; they are also starting to make recommendations.

One result of this has been direct cooperation between CalPERS in the USA and the UK-based Hermes Pension Fund management, both of whom are pursuing what Hermes calls "relational shareholder activism." Rio Tinto has also become exposed to an international group of investors who, in May 2000, were reported to be calling for the appointment of an independent non-executive deputy chairman "designed to make the board more accountable to shareholders."[5] Others, meanwhile, are more concerned that the companies they invest in should adopt ILO conventions relating to conditions in the workplace for all employees.

Companies that have implemented SHV schemes

There has been widespread interest in SHV systems and performance measurement approaches in the USA. These will typically be based around a combination of SVA and "balanced scorecard" metrics.[6] According to some estimates, over 5 percent of the FT 500 companies and about 8 percent of the FT Global 500 have now installed a SHV/performance measurement system and, in many cases, it has been the larger corporations that have taken the lead.[7]

Share price performance for over half of the sample of companies exceeded that of their competitors, suggesting that these schemes are worthwhile when it comes to showing improved relative shareholder performance. The introduction of external measurement benchmarks led the controller of Honeywell to say "I think what is changing more than anything is the expectation of returns. Being measured against outside forces rather than inside forces."[8]

These systems are introduced as a means of aligning strategy with SHV creation. As Charles Golden, CFO of Eli Lilly observed, "the most acute reason for a performance measurement system in our company was to avoid confusion about how day-to-day actions should follow from strategy."[9] Other companies that have implemented such schemes are Caterpillar, Mobil (now part of Exxon), and Dow Chemicals.

Much useful experience has been gained through the implementation of SHV systems in the USA. Most companies surveyed said that they are likely to implement SHV and performance measurement schemes in the future. This will take place as a response to shifts in their business environment, the development of new strategies, and as a way for new executive teams to "turn the tanker round."

The implementation process may not always be straightforward. As one manager of a US service company said: "The biggest challenge in implementing a ... system is to get people to think at the enterprise level in a standard way. The second cultural issue was that, previously, managers reported whatever they wanted to report on their own. In the new environment ... [managers] must report more consistent information."[10] There also has to be clear accountability for such a program, and internal IT systems have to be up to the job. Difficulties in measuring certain types of activity can cause problems in implementation, but there is general agreement that it is important to link programs to executive remuneration.

Broadly speaking, then, the use of SHV approaches, linked to balanced scorecards (see Chapter 12) and other techniques, is becoming more frequent. The USA is setting a trend other countries could do well to emulate.

The UK

With a stock market capitalization of over 150 percent of GDP, equity ownership has a strong tradition in the UK. Current stock market capitalization, as a percentage of GDP, remains the largest in Europe, and bigger than the USA's. London remains an attractive location for foreign companies seeking listings, and a lot of non-UK shares are traded in London, which has the reputation as the premier financial center for dealing in equities in the European time zones. Another important feature of the UK market is the strength of institutional investors.

One reason for this is the way pensions are funded. In the UK, employers' responsibilities for providing a pension are "hived off" to separately funded bodies – thus creating a vast pool of employer (and employee) contributions that have to find an investment home. Although funds have to be kept in liquid or semi-liquid form to fund pensions paid out today and tomorrow, much of the money is not required in the near term and is in long-term investments such as equities. The proportion of funds invested by the pension funds in equities (80 percent) is probably the highest in the world. Separating pension funding from the employer has meant that funds are not retained within the employers' businesses as they are in (say) Germany, but are invested in the financial markets.

While the subject of being inside or outside the Euro-zone remains controversial within the UK, the integration of European capital markets is continuing apace. The recently announced moves toward the creation of the iX stock market, which will combine the London Stock Exchange with the Deutsche Boerse is a further example of this. When completed, the market will be the third largest in the world measured on turnover (after the NASDAQ and the NYSE), and fourth largest when measured on total market capitalization, coming just behind the Tokyo Stock Exchange. The decision to use London as the primary center for dealing "blue-chip" stocks under UK regulations is also a confirmation of London's pre-eminence in this part of the market.

With the stakeholder approach not traditionally followed, British governments have preferred to allow well-developed common law rights to prevail. This has meant that companies have been freer to follow the shareholder model of maximizing the owners' wealth. And by taking an early initiative to privatize state-owned companies, the UK has widened the circle of equity owners.

Current valuation techniques

The traditional performance yardsticks used by investors in the UK (and indeed elsewhere) are dividend yields, price/earnings ratios and earnings per share – all of which have the advantage of being well understood. They are, however, somewhat simplistic since reported earnings are often manipulated by a combination of accounting practices and the exploitation of accounting anomalies by management. (These have been well documented by Terry Smith in his book *Accounting for Growth*.[11])

Return on invested capital (i.e. net operating profit after tax divided by invested capital) is becoming a key measure; the emergence of the SHV concept is reinforcing the message that companies have to improve their returns on invested capital as well as reduce their cost of capital. Similar economic factors, of course, have been putting pressure on return on equity capital in Europe.

In some respects, the UK has taken a lead in using some of the SVA techniques outlined in earlier chapters – maybe through a combination of greater financial disclosure by companies and an increasing need for a common measure of value that can compare one European company with another. Research commissioned by PricewaterhouseCoopers revealed that the majority of UK security analysts are now using future cash flows to value companies. They are doing this in a framework where the more conventional measures are still reported, but at their heart there now lies a well-developed cash flow model. In other words, cash flows are now starting to account for more in the valuation process than reported profits, and most of the better houses now use cash flow analytical techniques almost as a matter of course.

Why has this change occurred? In part it is due to European equities' under-performance, in turn attributable to low economic growth and increasing competition. Being accountable to their owners or providers of funds, investors have to achieve the maximum returns and are wary of companies that present no more than a facade of increasing profits and short-term increases in share prices (often attributable simply to a general increase in the market). They have also become disillusioned with managements' attempts at "window-dressing" lackluster performance in a tough low-inflation/low-growth environment.

Corporate governance

Owing to the strength of institutional investors in the UK, shares can be voted as blocs, and, in theory at least, some institutional shareholders could almost meet the definition of "stakeholders" as given earlier. Generally, though, while the top four or five institutions (say) may hold up to 50 percent of the available share capital in a mid-cap UK company, these shares are often treated in a "hands-off" manner. If performance suffers, positions are trimmed. Discreet pressure will sometimes be exercised with sustained under-performance, but the onus is often on investors to "vote with their feet" rather than become more actively involved in corporate management. This may have contributed to a situation where management has been relatively strong in the face of share-holder indecision or occasional apathy.

Disquiet about this has led to a number of recommendations, all designed to improve market transparency and set up conditions that continue to favor shareholder oversight into corporate affairs. Three committees – the Cadbury, Greenbury and most recently the Hampel committee – have produced weighty recommendations on how companies should govern themselves. A consensus has emerged:

● that in public companies there should be a separation of the chairman's from the CEO's role;

● that an adequate number, up to a third, of a board should be independent non-executive directors who can test management's decisions and remind them of their responsibilities to shareholders;

● that board members should be chosen in a reasonably open manner.

Shareholders are encouraged to take a "constructive interest" and test strategy and performance over time, but the door is left open for a more formal introduction of shareholder activism in the UK. Voting levels at AGMs remain mostly below the 40 percent mark, indicating a lack of interest by investors, many of whom are institutions.

Top management in public companies has usually been incentivized by a variety of share options schemes – or by phantom-type schemes (if private). Often, the targets that earnings had to reach before executive share options could be exercised have not been very demanding. But, as a result of the 1992 Cadbury Committee report on corporate governance, linked targets have been developed. These are:

● to use relative performance measures (i.e. comparing other companies in the same sector);

● to use total shareholder returns (i.e. dividends plus increase in share prices) rather than just an increase in share prices (which could be achieved by a general increase in the market) or raw increases in EPS (a figure often subject to manipulation by accounting treatments); and

● to have longer-term performance measures, so that benefits have to accrue to shareholders first over a period of time.

As a result, we are seeing more UK companies keen to put SHV measuring systems in place throughout their groups, in order to establish appropriate yardsticks by which management performance can be assessed before incentives are granted. Additionally, details of executive remuneration have to be made public in a company's annual accounts – in contrast to the situation in many European countries, where data protection laws prevent it.

What managements are doing

Some UK companies are now starting to embrace SHV concepts. Examples include Boots, Diageo, Tate and Lyle, and famously Lloyds-TSB. Of these perhaps the most well known and arguably the most successful has been Lloyds, the bank where SHV doubled every three years for nearly a decade. This paved the way for further mergers and acquisitions including the TSB and Scottish Widows, a life insurance company. Although the share performance has tailed off recently, it is hard to overlook the fact that the Lloyds-TSB group is one of the more profitably run banks not only in the UK but in the world, and has, almost uniquely in this industry, been able to combine competitive success with additional returns to the shareholders.

Tate and Lyle is another example of a company that has used SHV analysis to help improve share price performance. Too little attention had been paid to the management of working capital, with the result that the capital base of the company expanded far too rapidly and share price performance had suffered. Implementation of SHV improvement measures, including incentivization of management around a new SVA metric all helped to stabilize the situation during the late 1990s.

Diageo, formed out of a merger between Grand Metropolitan and Guinness, has also implemented an extensive SHV program. Started by the then CEO at Grand Met, the program was continued into the new merged entity. The company has set itself some ambitious goals and has an executive remuneration scheme tied to SVA measures. The initial problem was that the working capital tied up in the production of alcoholic drinks was large, and this was responsible for a long period of under-performance as the company struggled to service its extended capital base. Efforts are being made to reduce this. The SHV programs have also led to a reorientation of marketing strategy away from some of the lower-priced brands and towards the more expensive parts of the product range. There was also an extensive thinning out of the product/brand range itself as it became evident that some lines were just not adding value. These steps combined with a new executive incentive scheme provide a framework within which the company can move on to a new strategy, compete more effectively in its markets and still provide enhanced returns for shareholders.

National Power has also turned to an SHV/balanced scorecard approach to help motivate and improve the quality of its management and staff. SHV was one very important metric against which the company's plans could be compared and tested. Information on this topic was disseminated to a wide group of managers through regular briefings by the CEO. These broader shareholder goals were then used to establish goals for training and development programs for staff. The Investors in People program established a performance measurement framework which focussed attention on current business performance, sustaining and developing capabilities, influencing external stakeholders and sustaining an enabling culture and climate. Having devolved these plans down to individual departments, they were then aggregated up again on a functional and business unit basis, ultimately receiving board approval. These plans were then summarized as part of the company's performance contract with shareholders.

UK telecommunications companies, and the privatized electricity generation, distribution and supply companies, too, are focussing on improving the key drivers of SHV. In these industries government regulators use cost-of-capital calculations very deliberately to help them assess companies' underlying profitability when they set regulated prices.

Shareholder activism and responses to it

Some of the ideas of shareholder activism, promulgated by CalPERS in the USA (see above), have started to spread to the UK. The Hermes Pension Fund Management, for instance, is taking a longer-term and more activist view about managing its investments. In autumn 1998 it launched the Hermes-Lens fund designed to invest in mid-capitalization stocks with a policy based on "relational shareholder activism."

In corporate governance terms, Hermes stands fully behind the Cadbury and other proposals and thinks that a board should have three "vigorously independent non-executive directors on whom shareholders can rely for the independence of their judgement and who can act as agents for change should the need arise." Like CalPERS, it is pushing for greater openness and transparency in corporate reporting. This includes offering some conditional support for an incumbent management in case of a hostile bid, but not at any price. The fund reserves the right to take alternative action if shareholders' interests would be better served by so doing. In a statement of general principles, Hermes says: "A company run in the long-term interests of its shareholders will need to manage effectively relationships with its employees, suppliers and customers with regard to the common weal" which puts the case for SHV in the institutional investor context very well.

The desire for greater transparency from investors is being met, to some extent, by the companies themselves. Their agenda may differ to some extent, since the companies are keen to be seen to be good corporate citizens, in addition to demonstrating their shareholder value prowess. An organization called AccountAbility, set up in 1996, now has some impressive support from a variety of world economic and political organizations, but cites UK companies such as British Aerospace, BP Amoco, United Utilities, British Telecom, the Cooperative Bank, and Shell International.

Finally, it is worth mentioning that some organizations in the UK have taken a lead in moving much closer to what we call value reporting (see Chapter 12). One example is that of the Cooperative Bank – which is mutually owned, and so in the strict sense of the word is not a shareholder organization. Its "partnership" report provides a detailed and objective assessment of the bank's performance in relation to its stakeholders, and could be extended by other organizations that have shareholders. One positive side effect mentioned by the Cooperative Bank was that this report provided something equivalent to £1 million worth of free advertising to the bank and has helped generate significant volumes of new business.

Australia

Australia continues to have a healthy shareholder value culture. Market capitalization as a proportion of GDP was just under 80 percent in 1997, and some 40 percent of the population now owns shares – a sharp increase from a few years earlier. Institutional investors hold around half of their assets in equities contributing to a reasonable level of market turnover in securities.

Share ownership has been greatly enhanced by a series of privatizations and de-mutualizations, as Fig. 11.7 shows. All of the companies shown there have recently been floated, and have attracted wide public participation. This trend has continued with over 1.8 million additional Australians participating in the privatization of a further 16 percent of Telstra in 1999.

Indirect participation in equity markets through superannuation (pension) funds also continues its upward trend. Superannuation fund assets have increased to levels equivalent to 66 percent of GDP at the time of writing from 45 percent five years previously. This growth has been largely driven by legislation on compulsory employee contributions and favorable tax treatment of voluntary contributions. These contributions, which are based on a percentage of gross earnings, are set to rise by another two percentage points to 9 percent in 2002 and appear set to ensure continued solid growth in funds under management. Foreign equity ownership has remained relatively constant at around 32 percent of the market.

Shareholder activism is on the rise for institutional investors, who are increasingly prepared to collude in order to focus management attention on SHV. The role that institutional investors played in precipitating changes in

Australia public companies ranked by number of shareholders – December 1998	Million shareholders
Telstra	1.4
AMP	1.2
TAB Limited	0.6
National Mutual (AXA)	0.5
Colonial State Bank	0.4
Commonwealth Bank	0.4
BHP	0.3

Source: Reserve Bank of Australia Demutualisation in Australia January 1999

FIG 11.7 ● Australian public companies ranked by number of shareholders

leadership at the under-performing BHP represents a recent high-profile example of this phenomenon.

Greater shareholder activism may also be partly responsible for the small but steady rise in share buy-backs. These are a sign that shareholder pressure on management is mounting, and that it is sometimes expedient to give shares a boost by retiring the equity, possibly financed by additional debt, or by drawing down on reserves. This growth in share buy-backs was made possible by changes to corporate law in 1991. Since 1996, the value of stock repurchased has increased from 0.2 percent of market value to current levels of around 1 percent. This has been accompanied by a corresponding decline in the use of dividend reinvestment schemes, whose value has declined from a peak of around 1.5 percent of market value in 1990 to levels of around 0.5 percent.

The Australian equity markets over the five years to June 1999 have been solid by historical standards. Annual equivalent total shareholder returns over this period, as measured by a market accumulation index, have been in excess of 9 percent per annum. Although this performance appears much less impressive when compared to the results achieved in North American and European equity markets over the same period, it must be noted that metals and commodities prices – which have a large weighting in the Australian indices – were weak for most of this period.

Developments in SHV application

A recent PricewaterhouseCoopers survey examined the top 100 value-creating companies in Australia using the MVA measure (see Chapter 6) and found the best-performing value creators at opposite ends of the corporate spectrum. One group consisted of small agile and creative organizations operating in markets with numerous opportunities to diversify and expand. Companies in this group demonstrated by far the highest performance in terms of value creation, having between A$30 million and A$70 million of capital employed and scoring an average relative MVA of 3.36. At the other end of the spectrum, large, economically powerful businesses employing over A$3 billion of capital were, as a group, the next best performers achieving a relative MVA of 0.64. The underachievers tended to be the middle range of companies with market capitalization ranging from A$400 million to A$600 million, many in capital-intensive businesses in highly competitive markets. While these companies appear to be delivering efficient results in product markets, their lack of identifiable competitive advantage results in under performance. They only achieved an MVA figure of 0.15.

The survey also confirmed the increasing importance of SHV metrics as benchmarks for assessing and managing corporate performance. In 1998, among the top 100 value creators, the use of measures such as SVA, MVA and TSR exceeded the use of EPS by a factor of more than two to one. A year later, this ratio had increased to more than five to one.

SHV measures still have a way to go before they are generally accepted, but some of Australia's largest and most successful value creating companies, including Telstra, Lend Lease, Fosters Brewing Group, ANZ Banking Group, Coles Meyer, Westpac Banking Group and the Commonwealth Bank, have adopted such metrics. Companies have most often favored economic profit over measures such as CFROI, with simplicity of calculation being the reason most often cited. But surprisingly little was said by survey respondents about the use of metrics in executive remuneration schemes. And as yet there are few companies that have been able to drive the value agenda down into the operational front line.

Canada

With stock market capitalization just under 80 percent of GDP, and with 37 percent of the population owning shares, Canada organizes its financial affairs sympathetically towards shareholders. The proportion of assets invested in equities by institutions was recently recorded at 25 percent, which is on the low side. However, this proportion has been rising as interest rates have fallen, leading to a switch out of bonds and into equities.

The Canadian equities market is primarily characterized by the influence of two key factors: natural resource (e.g. oil and gas) prices, since the Canadian economy is still considered commodity-based in many respects; and the economy of the USA – the USA is Canada's largest trading partner. In addition, for some companies with large operations in Quebec, share prices can be adversely affected by uncertainty over that province's political future as part of, or separate from, the rest of Canada.

Currently, the Canadian public equities market comprises five stock exchanges: the Toronto Stock Exchange (TSE), the Montreal Stock Exchange (MSE), the Vancouver Stock Exchange (VSE), the Alberta Stock Exchange (ASE) and the Winnipeg Stock Exchange (WSE). The largest exchange, the TSE, is also the tenth largest in the world and the third largest in North America. It accounts for approximately 90 percent of the value of the shares traded on the Canadian exchanges and it has over 1,400 listed companies with a total market capitalization greater than C$1 trillion. The TSE 300, a market capitalization weighted index, is the general benchmark for the Canadian equity markets with its predominant sectors being natural resources, financial services, industrial products and utilities, which collectively make up more than 75 percent of the index. The performance of the TSE in the last five years has lagged behind the robust US market primarily due to the decline in commodity markets in the late 1990s. The returns for the TSE 300 and the S&P 500 are shown in Fig. 11.8.

The Canadian exchanges are currently planning to restructure: changes proposed include the appointment of the TSE as the senior equity exchange in Canada, shifting the derivatives trading market to the MSE, and combining the ASE and VSE to become the Canadian Venture Exchange. Although the Canadian equity market is growing, it is still relatively small in comparison to the world's equity markets – trading on the Canadian exchanges accounts for approximately 2 percent of global equities, a percentage has been declining in the past decade.

Who owns the shares?

According to a 1996 TSE study, 37.5 percent of the Canadian population (approximately 7.5 million people) participated in the Canadian equity market either by direct investments in common or preferred shares, or indirectly by investing in stock mutual funds. Also at that time, share ownership was the second most popular investment after home ownership, a dramatic increase since 1983 when equity assets ranked fifth behind investments in homes, Canada Savings Bonds, guaranteed investment certificates (GICs) and real estate excluding homes. The popularity of equity investments follows that of the USA.

The growth in equity investment in Canada has been driven by a number of factors, including:

- the prevalence of large pension funds especially among public sector employees;

- the popularity of investing in mutual funds due to increasing participation in Registered Retirement Savings Plan (RRSPs), which are individual retirement savings plans for which the government allows an income tax deduction for contributions. In 1996, 55 percent of Canadians owned RRSPs (Government regulations restrict foreign content to 20 percent of overall fund assets);

- the favorable performance of the stock market and increased knowledge about Canadian investment choices; and

- the continued existence of low inflation and increased fiscal responsibility by the federal government, which has resulted in low returns for bonds, once the preferred investment vehicle.

As for the Canadian institutional investment community, the number of brokerage houses has declined dramatically in the last ten years through industry consolidation. Recent changes that have impacted the community include the fact that chartered banks are now permitted to purchase investment banks; and that life insurance companies have been able to de-mutualize.

The Canadian investment community has traditionally analyzed companies using the price/earnings or net asset valuation approaches; however, the use of

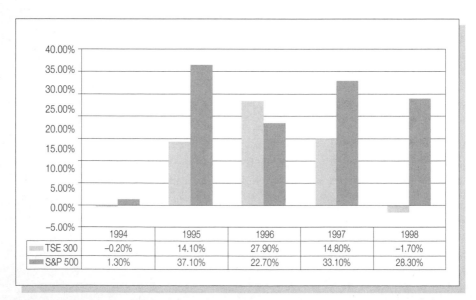

	1994	1995	1996	1997	1998
TSE 300	−0.20%	14.10%	27.90%	14.80%	−1.70%
S&P 500	1.30%	37.10%	22.70%	33.10%	28.30%

FIG 11.8 ● **TSE versus S&P 500 indices – total return**   Source: Bloomberg

valuation techniques involving a multiple of cash flow or EBITDA are increasingly being applied. As the US and Canadian institutional market participants become more closely involved in each other's market, a focus on increasing shareholder value, through tools such as SVA, will likely increase.

Corporate governance

Canadian capital markets have prided themselves on being fair and relatively efficient, and as a result, corporate governance has become a far more developed concept than shareholder value management (SVM) in Canada. It has been noted that the appearance of fairness is more important than SHV. Many companies have set up corporate governance committees, and the Canadian exchanges have also provided guidelines. Although compliance with these guidelines is not mandatory, it is highly recommended that public companies disclose their corporate governance practices and, if they differ from the guidelines, explain why.

Increased shareholder activism among provincial government-sponsored pension plans has been influential in encouraging companies to seriously consider corporate governance issues. As the size of the Canadian equity market grows and investor participation increases, corporate governance will be likely to be further entrenched among the public companies.

Warming up to SHV management

SHV methodologies have yet to make a significant impact on the overall Canadian market, despite the widespread adoption of such principles in its neighbor, the USA. However, as more Canadian companies become inter-listed on both Canadian and American stock exchanges, and US investment banks demand increased disclosure and usage of alternative measures of performance, acceptance of these techniques is visibly increasing. For example, in the past year, one of Canada's leading breweries, Molson, announced its intention to adopt a SHV management system as a strategy to develop a competitive advantage.

The Canadian media have also paid more attention to the topic of shareholder value. *The Financial Post* recently published an annual survey ranking the top 300 Canadian companies as measured by "market value added" (MVA).[12] The two sectors that dominated the top ten rankings in 1998 were telecommunications/high technology firms and financial institutions. Nortel Networks, a telecommunications giant in Canada, has been ranked number one for two years running, and the banking industry overall has been increasing operating profits and economic profits since the mid-1990s.[13]

Not only has the press increased its awareness of SHV measurements available; a number of Canadian institutional money managers have also set up research programs identifying companies that create value by investing in new ventures whose returns exceed the cost of capital.

However, though most Canadian companies say they recognize shareholders' interests are important in setting corporate strategy, few have attempted to quantify the economic value of their equity or measure the impact they have in its business decisions. This is also revealed in a recent survey of US money managers, which noted that Canadian public companies are far behind their US counterparts in managing shareholder concerns.[14] As the capital markets become more global, however, and as investors of Canadian equity become more sophisticated and/or demanding, SHV measures are likely to become more prevalent among Canadian boardrooms and investment analysts.

The Netherlands

In the spirit of the emerging consensus on SHV, we have grouped the Netherlands with other "shareholder-friendly" countries. As with others, the country's market capitalization is over 100 percent of GDP, and around 44 percent of the country's equities are in private hands, with pension fund assets around 85 percent of GDP. There is a vibrant market for shares, emphasized by the open nature of Dutch markets. Moreover, a disciplined and consensual attitude towards wage and income determination in the Netherlands has improved economic and corporate performance by preventing production costs from rising faster than productivity.

The commitment to SHV, however, is in some ways still incomplete, and in many ways the Netherlands can be thought of as a half-way house between more established Anglo-Saxon SHV countries, and stakeholder economies.

There are two important features of Dutch economic and financial life. On the one hand the country's relatively small size means that it is a classic small economy open to international trade: around 30 percent of the quoted shares on its stock exchange are owned by foreigners. Being home to some of the largest and most international companies in the world, it is interested in integration into the world economy. On the other hand, there is a tradition of consensus and local control that is less keen to involve outsiders. SHV management is caught between these two sometimes opposing streams in Dutch society.

This can be illustrated by looking in more detail at the two main forms of corporate organization in the Netherlands, the NV or *naamloze vennootschap* (anonymous limited company), and the BV or *besloten vennootschap* (closed limited company). Listed NVs are equivalent to the plc, incorporated, or AG structures seen in the UK, USA, and Germany respectively. However, unlisted NVs are much less investor-friendly; and even though the NV format is intended for large public companies, it is not always a good vehicle for representing shareholder interests.

All companies with more than 100 employees have to establish a council (similar to the German *Betriebsrat)*, which is entitled to be informed and consulted on many major corporate decisions, especially those involving labor and employees. In the case of larger companies with share capital and reserves of at least Fl25 million, a supervisory board also has to be established. This board has taken on many of the functions exercised by shareholders in other countries – for instance appointing and dismissing the management board and drawing up the annual accounts, which are then subject to shareholder approval. At the moment it is fair to say that this regime significantly dilutes the rights of shareholders, who have very little say in making changes to the supervisory board.

Additionally, voting control can be limited to particular classes of shareholders for NV companies, for instance by setting up an *administratiekantoor* (administration office) or AK that holds the original shares and issues share certificates. Certificate holders' rights can then be restricted to the receipt of dividends; their voting rights are exercised by the AK. Other certificate holders retain the right to attend and speak at shareholders' meetings, and can challenge management and supervisory board decisions. Certification of shares is a useful "poison pill" preventing hostile takeovers. A further variant of this is the use of preference shares that can be given special voting privileges. When these shares are in "safe" hands, they too constitute a powerful defense against unwelcome external bids.

While the statutes of NVs can limit the free transferability of shares, a BV's statutes must restrict such transferability (except possibly for transfers to other existing shareholders, close family and the BV itself). This makes the company takeover-proof, and also makes takeovers considerably more difficult for NV companies. Listed NV companies are required to have bearer shares, the transfer of which cannot be limited. (It is noteworthy that when BVs were introduced in 1971, some 90 percent of existing NVs converted into the more impregnable BV form.)

Share buy-backs are also more difficult to achieve in the Netherlands for NVs. A BV can acquire up to 50 percent of its own issued capital, but an NV can only buy back up to 10 percent of its shares without getting special shareholder approval. Incumbent shareholders of NVs have pre-emptive rights on new issues, which is not the case for BVs. For listed companies there are various control "triggers" that are activated when 5, 10, 25, 50, or 66.67 percent of issued capital changes hands.

Winds of change?

The complexities of Dutch corporate law have contributed to some "stakeholder" type behavior in the past. Firms have often owned significant blocs of shares in each other and, with hostile takeover activity unlikely, incumbent managements, protected by their supervisory boards, have concentrated on things other than creating SHV.

In 1997, a commission on corporate governance investigated the role of shareholders in corporate decision-making. It produced a list of 40 recommendations designed to enlarge the influence of shareholders and covering a wide range of corporate governance issues, from the way companies should use and disclose employee share option programs to a recommendation for more independent and critical supervisory boards. This commission's proposals have stimulated public discussion in the Netherlands on SHV management and on the validity of its ultimate goal, maximizing shareholder wealth. But there is as yet no real consensus about reconciling the interests of shareholders and stakeholders.

There are several reasons for this public suspicion concerning the ultimate benefit of shareholder value management. Maximizing SHV seems one-dimensional and so non-consensual, and Netherlands public opinion does not appreciate that shareholders are residual claim holders whose wealth can only increase after the other stakeholders have had their share.

SHV is also frequently associated with the sometimes rather insensitive introduction of stock option programs. Although designed to align the interests of management with SHV, such programs have often been seen as a "perk" aimed exclusively at senior managers. Owing to favorable taxation, surging stock markets and a lack of restrictions on exercising the options, stock option holders were able to realize huge profits without having to do very much. At a time of wage restraint for other employees, stock option plans, and hence the SHV approach, have been seen as being socially exclusive and hence unfair, undermining the Dutch "consensual" model.

Board members of Dutch companies, especially those operating on a multinational level, realize that they have rather more limited choices. They are under continuous pressure from the international financial markets to improve performance. Introducing and implementing SHV management is one effective way to change strategy. Dutch companies not only have to respond to heavy competition in their own markets, but also have to meet the exacting demands of globalized financial markets and reposition themselves to deal with the euro.

The pressure mounts, and some respond ...

We offer three recent examples of corporate response to the challenges posed by SHV. In the first case Unilever (jointly owned and registered in the Netherlands and the UK) has been seeking ways to increase its performance. Its shares have languished as the value of its brands has not brought the rewards investors are looking for. In response to this, Unilever decided to sell its speciality chemical division to ICI for around Fl15 billion.

The original management intention was to use the proceeds of this sale to acquire more companies and increase growth. It was expected that, within two to three years, suitable candidates for acquisition would be found – but, for a variety of reasons, none were found. Instead, unusually for Unilever, a decision was made to return these funds to shareholders via a "super dividend." This is one of the first occasions when shareholder interest has been clearly put ahead of management interest.

Another example is that of the state-owned KPN. Following the lead of other countries, in 1997 it was decided to separate the postal from the telecoms side, thus allowing the two separate businesses to focus on their core activities and facilitate the construction of international alliances. The increase in transparency made their shares more attractive. Again, this was a radical step away from consensual stakeholder management towards a situation where SHV management could be effectively introduced and implemented.

The story of the break-up of Vendex is a further example of more value being obtained for investors by the splitting up of various divisions rather than by trying to run them as a coherent group. At the start of 1998, Vendex International NV had activities in department stores, speciality stores, temp agencies, and in food retailing. During 1998, the company split into three separate companies – Vendex NV operating the department and speciality stores; Vedior NV, which took on the temping agency services; and Vendex Food. The third company, which operated the food retailing side, promptly merged with another company, De Boer Unigro, to form a new company, Laurus NV. This last example shows how diversified groups can prosper more when their various component parts are floated off and allowed to make their own decisions.

At the moment it is not entirely clear how the debate will go, but these examples show that time and the pressure of change probably favor the SHV approach in the Netherlands. There is still scope for a more "Dutch" variant that will try to maintain a high degree of consensus. Maybe there will be a gradual realization that more weight should be given to SHV issues and performance requirements, but not at any price. Entrepreneurship combined with social responsibility could be the right description, and as such would represent a continuing of a middle way between stakes and shares, but veering more towards the SHV approach over time.

Sweden

Sweden too is a country with a long history of stakeholder traditions. Yet in many respects the earlier trends towards greater "SHV friendliness," identified in the first edition of this book, have continued apace. Stock market capitalization is now over 100 percent of GDP, and nearly half the population own shares. This is probably the highest proportion in the EU/OECD area, and possibly the highest proportion anywhere in the world. Sweden is, in our opinion, firmly in the camp of the shareholder-friendly countries.

Around 25 percent of all shares are held by private households, with the rest split between institutional investors, such as insurance companies and pension funds, and foreign institutional investors. There is still a strong residue of stakeholder power in terms of the proportion of equities owned by the government (11 percent) and corporates (19 percent). Corporate shareholdings represent complex cross-shareholding arrangements between firms, as well as entrenched "stakes" by dominant stakeholders. There are signs, though, that these two blocs are likely to be made available to a wider shareholding community in the near future, and this will have a large impact on the industrial and financial landscape.

In 1999 there were $52 billion worth of mergers in Sweden. This has been led off by a restructuring wave in the Wallenberg group, which has freed up its stakes in Stora and Astra. Volvo cars were also sold to Ford for $6.5 billion, which would have been unthinkable as recently as six years before, when a similar plan to sell to Renault was blocked.

The significance of these moves in the Swedish context cannot be underestimated. Wallenberg's holding company, Investor, holds dominant stakes in ABB, Ericsson, Electrolux, Atlas Copco and Gambro. In all, it owns a dominant share in companies that constitute 40 percent of the entire Swedish stock exchange. But, interestingly, Investor itself is under pressure. It recently turned in a negative performance for the year when the Swedish market itself managed a 13 percent gain. The Investor group habitually sells at a 30 percent discount to its book value, which opens up a window of vulnerability. There has been a change of the guard at Investor as a younger scion of the Wallenberg family, Marcus Wallenberg, has taken over the top management position. It is increasingly likely that the protected network of voting shares that underpins a lot of the Investor empire is starting to unravel.

Two recent developments underscore this. A hostile bid for Scania, the Swedish truckmaker that is part of the Wallenberg group, was made by the Volvo CEO Leif Johansson, backed by 13 percent of the shares voted by Swedish fund managers. They were disgruntled by the lackluster performance of Scania's stock after its initial public offering in 1996. As it happened, the initiative did not carry the day, nor did it overcome serious anti-trust concerns at the European level. But, it has meant that, as the major shareholder, Investor now has a strong incentive to take steps to keep Scania's share price high.

Martin Ebner, of UBS fame (see below, under Switzerland), has also entered the fray as a stalker for ABB, and has a stake large enough to justify a seat on the board. ABB's share price has languished, and Ebner's presence was sufficient to put up the share price on the rumor of radical re-structuring to come and of a simplification of the share structure. All of which indicates a change in the fundamental attitudes to running large public corporations. While there are rumors that Investor could substantially reduce its stakes in Swedish companies, this could rather be a prelude to a further diversification of their portfolio. High personal taxes and global competition are forcing Swedish companies to become ever more international, to the extent of changing their domicile. Ericsson has re-located many headquarters functions in the UK, simply to be able to offer competitive salaries and bonuses that would not be gobbled up by Sweden's very high marginal personal tax rates. Indeed, it is noticeable that SHV has taken root as a theme and focus of management attention at several Investor-controlled companies, including SCA, Atlas Copco, and more recently Electrolux.

And the markets ...

Sweden's financial markets are also progressing rapidly. In 1999, OM acquired the Stockholm Stock Exchange. OM was already operating a number of option exchanges including the OM London Exchange and its other business is to develop and sell advanced stock exchange systems with installations in countries throughout the world. OM Stockholm Stock Exchange does not believe in European stock market alliances and instead it focuses on a technology driven, low-transaction cost model. Norex is being built up to include the Stockholm and Copenhagen stock and option exchanges, with plans to link up

Oslo soon. Although Helsinki is still not keen on entering this arrangement, the three smaller Baltic states are planning to link up in the future. This could well bring forward the day when OM succeeds in its intention to become the independent European stock exchange alternative. Finally, it is worth mentioning that rules will shortly be introduced on the market to allow share buy-backs. Shareholder activism is alive and well in the form of the Small Shareholders Association.

Switzerland

Switzerland has a thriving shareholder culture, enhanced by substantial foreign participation. Stock market capitalization is around 150 percent of GDP, which partly reflects the global importance of many Swiss companies as well as the attractions of Switzerland for foreign investors. Only 13 percent of households own shares and so most shares in Switzerland are owned by institutional investors. However, those few households in Switzerland that own shares own a lot of them, and they account for around 30 percent of all shares owned, and are the second most important sector after foreign institutional investors. Just over 21 percent of equities are owned by domestic institutional investors such as pension funds and investment trusts. Institutional investors hold a relatively high proportion (50 percent) of their assets in equities – which creates a reasonable demand for share transactions. Industrial cross-shareholdings remain an important factor in Switzerland and account for around 16 percent of shares owned.

Switzerland still has a two-class shareholder system with registered and bearer shares. These are not generally allocated equal voting rights, and there are still several companies that put an upper limit on the number of voting shares. Nestlé falls into this category, where only 3 percent of share votes can be voted by any individual investor whatever the actual size of the shareholding. These arrangements mean that the market for corporate control in Switzerland is still relatively limited, but there are signs that it is opening up.

Shares where voting power is limited trade at a discount to those where it is not, as Fig. 11.9 shows. Discounts of between 5 percent and 30 percent are possible. Under certain circumstances, large discounts can be an invitation for outside bidders to redouble their efforts to overcome the barriers to takeover, since the amount of "locked up value" can become too large to resist.

There is a tendency for companies to merge their two shares into one class, often the registered type of share that is easier to control. Doing this helps improve the marketability of the shares, since the price of individual shares in

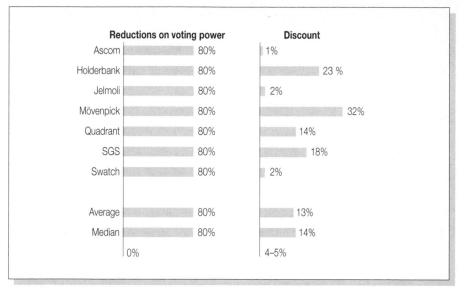

FIG 11.9 ● Discounts for loss of voting rights in selected Swiss companies

the "double" system in Switzerland can be surprisingly high. Two recent converts to a single class of share are ABB and UBS.

These two corporations are interesting for other reasons, not the least because a single investor, Martin Ebner, has been heavily involved in pushing SHV higher up the boardroom's agenda. UBS, a paragon of Swiss corporate life, ultimately succumbed to a determination to push up its own SHV-generating abilities, and merged with SBC. As we saw in the previous section on Sweden, ABB too is being encouraged to take a more positive view of shareholder value, led again by Ebner.

So, while there is no legal sanction against having two or more classes of shareholders in Switzerland, it is likely that market forces will encourage the replacement of multi-share types with one more tradeable and hence accessible instrument. This is turn will mean that Swiss management will be less sheltered from outside interference than before.

Management attitudes to SHV

There are still some significant areas for improvement in Switzerland. According to a survey conducted by PricewaterhouseCoopers,[15] only one-third of investors and analysts find financial reports very useful for communicating the "true" value of an organization. Equally, only one-third of analysts and investors think that Swiss companies are prepared to work proactively with them to provide better more meaningful information. The overwhelming majority of investors and analysts are concerned about the very high level of discretion companies have under Swiss GAAP in striking an earnings figure, and this tends to reduce confidence in those very numbers.

There is a fair amount of disunity among experts: many buy-side analysts, representing investors, have serious doubts about the abilities of sell-side analysts to understand the strategies of the companies they follow – perhaps a reflection of the weak quality of the information many analysts have to work with. Both analysts and investors are agreed, however, that there is a clear benefit to companies in improving the flow of information.

VBM in Switzerland

The importance of managing with SHV goals firmly in mind is something not yet clearly understood by all Swiss companies. A recent Pricewaterhouse-Coopers study[16] showed that over 60 percent of board members and senior management were compensated with schemes oriented around SHV targets, but this has not stretched very far into the ranks of middle management. There appears to be a slight difference in approaches used across industry and commerce. Financial services organizations prefer forms of FCF/DCF approaches, while industry has a clear preference for SVA/EVA approaches.

What has become particularly evident is that very few Swiss organizations are using SHV to compare and contrast the valuations being put on them by the market and consider what implications they have for their own performance. Only 20 percent of the industrial respondents in the PricewaterhouseCoopers survey admitted that they had done such an analysis.

The survey also found that Swiss companies fell into two large groups. At one end of the scale are what are called the "wizards" who have an above-average grasp of SHV concepts and an above-average development of the necessary accounting and information systems to ensure that they can keep a tab on the strategies they develop. At the other end of scale were a large number of companies (the "neophytes") who were just starting out on the value-based management journey. Several Swiss blue-chip companies came into this group, as did many medium-sized businesses.

Switzerland is now an island entirely surrounded by the sea of "Euroland." As markets become more transparent elsewhere in the EU, so it is very likely that Swiss companies will have to become more accessible to global investors who, as we know, require more servicing than domestic investors. Since Swiss companies have every intention to remain globally competitive, the Swiss are also likely to take further steps to liberalize reporting arrangements, which will further enhance the country's already enviable record for stability.

SOME STAKEHOLDER COUNTRIES

Most of the rest of the world's developed economies fall into the "stakeholder" category. This is not to say that there are no shareholders, or that equities are unknown in these countries – far from it. Many have extensive equity markets and show signs of moving towards a more "shareholder friendly" framework. But, for the time being, there are still noticeable differences between this group and those countries discussed above.

On average, stakeholder economies' stock markets are much less developed, with market capitalization coming to around 40 percent of GDP – see Fig. 11.5. A much smaller proportion of the population owns shares, which probably means that share owning is very much the prerogative of the rich. The percentage of shares owned by private households is also less than for the first group. What is even more significant is how the remaining shares are divided up. The corporates, through interlocking cross-holdings, account for around a third of shares owned. Governments own a larger stake, in this sample owning 7 percent of shares, while banks account for another 10 percent. The role of other institutional investors is correspondingly reduced.

As we have described earlier in this chapter, these are the countries where government and banks play an important part in keeping control carefully restricted to a select group of individuals and institutions. However, in several countries – Germany deserves a special mention here – moves are afoot to shift many of these arrangements towards greater transparency and openness. The experience of the shareholder-friendly countries' superior macro-economic performance over the last decade has not been lost on many observers in "stakeholderland." We are probably witnessing movements within a chrysalis as the SHV butterfly develops and matures – to emerge into the world in a not too distant future.

Germany

The 1990s were one of the less happy decades for Germany. After decades of unbroken prosperity and growth, the after-shocks of reunification left German industry with a high cost base and declining international competitiveness. Demands on government spending continued to be high; at one time, there was a chance that Germany, normally considered a pillar of financial rectitude, might not have been allowed into the Euro-zone. Rather than luxuriating in the feeling that the system "worked," local observers started wondering if there were lessons to be learnt from others, particularly in the field of SHV.

Typically for a "stakeholder" economy, only a small proportion of the German population owns shares (7 percent), and householders only account for 14 percent of shares. The great bulk of shares (42 percent) are owned by the corporates, either as savings for their own pension schemes, or as part of complex pyramid-like arrangements of interlocking shareholdings (known as *Schachtelbeteiligungen*). Banks and government between them own another 14 percent of equity. Insurance, pension and investment fund institutional investors are correspondingly under-represented. Foreign investors own just under 10 percent of the equity market.

The German economy is also about bonds; financial institutions only place around 12 percent of their assets in equities. This emphasis is a result of many factors, including tax rules that discriminate against equities for investment purposes, risk averseness by investors and the sometimes respectable investment performance from the bond side.

But there has been a long tradition that regarded shareholders as little more than a public nuisance. The German banker Carl Fuerstenberg, director of a powerful nineteenth-century Berlin trading bank, is reputed to have said that shareholders "are stupid and insolent; stupid because they buy shares and insolent because they expect a dividend."[17] This attitude has persisted: even in the recent past large corporations have been reluctant to release relatively non-controversial information to shareholders, leading to court cases where shareholders' rights to information were confirmed.[18]

These attitudes are starting to change, and in the last few years there have been a series of quite remarkable changes. For instance, just a year after the biggest loss in his company's history, Jürgen Schrempp, the CEO of Daimler-Benz, announced that the new goal would be "profit, profit, profit." He was referring explicitly to the fact that SHV was to be the guide for future company action. In Schrempp's opinion, focussing on this approach was the only way to bring the company back into a lasting profitable state.

The resulting decisions, to restrict Daimler-Benz to its core businesses and to dispose of loss-making segments such as Fokker and AEG, have obviously led to job cuts in these firms – cuts that the unions attribute solely to the drive for SHV. Accompanied as they were by decisions to move to a different form of more internationally acceptable accounting (see below), the decisions unleashed a storm of controversy. The company even felt it expedient to drop the phrase "shareholder value" for a while and replace it with the more neutral-sounding *Unternehmenswertsteigerung*, or increase in corporate value.

But the medicine started to work: Daimler started to improve. It was subsequently able to take over Chrysler and project itself onto the world stage as a long-term player in the automobile industry.

Daimler has not been alone. Siemens, another giant German firm, had languished for years with an underperforming share price. The group was floundering as smaller more nimble rivals quickly grabbed commanding positions in the new industries. Siemens spent billions shoring up positions in computers and integrated circuits, which did little more than freeze the company with a wide-ranging portfolio, a lot of which was losing money. As a pre-eminent example of stakeholding, there was a serious lack of decision-making at the center as conflicting interests between suppliers, customers and employees all had to be balanced off against each other. Shareholder interests were politely put on hold for several years.

Siemens has now started to use economic profit and target returns at corporate and divisional levels. Similarly, executive compensation is to be tied to economic profit targets, and SHV ideas are being propagated among employees. Even more radically, the portfolio has been trimmed. The semiconductor business has been spun off as Infinion, and the loss-making PC business Siemens Nixdorf has been sold as Wincore Nixdorf to KKR, the venture capitalist/MBO specialists. Resources have been freed up to expand into growth areas and the share price has lifted off. The markets have become much more enthusiastic: the multi-divisional Siemens has finally shown that it is able to take steps to preserve its future and reward shareholders at the same time.

The recent takeover of Mannesmann by Vodafone is yet another conspicuous example of how SHV and more liberal capital markets have been making their impact on Germany. The bulk of Mannesmann's shares were owned by foreign institutional investors, who were swayed by questions as to whose strategy would result in the higher long-term gain to shareholders. This was the first hostile bid launched on a large German multi-divisional company, and it will surely not be the last.

Markets liberalize too

Great efforts are being made to improve accessibility to the equity markets. The only legal form of corporation that can seek a stock exchange listing is an *Aktiengesellschaft*, or AG. An AG has three governing bodies: the annual general meeting of shareholders *(Hauptversammlung)*, a supervisory board *(Aufsichtsrat)*, and a managing board *(Vorstand)*. In the AGM, shareholders generally decide by simple majority. The supervisory board must have at least

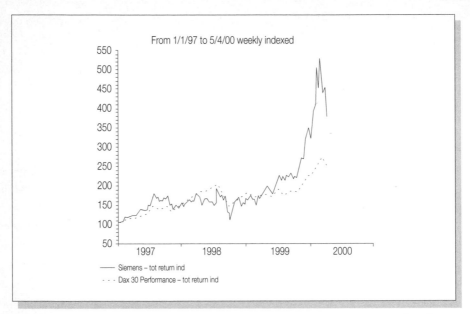

FIG 11.10 ● **Siemens share price improves with adoption of SHV**

Source: Datastream

three and at most 21 members, and includes worker representatives for all but the smallest AGs. The supervisory board elects the managing board. No supervisory board member may be on the managing board or in a position of similar executive power. In practice, however, the boards of affiliated firms generally share several members. For example, a subsidiary's supervisory board generally includes members of the parent company's managing board.

It has been felt that the rules surrounding listings on the main exchange are too onerous and, in an effort to increase the extent of equity markets, the *Neue Markt* (new market) was set up, specifically to attract small start-up companies. Listing rules have been relaxed slightly, the main innovations being that smaller amounts of money are required for an initial float; that accounts can conform to US GAAP (generally accepted accounting principles), the IAS (international accounting standards) system or to German GAAP; and that a company previously listed elsewhere and conforming to local EU regulations does not have to provide as much documentation.

This has already had an impact as Figs. 11.11 and 11.12 show, and there has been a steady stream of IPOs on the market, mostly in high-tech start-up areas. The *Neue Markt* looks as if it is becoming one of the premier markets in Europe for small companies to be listed successfully, and it may become a serious European alternative to a listing on NASDAQ in the USA.

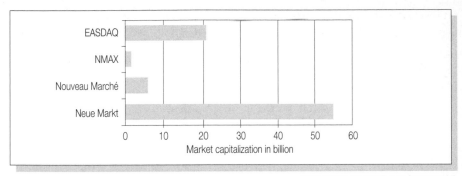

Source: Dresdner Kleinwort Benson, September 1999

FIG 11.11 ● **European "new market" market capitalization**

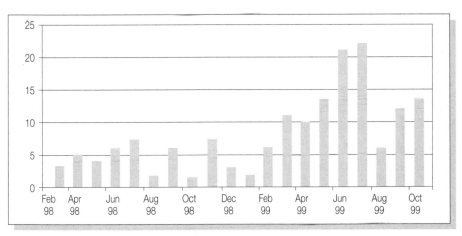

FIG 11.12 ● **IPOs in the *Neue Markt*, 1998–9**

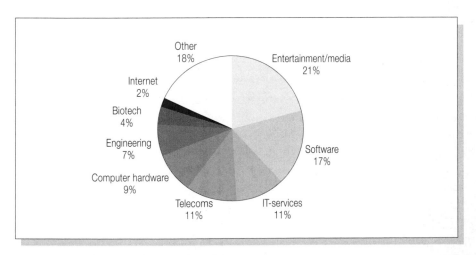

FIG 11.13 ● **Market capitalization of the *Neue Markt* by sector**

The pursuit of SHV is also being visibly assisted by changes in the tax rules on capital gains. One of the main obstacles preventing dominant stakeholders from liquidating their positions was a capital gains tax regime that reduced a lot of the benefit from turning stakeholdings into cash. This too is under review, and more liberal rules will very probably be introduced. This is likely to have a dramatic impact on the corporate landscape in Germany. One example of this was the intended merger between the Deutsche and Dresdner banks. Prior to the relaxation of the capital gains tax, this would have been utterly out of the question.

There are still hurdles

Considerable barriers remain, though. Although a strong tide is moving in the general direction of greater transparency and exposure to SHV ideas, there is still considerable resistance. One of the hurdles that remain is the variety of shares that can be issued. AGs must issue common stock *(Stammaktien)* with one vote per share. In addition, up to 50 percent of total capital can be preferred stock *(Vorzugsaktien)*, where each share receives a cumulative, preferential dividend. The preference can be defined, for example, in terms of seniority to the dividend claim of common stock or in terms of a larger dividend. Given the preference, these shares may be issued without the right to vote. Strictly speaking, however, these shares do have a (dormant) vote; the law requires each preferred share to have a vote if the preferred dividend is not paid for two years in a row. In addition, preferred-share holders may have the right to vote in matters of special interest to them. In addition, firms may issue *Genußscheine* (participation rights), that are very similar to US preferred stock. These participation rights have no voting rights attached and may be designed to be sufficiently debt-like to make dividends tax-deductible or equity-like to be included in banks' equity capital. This means that it is possible to open up differences between ownership and control.

Limits can be placed on how many shares an individual shareholder can vote, which, combined with cross-shareholdings and the interlocking nature of relationships between supervisory and management board members, can lead to voting "cartels," where a variety of groups can provide mutual support. German law also allows sizeable transfers to stakeholders once a coalition owns at least 75 percent of the votes. A 75 percent majority can make a binding tender offer to minority shareholders even though it is below market value. The 75 percent majority need not even be held by one party, since two or more large stakeholders can collude.

One of the most serious drawbacks for an active shareholder-driven view of the world in Germany is the absence of a funded pension scheme system.

Although there has been much discussion around this point, for the time being German pensions are still organized on an essentially pay-as-you-go system. Not only does this encourage investments in bonds, with steady income flows, over equities, but it also means that important long-term institutional investors play a much reduced role, and have a lower interest in equities.[19]

Banks on the other hand have a considerable interest in the corporate side, although primarily as suppliers of long-term debt. Banks can also vote proxy shares held in their possession, and this they normally do. Since these indirect shareholdings can sometimes be quite large, the banks' role is much larger than the size of their direct shareholdings would suggest.

Broadly speaking, banks tend to support the incumbent management of the firm, which means that there could be a conflict of interest between banks as suppliers of debt and banks as representatives of equity interests. Within limits, if a management strategy has as one of its outcomes increased indebtedness (with a consequent reduction in SHV), it is not clear whether banks, as representatives of shareholders, would be likely to object. Certainly, where there have been corporate shipwrecks, as with the Schneider affair, or more recently at construction company Philip Holzman, banks have been instrumental, first in receiving public blame and secondly in putting together rescue packages. These packages sometimes involve the open intervention of the government, in true stakeholder style.

The jury is still out on whether the banks play a positive monitoring role over management through their use of proxy votes. There is a suspicion that where banks represent a second or third largest block of shares, their intervention can sometimes be beneficial and protect the interests of minority shareholders (which might include themselves). The situation is less clear where the banks are capable, either singly or in combination with each other, to vote the largest share block. In any event, the banks are keen to show they are responsible corporate citizens and don't abuse their power – too openly, at any rate.

There are also other obstacles. Information on executive share trading, options packages and the like cannot be made available since it contravenes data protection laws. The granting of options also has to be very carefully constructed to minimize the tax consequences.

New accounting?

Conventional German accounting practice is aimed at protecting a company's creditors. It is also generous with allowing provisions and the formation of hidden reserves which makes it difficult to assess the true performance of companies. Hence the required "transparent" information is not made available to the extent it is in more shareholder-focussed Anglo-Saxon accounting procedures. But, as the large Germany-based multinationals increasingly tap international capital markets and need to attract large foreign institutional investors, the situation is changing.

For this reason, large companies are increasingly issuing their financial statements according to international norms. Bayer and Deutsche Bank are using IAS, while US GAAP are preferred by Daimler-Benz. In fact Daimler, which became a listed company on the New York Stock Exchange in 1994, was the first German company to publish accounts under US GAAP, followed by Deutsche Telekom and Veba.

As we have seen, IPOs on the *Neue Markt* are already allowed some choice on the accounting standards that they use, and this might be the beginning of a wider re-evaluation of the situation. Considering the importance to Germany of the international capital markets and global information requirements, improvements in this area would be very welcome for those interested in expanding SHV.

Managements are changing

Many *Mittelstand* companies, which started as family concerns but are now major industrial groups, retain a paternalistic culture that views SHV as a fad. For them, there is too much emphasis on equity investors. Nevertheless, SHV ideas are gaining ground and encouraging a closer look at Germany as an economic and financial center.

A recent study[20] correlated the total shareholder return of the top 30 German companies with German institutional investors' views of the degree to which these companies concentrate on SHV enhancement. Key investors, it found, increasingly prefer companies that focus on SHV – by which they mean companies that pursue a clearly defined strategy; that understand what "creating shareholder value" means; that have excellent investor relations; and that achieve a good shareholder return.

Other aspects of the SHV concept are also becoming visible in Germany. Lately, some companies have thought of introducing management bonus systems based on share ownership as well as stock options. Such a benchmarking system, which is also comprehensible to outsiders, is only available to management because SHV measures exist.

Share repurchases are also a new idea in Germany. Until recently not allowed under German law, they enable German public companies to have the same opportunities as "Anglo-Saxon" companies.

Most of the Dax 30 companies have paid lip service to SHV ideas in their annual reports. Several have gone as far as starting a SHV initiative, although relatively few of them have gone the whole hog and started to implement such an approach across the entire organization. The following is a selection of relatively high-profile companies that have taken steps towards installing and implementing a SHV measurement system.

● **Veba** has applied a CFROI approach at the consolidated holding company as well as at the business unit level. It is on record as being interested and committed to shareholder value creation, but share price performance has been distinctly mediocre. The recent merger with VIAG, a similarly diverse holding company, has added, rather than reduced, market worries on the value creating score.

● A similar story can be told of **Bayer**, where another CFROI scheme has been started, with as yet relatively little positive impact on share prices. As yet this is not linked to executive compensation.

● Several companies have adopted an economic value/EVA approach to shareholder value. **Daimler** and **Siemens** are the two best exponents of the approach. Siemens (see above) has experienced much the greater uplift in its share price, while Daimler Chrysler has had to convince investors that it is still a good German company rather than an average US company.

● **Lufthansa** has a well-developed SHV approach, and performance has distinctly improved. Economic profit measures are applied at the corporate level, and shareholder value methodology is being used to help allocate capital to the various business units.

● **Deutsche Telekom** and **Metro** are two other well-known German companies that have started to use SHV thinking in their management practice.

● Although less committed to implementing SHV measures, **BASF** has introduced stock option schemes for top management, and is looking for authorization to buy back some of its shares.

German companies are being forced to adapt to harsher and more competitive circumstances. The euro is bringing about a much greater degree of transparency, and by removing currency risks within the Euro-zone is making it easier for investors to discriminate between poorly and well-performing companies. In the past, German companies had probably been beneficiaries of a strong currency that rewarded foreign investors with currency gains, and punished domestic investors who strayed abroad.

As part of a "weak" currency area, things look rather different. Domestic investors may well be more inclined to look more closely at other EU or non-EU companies, especially if they are more focussed than the, often highly diversified, German blue chips. Foreign investors may be less interested in keeping German shares for their longer-term currency gain potential, and rather more because they are becoming increasingly cheap, and so present an opportunity for others to break into what is still Europe's largest national market. Some US investment banks are realizing that SHV thinking is a likely prelude to a chain of divestments and other M&A transactions that present very tempting opportunities.

Of course, this is all taking place in an environment where some of the traditional stakeholders such as banks and the government are finding their own roles more and more constrained: they can no longer provide long-term finance to their corporate stakeholding allies in the manner to which they were accustomed, and in the manner that is increasingly necessary to finance extensive restructuring in industry. The barriers to hostile takeovers have fallen.

We think, therefore, that the combined impact of higher foreign share ownership for German corporations, combined with a review of current pension funding arrangements, will lead to a much more active market for corporate control and mergers and acquisitions in the future. The German corporates may start to show the rest of the world how effective SHV strategies can be – especially if they then go on to master the approach more rapidly and more thoroughly than others.

France

SHV in France is slowly becoming more acceptable, but the drive to reform looks less intense than in Germany. As with so many other areas of life, the possibility of a "Gallic" variant cannot be ruled out.

In many respects France is still locked in the grip of stakeholderism. This can be illustrated by the fumbling that went on with respect to the Société General/Paribas/BNP banking merger and takeover. The original idea mooted was for a "merger," but more realistically a takeover of Paribas by Société General. Rather than allowing things to develop so that institutional investors (many of whom are foreign) could make up their minds more or less independently, BNP decided to intervene with a counter-bid. Very quickly the government was drawn into the fray. In the ensuing stand-off, there was at least the possibility that a non-French bank could enter the contest. However, any ideas of a European reorganization of the clearing banks, leading to the emergence of a multinational banking group motivated by the interests of international shareholders, were quickly squashed by the government and central bank. The only options allowed were between the French bidders and it was BNP that finally won the day. The whole affair bore the imprint of many different stake-holder fingers, and few would claim that the outcome reflected well either on the French banking establishment or for the creation of SHV.

The stakeholder nature of the French economy and finance can be seen in other ways too. Stock market capitalization is around 40 percent of GDP; 10 percent of the population owns shares. Private households account for 19 percent of equity ownership, while the great bulk of shares is owned as part of complex cross-shareholdings by industries. Insurance companies and pension funds are under-represented and it is foreign shareowners that constitute the third largest group. Banks and the government own modest amounts of equity.

The prevalence of pay-as-you-go pension schemes is reflected in the very small value of pension fund assets as a proportion of GDP (3 percent). Institu-tions are far more inclined to invest in bonds and property; equities account for around 20 percent of their assets. All these figures are typical of stakeholder countries.

One of the major features distinguishing the French system from the "Anglo-Saxon" model is in its broader view of a company's social responsibility. The direction of a French publicly listed company is not determined exclusively by its profitability and duties to its shareholders; instead it depends on objectives more broadly defined by both managers and owners.

French corporate law also makes it relatively easy to separate the ownership of shares from the exercise of voting power in both limited liability companies (*sociétés à responsabilité limitée* or SARL) and in publicly quoted companies (*sociétés anonymes* or SA). These companies can issue ownership certificates without voting rights: in particular they can issue *actions à dividende prioritaire* (ADPs), which give the right to a dividend stream without any voting right. This type of shares can be created when an increase of capital or a conversion of shares occur. ADPs cannot represent more than 25 percent of the total share capital. Companies can also split out the voting from the income stream "rights" on a share. So a company can issue certificates of investment (*certifi-cats d'investissement* or CDVs), which embody a right to future dividend streams; it can also issue certificates of voting right (*certificats de droit de vote*, or CIs). Both types of certificates are issued simultaneously when an increase of capital or a splitting of existing shares occurs. CDVs are distributed among voting shareholders proportional to their voting rights. CDVs are not transfer-able, but CIs are. CIs cannot represent more than 25 percent of the capital.

After seeking shareholder approval to change the company's statutes, other ways of controlling votes can be found. For instance shares with double voting rights can be issued to "faithful" shareholders, defined as those who have held the shares for a minimum of two years. Preference shares can also be issued with advantageous access to dividend streams in return for limited voting rights. Voting caps are also allowed under French law, so that a CDV might only be able to mobilize an upper limit of CIs. Control of voting rights is then reinforced by the nature of the French corporate system, where the public sector has greater importance, and bank loans are preferred to equity financing.

Change through the back door?

The "stakeholder" approach is rooted in the reconstruction period after the Second World War, as well as in the nationalization of the banks at the beginning of the Mitterrand presidency. These large nationalized groups were expected to meet several objectives, only one of which was the financial goal of earning an adequate return. Employment creation, innovation and supporting regional policies were other aims, sometimes rated higher than creating an adequate return for shareholders.

But, as we have stated, foreign investors now own a substantial proportion of French equities, and they are demanding greater transparency, better information and a more level playing field for their investment decisions. This has led to growing pressure on French corporates to improve their shareholder performance. As a result, French companies can now choose which GAAP they wish to report under. Large corporates wishing to attract foreign investment – including over half of the CAC40 – tend to choose US GAAP or IAS, and most report in French and English. New legislation has made share buy-backs easier: a buy-back program of less than 10 percent of share capital every 18 months is now permitted.

The French stock markets themselves have been changing, with the aim of surviving into the new millennium and becoming better established players in Europe. In February 1996, the New Market *(Nouveau Marché)* was launched. A full exchange in itself with its own rules and members, it is aimed primarily at listing high-technology firms and others with a high-growth potential. More recently, there have been efforts to merge certain derivative markets with the Germans, and to set up a new joint equity market with the Dutch and the Belgians.

Other areas have seen changes, too. Liberalization has taken place in the telecommunications markets, and competition is likely to affect electricity markets in the foreseeable future. As the state withdraws, so private enterprise and shareholders enter, leading perhaps to more cross-border mergers, and with them a duty to become more transparent. Recently the desire for greater transparency spilt over into an area normally known for its secrecy. This was triggered by undisclosed pay-outs to a senior executive at Elf-Aquitaine, who left after Elf was taken over by TotalFina. CEOs are now pushing publicly for greater disclosure about such pay-outs, which are not normally made public.

Some reforms are supportive of greater shareholder-friendliness, even if that is not their explicit aim. Profit-sharing schemes have been promoted by the government, and, since 1990, share-based profit-share schemes have been made compulsory for firms with between 50 and 99 employees. Stock options too are possible, although their fuller use awaits better tax treatment. At the moment selling options within a five-year period attracts tax at 50 percent, which only falls to a rate between 20 and 30 percent later. Despite this more companies are introducing stock options.

Corporate governance

The French business and financial community are addressing themselves to matters of corporate governance such as the need for:

- a more representative selection of individual shareholders with expertise sitting on the boards of large companies;

- an improvement in the core shareholder system that was established at the time of the 1986 privatization and then expanded;

- more effective controls on top management – despite a clear definition of the respective powers that various management bodies have in French *societés anonymes* (public limited companies).

This emergence of the concept of corporate governance is a result of shareholder lobbying and scandals related to management misbehavior. A committee set up by two employers' federations under Marc Viénot, president of the Société Générale bank, reported in 1995 with a series of recommendations that included a limit on the number of directorships that could be held, and the appointment of at least two "independent" directors on every public company's board. It also recommended the establishment of committees to deal with board appointments, audit and directors' remuneration. French companies were given a choice of a one-tier or two-tier board; 98 percent have opted for the unitary system. French corporate law still does not distinguish between non-executive and executive directors, and great authority continues to be vested in the role of company president.

The Viénot report did not criticize the practice of cross-shareholding, common in French industry, which has the effect of protecting an incumbent management from suffering the consequences of poor performance, or from takeovers. Nor did the report result in any obligations to comply with its recommendations. One observer notes that "every company I have ever questioned has refused to indicate which [Viénot report] recommendations it has not followed and why."[21] Nevertheless, recent privatizations have led to a reduction in the strength of core shareholders (*noyaux durs*), the small clique that sits on the boards of virtually all large French groups.

Market pressure in France is also increasingly favorable to shareholders. There are two main reasons: the first is the privatization of major financial and industrial firms in parallel with the deregulation of their markets and increased competition. As most of the privatizations have so far been a disappointment – privatization stocks have substantially underperformed in most cases – both the state and the management of the privatized companies need to focus on value.

The second reason for the improving climate for shareholders is the internationalization of the French stock exchange. Foreign investment has increased dramatically in recent years, and these foreign investors are asking for more transparency.

Indeed, the signs are that investors are beginning to find their voice and urging businesses to be more responsive to shareholders. And businesses are beginning to respond. In this trend, foreign institutions, which in the past have maintained a low profile, are an important force. Moreover, French stocks have to raise their image as they attempt to widen their shareholder base by diversifying risk and going global.

The pension fund factor

Perhaps one of the biggest problems for a more SHV-oriented approach in France lies in public attitudes to the funding of pensions. As in Germany – where the term *Generationsvertrag*, or contract between the generations, summarizes the idea of the pay-as-you-go system – so the French government continues to refer positively to the idea of *repartition*. Here too the current generation is called upon to support the elderly.[22]

The difficulty here is that the current scheme is widely recognized to need urgent topping-up if it is to continue to provide the same level of benefit in the future as it does now. Over the last few years there has been some tinkering with the system, essentially to lengthen the contribution period to 40 years and reduce the pay-out ratio. Many think that these reforms are insufficient, but for the time being the government is not really willing to overcome considerable political obstacles to changing the system. From a SHV point of view, though, a shift in the direction of a funded pension system would probably unleash a considerable force for reform and renewal in French corporate life.

SHV at work

In 1995, the Vivendi Group (previously Compagnie Générale des Eaux) was 190th in an MVA ranking published in the magazine *L'Expansion*, with a negative market value added of FFr17 billion. By 1998, the group ranked fourth and displayed a positive MVA of FFr132 billion, despite having had a negative EVA™ over the intervening period.

This performance was mainly the result of a sweeping change in the activities of the group. Prior to the accession of the new CEO, Jean-Marie Messier, the group was mainly concentrated on services to local institutions and municipalities, such as in water distribution, waste collection, building and construction. It was beginning to invest in telecoms and held a significant minority interest in the communication field in a company called Havas. Its service activities were highly profitable but had limited growth prospects. Even though the group displayed a willingness to invest its profits from its historical activities into other areas, it did so in a rather uncoordinated fashion.

The arrival of Messier gave a much firmer shape to the company's future strategic orientation. A new appraisal led the group to make many divestitures in the field of services, which lifted the company's global profits. These profits were then effectively re-invested in the communications area, where some important, probably dominant, shareholding positions were built up:

● Telephone: Vivendi was the main shareholder of the second largest telecom operator in France in 1999, behind France Telecom, with Cégétel and SFR.

● Television: Vivendi became the main shareholder of Canal Plus, the first pay-TV channel in France, as well as Canal Satellite, the country's first TV satellite service.

● Communication: Vivendi merged in 1998 with Havas, a significant actor in the publishing, advertising and multimedia areas (AOL France).

Initially this focussed strategy was greeted positively by the markets, showing that they are receptive to plans likely to meet shareholder expectations. It might have been better if the strategy had rested there but, later in 1999, Vivendi stock suffered from a significant setback. This was due to the announcement of a further round of expansion, including acquisitions in a wide range of industries such as water, television, the internet and publishing. This exposed the company to the wrath of its shareholders who began to realize that rather than investing in a well-focussed corporation, they were actually exposed to a widely diversified conglomerate – and conglomerates are unfashionable and tend to trade at a discount to the rest of the market.

This example emphasizes that it is not always the increase in profits, or the decrease in capital employed, at short term, that necessarily creates value. Rather it is the effective communication of a clear and convincing strategy to the market, understood by the investors and effectively realized by the management that contributes above all else, to the long run creation of value.

OTHER EUROPEAN MARKETS

While we believe SHV concepts are gaining ground in Europe, their take-up varies from country to country, as we have seen; often it can depend on particular tax and other legislative environments.

For instance, if a company's cash flow figures are readily available, SHV analysis may be easier to introduce. Such is the case in **Spain**; there, cash flow information became compulsory in annual reports from 1990 onwards, making it common to evaluate company performance by means of cash flow analysis. All the same, the level of cash flow information varies in quality depending on the particular industry or sector. SHV has been introduced in some major Spanish banking and electricity companies – although only in terms of the share price.

In many respects, Spain is a "stakeholder" country. Nearly a third of the population own shares, and market capitalization also comes to around one third of GDP. Evidence suggests equities play a relatively minor role in the portfolios of financial institutions. Optimists take the view that the country is potentially on the threshold of a much greater involvement with equities. Recent developments, however, have been disappointing, and could set back SHV initiatives in the country.

At the time of the privatization of Telefonica, the country's largest telecom operator, it was decided to create a stock options program that did not put a cap on the upper value of the options. As the share prices rose, so many senior managers of Telefonica benefitted greatly. Unfortunately this coincided with an extensive program of lay-offs and cut backs, all designed to increase the future competitiveness of the group. The coincidence of these two events proved too much for many public observers, who associated the stock options' munificence with the niggardliness of the treatment handed out to long-serving employees.

In response to this, the government introduced a much less favorable tax regime for stock options, making them less attractive in the future. This has had the rather unfortunate effect of separating SHV's remuneration aspects from its performance-enhancing side. Part of the recent downturn in stock prices was associated with the lack of any fundamental plan or strategy by the company to support the previous equity rally, so once the buying spree was over, there was little "fundamental" support for equity valuations.

Few companies in Spain are actively pursuing SHV programs. This is despite the introduction of the euro, which is likely to force Spanish companies into having to pay much closer attention to maximizing value, if only to avoid their own stock exchange becoming increasingly marginalized in the years to come.

Particular markets may have particular characteristics relevant to SHV. Take **Norway**, where the Oslo Stock Exchange is the home for the equity of extensive shipping and offshore construction companies. These industries, as well as the oil and gas industry, are extremely capital-intensive and naturally have large non-cash items in their accounting records. Because of this, the Norwegian marketplace has long recognized that earnings multiples are of limited use. The historically low relative market capitalization of technology and service and trade businesses, and the relatively high relative market capitalization of capital-intensive industries has forced institutional, private financial and strategic, and industrial investors to focus on relevant cash items rather than accounting information.

In **Finland,** as elsewhere, increased internationalization has meant that the price formation of many of the country's central stocks is exogenous to Helsinki Stock Exchange. Companies are more likely to consider the opinions of shareholders when they have large numbers of international investors. For instance, after Nokia's management announced it did not intend to sell off the company's TV business division, despite its dismal performance, growing outside pressure forced Nokia to concentrate on its core business. The company divested after all, and Nokia stock soared on the announcement.

The Finnish stock market is notable for the large number of companies with dual-class share structure. It is not exceptional for shareholders with, say, 14 percent of total stock to have 80 percent of votes. Not surprisingly, hostile takeovers have been a rare phenomenon in Finland. But new legislation has increased the power of minor shareholders by requiring a majority of votes in every share class at shareholders' meetings.

JAPAN
....

SHV rising in the East?

Together with Germany, Japan was one of the post-war *Wunderkinder*, and for decades dazzled the world with rapid growth, rising living standards and enormous balance of payments surpluses. Briefly the Japanese stock market became the largest in the world by capitalization, and people spoke of a "wall" of Japanese money that was going to push the country into being the major arbiter of the world's economy in the twenty-first century.

Then the bubble burst, and a collapse in equity and property prices set the scene for a decade of stagnation and recession. Economic growth rates collapsed and the banking system became steadily more insolvent, acting like a huge ball and chain. The banks' weak solvency meant that they could not finance expansion even where it looked sensible. Excess savings drove interest rates down to virtually vanishing point, and for a while it looked as if there was very little anyone could do. All the time, foreign pressure was building for further deregulation and market liberalization as a means of freeing up structures that looked increasingly ossified.

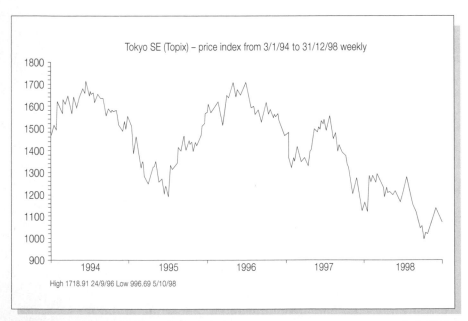

Tokyo SE (Topix) – price index from 3/1/94 to 31/12/98 weekly

High 1718.91 24/9/96 Low 996.69 5/10/98

FIG 11.14 ● **Loss of SHV since 1994**

Source: Datastream

At the time of writing, however, there are signs that the Japanese economy is moving forward again: gradual reforms, we believe, are making SHV a more viable proposition than before. Although there are still some striking differences from other countries, there are also many similarities, and we want to argue here that Japan too is converging on the emerging shareholder value consensus.

The halving of value of the stock market has not been a great incentive to hold shares, and only around 9 percent of the population are shareholders in Japan. At 58 percent of GDP, the equity market capitalization is very similar to other stakeholder economies. The largest bloc of equity holders consists of the corporates (31 percent), and this represents (in large measure) the cross shareholding arrangements referred to as *Keiretsu* and *Mochiai*.

The purpose of the cross-shareholding system is to promote stability and to protect companies from takeover. *Mochiai* shareholding patterns usually involve bank-financed purchases of newly issued shares. As the proceeds from issuance are generally used to purchase new shares or to repay bank borrowings for the purchase of shares in another group, no equity capital is raised by the transaction. These patterns became more common in the 1960s due to a combination of two factors: the desire for protection from foreign competitors following the opening of the Japanese economy when it joined the OECD in 1964, and the need to support equity prices during the brokerage recession of 1965.[23]

Over time, cross-shareholdings have increasingly come to define reciprocity in business relationships, with their level increasing or decreasing according to the intensity of those relationships. This system has contributed significantly to the closed nature of the Japanese market. Thus, life insurance companies or banks purchasing shares can expect to receive business in the form of insurance sales or loans from the companies in which they invest. Member companies of Japanese industrial groups such as Mitsui and Mitsubishi can expect to receive financing in the form of bank loans for strategic rather than economic reasons. Some analysts have gone so far as to suggest that financing costs related to such investments should be considered selling, general and administrative (SGA) expenses. More significantly, these member companies could expect to receive financing in the form of loans from the group bank for strategic rather than economic reasons.

The other major groups owning shares are private households (22 percent), followed by the banks (13 percent). Insurance, pension and foreign investors all account for around 10 percent each. But as with the other stakeholder economies, the role of institutional investors is proportionately lower than with shareholder-friendly countries. Institutions hold 18 percent of their assets in equities, again about average for a stakeholding country. In absolute terms, however, Japanese institutions still dispose of a very large volume of assets, second only to those in the USA. This gives added importance to understanding what has happened in Japan, since relatively small changes in behavior there can have large repercussions elsewhere in the world financial market. For all its difficulties, it is still the largest creditor nation in the world.

The winds of change

The *Keiretsu* system has very often run on the basis of a "house" bank providing finance. During the depression years it became increasingly clear that when all the members of a *Keiretsu* faced problems, they could overwhelm the house bank, which would not be able to honor its commitments to the group. Seen from another, and increasingly urgent point of view, the bank would not be able to meet its own commitments and succeed in creating value for its shareholders. The old structure limited the direct shareholdings of the bank in the other members of the group to 5 percent, but of course the other members could hold shares in the bank and in each other (see Fig. 11.15).

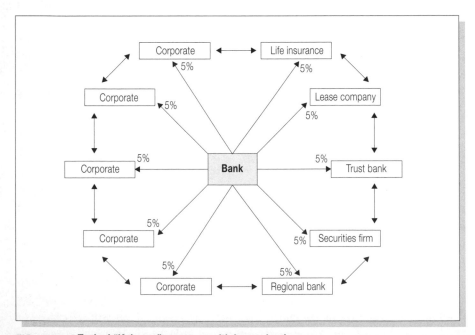

FIG 11.15 ● **Typical "Keiretsu" structure with house bank**

Recent reforms have allowed the creation of a more effective holding company structure. It is now possible to create divisions that can then have their own subsidiaries. Anti-trust rules still require that the divisions don't hold more than 5 percent of the shares in their subsidiaries. This change might seem rather academic, but it is not. The creation of the legal entity of the "holding company" has brought a lot more transparency into the otherwise rather murky world of the *Keiretsu*. The holding company's primary purpose is to hold shares that have to generate a sensible return for the owner. If the division fails to do this it is now much easier to divest.

The existence of a holding company weakens a relationship established through the cross-holding of shares among Japanese companies. Historically, Japanese companies have held other companies' shares for the purpose of strengthening business relationships and have not really looked for investment return or indeed exercised their voting rights. Cross-shareholding has supported the existence of silent shareholders for a long time. A holding company structure, on the other hand, introduces and permits a more rational grouping of companies. Companies that hold a common interest in business will be governed under the same holding company.

After the bursting of the "bubble," the holding company structure is making it much easier to sell shares in unprofitable subsidiaries, and use the proceeds to cover losses in core businesses, or to make larger investments in these areas, in the hope that they will return to a robust profitability in the future. Although this does not seem particularly new, it does represent a considerable shift in the way Japanese companies can do business with each other. It will also lead to a much more active market for corporate control.

This process will be assisted by further changes in the regulations affecting banks. A series of bank mergers, in addition to the injection of significant sums of money by the government into the banking system, is starting to make a realignment within the Japanese financial services industry more feasible. The banks can, to some extent, distance themselves from some of their worst invest-ment decisions and channel resources into areas that will be of more direct benefit to their own shareholders, rather than supporting a wide range of unprofitable activities.

Although there are welcome signs of change, there are still areas where the reform process has yet to begin. One rather quaint custom, and one that militates directly against more participation by shareholders, is that most corporate AGMs occur on the same day. For instance, in 1999 just over 88 percent of all the companies listed on the Tokyo Stock Exchange decided to have their AGM on the same day, namely June 29. This makes it very difficult

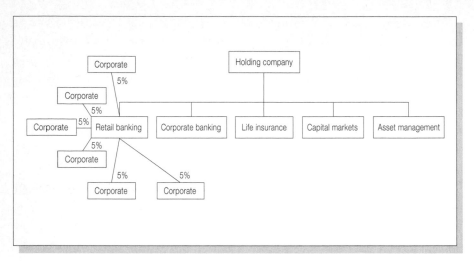

FIG 11.16 ● **Revised Japanese holding company structure**

for shareholder groups seeking to express their views from being present at more than one AGM. Despite suggestions that the date could be shifted to a weekend (which might encourage a higher participation by small investors), signs of change in this important area remain scarce. It would be a welcome gesture for SHV if the larger corporations could set an example and have their AGMs at times and places better suited to the shareholders rather than to the wishes of management.

Accounting rules

Japanese accounting rules are rather more flexible than in some other jurisdictions, making the interpretation of financial statistics more difficult. There are issues, notably in relation to consolidations and the treatment of unrealized gains and losses (both on and off the balance sheet).

At present, Japanese regulations do not permit the filing of consolidated tax returns. Consolidated financial statements are not required for uniform commercial code purposes. Due to this, and to their historic goals of growing the scale of their businesses, Japanese managements appear to have focussed on aggregate parent-company pre-tax earnings results rather than on consolidated net income on a per-share basis. Furthermore, there is flexibility for Japanese group companies to determine which subsidiaries are to be consolidated – thus allowing them to record (and hence push) losses in unconsolidated subsidiaries.

This problem is further compounded by the accounting treatment for unrealized gains and losses, i.e. a failure to mark-to-market. Readers of the financial press will no doubt be familiar with the topic of problem loans at Japanese banks. Commentators have questioned whether the amount of unrealized gains on securities holdings (*mochiai*) or land purchased many years before will be adequate to cover estimated losses related to bad loans. Accounting rules at the moment make it difficult to revalue assets, so that the "work out" period to write off the value of investments is sometimes quite long. Due to the difficulty of obtaining true figures, a number of foreign investors stopped investing in Japanese bank stocks despite the fact that they represent over 20 percent of the stock market's value. Japanese life insurance companies also took a similar view: they have announced they will not purchase additional shares in banks that are seeking to shore up their capital position until they address the problems of bad loans by reducing risky assets.

PricewaterhouseCoopers experience shows a number of significant differences between the accounting treatment prescribed under Japanese GAAP and US GAAP, the *de facto* global standard. Differences may arise in the following areas: pensions and employee benefits, leases, consolidation versus equity accounting for investments, financial instruments, and business combinations. There are also other differences in accounting principles which may have a significant effect for individual companies.

SHV-oriented companies

During the past few years, increasing numbers of Japanese companies have adopted the idea of shareholder value. They began with ROE, trying to measure their investment efficiency on shareholders' capital; the majority of Japanese companies continue to report their ROE figure, believing it "proves" their management is SHV-oriented. Fortunately, some leading companies have become aware of the shortcomings of ROE and have already taken steps to plan, manage, and measure their business performance in terms of economic profit (EP) and free cash flows (FCF). Some now link their compensation scheme to those measures in order to enhance their SHV.

These changes in Japanese corporate behavior are largely attributable to prolonged economic weakness and some regulatory changes. When banks ran up huge bad debts during the recession, their corporate customers could no longer rely on the banks for easy cash. Companies were left alone to manage their own cash flows if they wanted to survive – which they did. Japanese companies became much more aware of the necessity of managing expenditures and investment in accordance with the cash generated. As banks could no longer be relied upon to provide additional funding, so the capital markets became a more important source of finance.

This has led to a number of companies adopting different valuation and performance metrics and starting to apply some of the lessons learnt elsewhere with SHV. For instance, Hoya, a producer of crystal glass, glasses, lenses and semi-conductor photo masks, announced in fiscal year 1999 that it was going to apply economic value added (EVA) to measure its business performance as a group and to allocate resources through corporate budgeting. By generating higher returns than expected in the stock market, it aims to increase SHV. Hoya also plans to use EVA in measuring the performance of its subsidiaries and its business units. Management teams in Hoya are now expressly looking at issues such as how to calculate the theoretical share price, how to increase its value and how to manage free cash flows in a long-term plan.

Hoya modified the original EVA in a way to fit their unique needs, calling it SVA. They claimed to put more importance on SVA rather than ROE, and to reject new investments or capital expenditures if they lower SVA, even though ROE might increase in the short term. "ROE does not reflect the cost of capital," one of the company's top executives said. "It might be able to measure capital utilization, but it is not able to measure corporate value to our shareholders." If Hoya successfully increases SVA in a long run, ROE will increase as a result. They believe SVA and ROE are not contradictory measures.

Other companies moving in the direction of SHV include Kao, a producer of personal care, household, and sanitary goods and synthetic products. It intends to use EVA to measure its value and to apply it to its business performance measurement, corporate budgeting and incentive scheme for executives. EVA serves as a critical tool for matters such as divestment from a business. Kao's view is that EVA is a better measure as a group management tool since it is an absolute figure, which could be added or subtracted and factored into smaller components. On the other hand, ratio measures such as ROE are difficult to use since they cannot be simply added together. Kao intends to look at EVA on a geographical and on a strategic business unit basis.

Matsushita Electric Works (MEW), a sister company of Matsushita Electric Industrial and a producer of lighting apparatus, housing materials, electric equipment, and electronic materials, introduced a new EVA performance metric in 1998. The chairman pointed to the risks of using ROE alone and advocated an idea of "expanded reproductive ROE," which has crystallized as MEP or Matsushita economic profit and is used to identify value-destroying units. One of the top executives has also pointed to the shortcomings of ROE as a measure by explaining that ROE can be manipulated without increasing profits at all by decreasing capital investment. MEW claims that accounting profit-based management tools are no longer appropriate, and aims to strengthen its competitiveness and profitability under a management that takes capital efficiency and SHV seriously. Before adopting MEP, MEW cleared all internal funds accumulated in business units, and calculated net operating capital, which consists of fixed assets, subsidiary investment, and shared working capital. MEW has expanded the amount of reporting done on cash flow, and provides statements of cash flow for each SBU according to SEC guidelines. Free cash flow also enters into its deliberations.

Sony, too is moving into more SHV-based metrics, based primarily around EVA. Its system primarily addresses the question of executive remuneration. Other companies that claim to use SHV include Asahi Chemicals, TDK, Nakamoto, Jeans Mate, Konami, Asahi Beer Brewery, Kawasaki Steel, Matsushita Electric Industrial, Orix and Sanwa Shutter.

HUNGARY AND OTHER EASTERN EUROPEAN COUNTRIES

SHV in Hungary continues to develop. Perhaps not as fast as first hoped for, but nevertheless in a broadly positive direction. Stock market capitalization is just under 30 percent of GDP, a ratio that has been fairly stable over the last few years. There are now 55 firms quoted on the market at the time of writing, compared with 23 five years before. All the same, the overall size of the market is comparatively small – it is valued at US$13 billion, with a daily transactions volume of US$52 million.

The reasons for a country such as Hungary utilizing and benefitting from an SHV approach are as important as ever. The economy is growing relatively fast – nearly 4 percent a year – but a lot of this is coming from a large government deficit of nearly 5 percent of GDP. There is a current account deficit also of around 4 percent of GDP which is covered by additional borrowing and by a small inward flow of direct investment. This supplements a stock of foreign investment that is estimated at around US$20 billion. There is evidence of a two-tier economy, with a foreign-owned sector that currently accounts for around one-third of GDP and for 25 percent of private sector employment. This sector has been growing rather faster than the domestically-owned companies, in part because local companies find it much more difficult to get the necessary finance. Small and medium-sized companies only account for 4 percent of loans advanced by the banking sector, and they have yet to gain significant access to the equity market. So, although additional investment in infrastructure, industry and commerce is necessary, a lot of this will have to come from either foreign or domestic investors. Last year there was not a single IPO in Hungary, and so attention has been focussed on privatizing some of the remaining government-owned assets.

Currently, the government is likely to retain some significant holdings in industry and commerce but, in other cases, private capital is expected to play a larger role, even though the state will continue to have the last say through possession of a "golden share." For instance, under Hungary's 1997 privatization act, the government, through the state property agency (a largely passive shareholder), will keep "golden share" stakes in 98 companies. This will include companies in the energy, telecommunication and agribusiness sectors.

Measures to de-regulate industry and create the conditions for successful privatization are being introduced. For instance it has been announced that 15 percent of the electricity generating market will be open to new producers, accompanied by a reform of electricity tariffs to make them more transparent. There was a similar move to de-regulate the price of domestically produced natural gas (cheaper than imported gas) – a prelude to re-structuring the main gas importer and distributor MOL, which is being encouraged to operate more closely along SHV lines.

In telecommunications, the government holding agency, APV Rt, sold its remaining stake in MATAV Rt, although the government retained a single "golden share." The Social Security Funds are also thinking of privatizing their holdings in several companies, including the pharmaceutical companies Human and Richter, as well as their holdings in a savings bank, OTP, and in a property company. Steps are also being taken to privatize some of the state-owned banks.

Other changes that will create liquidity and volume in the financial markets in the long term, and so enhance the role of institutional investors, are afoot. These include the tentative emergence of mortgage banks. At the moment the market is held back by some legal difficulties, but the initial launch of mortgage-backed securities in 1999 attracted strong institutional interest and is a harbinger for the future.

Another major area of reform lies in the field of pensions. Here good intentions on the government-side have encountered political reality. It was intended to have three legs or pillars to the pension system: first, a modified "pay-as-you-go" system; second, a fully-funded and mandatory "pillar" forming the core of a state based pension; third, a voluntary fully-funded sector operated by private pension funds and regulated by an independent supervisory agency. The impact of these schemes will be to mobilize the nation's savings more effectively and channel them through institutional investment organizations. Unfortunately, the reform of the second state-funded "pillar" has been postponed, as the government was reluctant to incur unpopularity through a rise in employee contributions. With improving general economic conditions it is hoped that these reforms will eventually be carried out.

The situation we have described in Hungary is fairly typical for the "Visigrad" countries – those (Poland, Hungary and the Czech Republic) who are seeking to join the EU in the near future. All of them face extensive adjustments as they adapt to EU conditions, and one of these adjustments is to improve their capital markets. Previous inflows of foreign capital have by and large diminished, requiring greater attention to be paid to tapping into domestic sources of saving to finance corporate development. SHV approaches offer a useful way of understanding what large state-owned, but soon to be privatized, companies have to do to survive and prosper in the new conditions. When these initiatives are tied to other macro changes that enhance the role of equity investors, then favorable conditions will have become established for future expansion of equity ownership in this region.

EMERGING MARKETS

So far, this book has been concerned with countries that have well-developed financial markets, where changes in corporate performance can be reflected and acted upon by an independent and well-informed financial community. Clearly, under such conditions the SHV approach works best. But it would be erroneous to think that these are the only countries where it can be used.

Emerging markets are so called because they are markets where the underlying conditions for SHV are in the main improving, in accordance with the increase in globalization and the pressure on all companies to improve their performance that we have emphasized throughout this book. Various rounds of de-regulation, trade liberalization and, importantly, the freeing of capital flows mean that many countries that were previously backwaters are now being brought into the main currents of world financial markets. At first sight this trend might only have an effect on some of the larger companies, but with time it spreads more widely within a local economy. We will begin this section by looking at a hypothetical emerging market, modelled on an actual case in the New World. This will be followed by a closer look at developments in Singapore and South Korea and finally India – not perhaps a country that springs to mind for SHV enthusiasts, but one where interesting things are starting to happen.

The new emerging world

Corporate structures in many parts of the world have grown up in a rather topsy-turvy fashion. When currencies are not convertible and extensive trade barriers remain, there is often a shortage of investible funds. Furthermore, a lot of money generated from foreign trade is parked offshore in hard currency accounts and does not flow back to the benefit of the domestic economy.

Under these circumstances, companies develop in a different pattern than in the West. Very often there is little competition. A domestic company making goods for a small local market demands and gets trade protection; working behind high tariff walls, it has no incentive to become more efficient. Where it is profitable, it also finds that there are no obvious places where it can expand. So, when another domestic opportunity arises, often in an entirely disparate industry where no synergies exist, the company invests and again, armed with tariff protection, starts to operate in completely unrelated areas.

Similarly, a country will have import controls, accompanied by the issuing of import licenses. Here a local company requires two things: an agreement with a foreign supplier and, probably more importantly, an agreement from the government giving the firm the right to exploit the local market. The foreign supplier is frequently not interested in developing the market itself, owing to trade and other barriers, and may license production – which often comes down to deciding to work with a financially solvent partner. This too can lead to the formation of highly diversified groups in a local market, a process driven largely by the issue and allocation of import licenses. Large domestic companies are financially able to bid for and obtain a license, but otherwise bring little product expertise. The end result is lot of inefficiently run operations monopolizing a local market. Consumers are charged high prices, the company has acceptable margins in some areas, but there is very little growth in the market overall.

The existence of such large, multidivisional "conglomerate" companies in sometimes quite restricted markets is becoming progressively less tenable. As tariff barriers and capital controls are lifted, so markets become more open and barriers to entry are falling. If you are an incumbent firm you are faced with more choices than before, and also the probability of more competition. Competitors will no longer need to be actually located in your market, but can supply from outside. If their product is superior to yours, a process of "cherry-picking" takes place. The more attractive parts of the market, those with either higher growth or higher margins, are conquered by your competitors, leaving you with a smaller market share but still burdened with costs established on the back of much higher volumes.

Capital market liberalization means that alternative forms of finance become available; more tellingly, performance expectations tend to rise. Local stock markets have to adjust to the fact that they need not only to attract new funds, but also to retain the ones they already have. Long traditions of insider trading and the placing of share packets with "strategic" shareholders also have to change as outsiders insist on greater transparency. Local financial institutions may have to take a more hands-on approach in managing their affiliates and subsidiaries to ensure that they attain internationally acceptable performance levels.

Where macro-economic conditions improve, with falling inflation rates and reasonably stable and convertible currencies, so the assumption that foreign investment will always provide a higher return also needs to be re-examined. Greater price stability and lower interest rates make the market more transparent and may also mean a domestic portfolio could actually out-perform one in formerly favored foreign markets.

All of which may create ever greater challenges for the multi-divisional incumbent, which will have to focus its attention on a smaller range of activities. More efficient capital markets make it possible for other domestic players to build up specialisms in one area. More efficient goods markets mean that foreign producers can compete in the local market on much more even terms. In such circumstances, many existing incumbents face extinction unless they can radically improve their performance – and it is here that the application of SHV analysis can be very useful. It enables managements to understand the size of the performance challenge, and encourages them to seek out solutions before they are overwhelmed by the shift to a more de-regulated and competitive environment.[24]

A new market for corporate control is also created by market liberalization. Existing groups may need to be broken up to release talents currently hidden within large bureaucracies, and new groups can form that push previously underperforming assets into new combinations, allowing them to compete more effectively in both domestic and foreign markets. Companies can also free themselves from the constraints imposed by a small domestic base, investing greater amounts and thus achieving critical volume and scale effects.

Such changes will go against the grain of years of experience and practice. But they also signify a new playing field, where existing incumbents have opportunities to dispose of the less attractive parts of their portfolio and make serious efforts to convert themselves into medium-sized global players in a smaller range of industries and products. SHV analysis provides a very effective way to get these messages across.

Eastern Asia

In the 1980s and early 1990s the fastest-growing economies in the world were to be found in east Asia. It was the region where formidable new products and links to the global economy were being developed and where nothing could ever go wrong, it seemed. But it did.

In 1997 and 1998 there was a massive retrenchment; stock markets in the area lost a huge amount of value. At the time, it was feared that this might trigger a worldwide recession. So far it hasn't, but the experience has left some scars. The theme of SHV, previously written off as a Western curiosity has taken on greater significance.

As a region, south and east Asia had been dependent on capital inflows. These reached such a magnitude that local economies could not effectively absorb the funds, which leaked out into the economy in the form of property speculation and into dubious loans for highly uncertain and speculative projects. When the capital inflows stopped, local economies found it very difficult to sustain the valuations their equities had reached, and rapidly what had gone up came down.

Many of the characteristics of emerging economies, such as the large unfocussed conglomerates described at the beginning of this section, are to be found in east Asia. This region has had to learn that more discipline is needed in the way corporations are run – in other words, there is a corporate governance issue. The "cronyism" that typifies many corporate relations is difficult to reconcile with the more open and transparent systems developed in the shareholder economies, and there is a need to introduce reforms in this area. There is also a fair degree of state ownership, and close associations with banks that frequently play a secondary role to the industrial conglomerates. Chan Wing Leong, the CFO of Sembawang, a Singapore-based conglomerate, summarized how one of the stakeholders in such a system might react:

> Our primary shareholder, the government, has a different sense of shareholder value than just share price; moreover, it appoints the chief executive and the chairman of the board. If there are three consecutive quarters of declining profits, the government will be less concerned about the declining share price and more concerned about why the profit is decreasing – what is the underlying problem? Of course, the government

will be disappointed if the share price falls, but it will not take drastic
action to remove the entire board just for that. Let's just say they are more
forgiving than others!

Other stakeholders, notably the banks, would have also been lenient in the
face of a downturn in performance in the past, concentrating instead on
growth and volume. This luxury is now coming to an end, and sustained
periods of underperformance will be more closely scrutinized than they were
before the crisis.

At the time of writing, equity prices have recovered and, on the surface at
least, much has returned to normal. We shall see as we examine two Asian
economies, Singapore and South Korea, that beneath this surface, changes are
going on that should pave the way for greater transparency and an application
of SHV approaches.

South Korea

The crisis of the late 1990s has left several scars behind in South Korea, not the
least in efforts to reform the *Chaebol* system. As a member of the OECD, South
Korea is dismantling many of its earlier barriers to capital flows, and so the
question of greater transparency and investor protection has taken on extra
importance. De-regulation is a general trend that is likely to be accelerated in
the future in areas such as floating foreign exchange rates (the Foreign
Exchange Control Act), and liberalizing the stock purchase limit for foreigners.
There are a few remaining barriers for investors from abroad in the Korean
financial market. Foreign equity ownership is still concentrated in managed
funds, but with time there is likely to be more direct foreign ownership of
Korean companies.

As a result of the crisis, the distinction between ownership and management
has become more important. As a means of improving transparency, government now requires the corporate sector to adopt accounting principles in line
with international standards. They are also required to have more outside
board members, assure the rights of minority shareholders and introduce other
control programs. Some changes are of a longer-term nature, related to more
general transformations in the external political and social environment. For
the time being, though, the changes achieved in areas of corporate governance
and SHV are an important part of the renewal of Korean financial and industrial life.

These changes can be seen even more dramatically in the case of the
Chaebol, the large industrial Korean conglomerate companies. At the moment
they are trying to reduce debt and rationalize their portfolios, divesting their

non-profitable activities. The government has even gone so far as to start to dismantle one of the largest *Chaebol*s. We think it might be better if the *Chaebol*s could undertake these steps themselves, rather than being forced to do it.

Banks and *Chaebol*s have been loosening their ties, with more of the risk being transferred to the banks. In the future a *Chaebol* will no longer have access to cheap credit, and hence will not be able to adopt the "volume or bust" strategy. These changes will also mean that greater attention will have to be paid to the shareholders.

In the eyes of many, "shareholders" meant the interests of the dominant *Chaebol* shareholders, and small minority shareholders were generally ignored. Indeed, although Korean business law focussed on the rights of creditors, in practice these were often subordinate to the interests of larger stakeholders. After the crisis this situation has started to change. The recent "minority share-holders' rights movement" is an example.

Jang Ha Sung, a professor at Korea University has been in the forefront of this. Focussing on shareholder rights and SHV under the banner of an independent civic group, People's Solidarity for Participatory Democracy, he has targeted a number of *Chaebol*s that have mismanaged their funds. He set out, for example, to stop SK Telekom, a profitable part of the SK *Chaebol*, from bailing out weaker sister companies, and succeeded in securing the appointment of outside directors and amending the company's articles to increase transparency and impose a ceiling on deals with other SK companies. Over 50 percent of the stock was held by foreigners – a useful situation, as it happened: "Domestic institutions … were unhelpful because they were affiliated to the *Chaebol* or owned by the government, whose bureaucrats are over-friendly with big-business."[25]

Lawyers and accountants have been giving their services free for Professor Sung's group, which would like to extend its fight to the big five auditing firms who, he believes, "contributed to the Asian crisis by franchising their names to weak local auditors." Meanwhile, to avoid spending indecent amounts of time in court, the managements of most companies are now paying more attention to SHV.

As interest rates come down in South Korea, there is a growing pool of private retail investors who are keen to tap into the equity market in order to earn higher returns on their savings. This too is going to make companies think more closely about both their dividends and the capital appreciation they can achieve. Companies that have tried an SHV approach include one of the country's biggest companies, the LG group, which introduced value-based management in 1995, and now uses it to assist in making investment decisions. The company also uses an SVA methodology to evaluate the performance of its strategic business units.

Singapore

The two crisis years of 1997 and 1998 saw a fall of 24 percent and 7 percent respectively in equity values in Singapore. Although stock prices have more than recovered this ground since then, there are now moves afoot to increase the importance of SHV in improving performance.

The Singapore government has been proactive in encouraging the private sector to focus on SHV. Its main investment-holding arm, Temasek Holdings (which has a significant majority stake in all the top-listed companies in Singapore), recently adopted an active shareholder stance.[26] This in turn has given rise to regular press announcements by government-linked companies of restructuring plans, proposed M&A and share buy-backs as actions needed for shareholder value enhancements.

Some of the changes that have taken place in Singapore to enhance corporate governance and provide an SHV-friendly environment include new legislation to allow share buy-backs. From the end of 1998, companies, with the approval of shareholders, have been able to buy back up to 10 percent of their shares.

Since then, cash-rich companies have begun to announce various share buy-back schemes which they perceive as a way of improving SHV. Singapore Press Holdings (SPH) has implemented a successful capital reduction plan that paid S$500 million to shareholders. It also bought back up to 10 percent of its shares and arranged a tax credit for investors that sell their shares to SPH. Singapore Telecom (SingTel) also announced recently it would return S$2.5 billion to shareholders by buying back shares and paying a special dividend. (Both SingTel and SPH are government-owned companies.)

In another change conducive to SHV, banks have been allowed to lower their capital adequacy ratios from 12 to 10 percent. It is envisaged that the excess capital will be returned to shareholders, thus providing an avenue to increase SHV.

Mergers and divestitures

In the past year, two major bank mergers have occurred (Keppel/Tat Lee and DBS/POSB banks). The press releases for both these mergers cited SHV enhancement as one of the reasons, possibly through economies of scale and increased business opportunities. More such mergers are anticipated, especially in the shipbuilding industry – where huge conglomerates are involved – and in high technology. In terms of divestments, SingTel's recent sale of Netcom (a Norwegian mobile phone company) has contributed to its overall SHV enhancement by enabling it to focus on its core strength, the Asia-Pacific market.

With the worst of the economic crisis over, we can now expect to see companies focussing on growth and profitability to maximize value creation down to their operating levels. Companies in Singapore are beginning to exhibit greater transparency and conducting investor communication programs. Others have announced their decisions to focus on core competencies; shedding subsidiaries that are not in line with the new objectives. There is also a greater acceptance of a link between SHV improvement and compensation for senior executives. One particular company, Singapore Technologies, implemented EVA in the early 1990s but found that big improvements at all levels were made only recently when they started to link executive compensation to SVA/EVA and its key performance indicators.

Asian CEO interest in shareholder value is gaining ground largely as a reaction to the 1997 crisis, and a determination not to let it happen again. Indeed some analysts have gone so far as to say that the crisis was actually a "blessing in disguise," since it now means that Asian CEOs will increasingly be evaluated on their SVA rather than the size of their balance sheets, as was the case in the pre-crisis years.

India

Since independence in 1947, the government has played a dominant role in the Indian economy. Until recently economic policy, formulated in a series of five-year plans, followed policies of import substitution and a heavily protected trade regime, with extensive public ownership of productive capital and a complex of controls and regulations governing the activities of the private sector. In addition, restrictions were placed on foreign ownership of businesses.

In the 1990s, mounting budget deficits and foreign exchange crises prompted the government to start a process of economic liberalization, allowing foreign institutional investors (FIIs) to invest in Indian equity and debt and Indian corporates to raise funds from abroad.

The Indian capital market therefore grew very quickly. The market capitalization of the Mumbai Stock Exchange (which represents 90 percent of the total market capitalization of the country) quadrupled from Rs1.1 trillion at the end of 1990–1 to Rs4.3 trillion at the end of 1996–7. The number of listed companies on the 23 stock exchanges in India grew to around 9,000 by the end of March 1996, from around 4,300 in 1985.

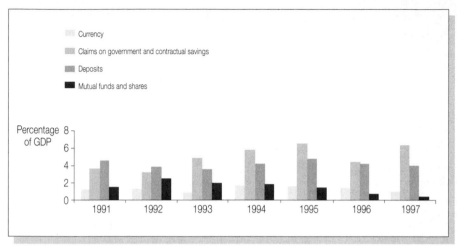

FIG 11.17 ● The Indian context, 1991–7

Although this may have seemed like a false dawn at the time, the seeds of an idea had been planted. In particular there have been a series of IT start-ups, capitalizing on a pool of good computer-literate programers and system developers centered on Hyderabad and Bangalore in south India. More importantly they have prospered.

This development has made people sit up and take notice. Suddenly there was a group of Indian companies, based in India, providing super-returns to equity investors in India. The government was barely to be seen in all this, except in one very enlightened way. There had been a de-regulation of the computer industry, and there were virtually no import restrictions. The market was galvanized into action as less dynamic sectors suddenly found that investors' appetites had been whetted. The equity market started to fulfill its purpose, that of allocating capital to those companies with the expectations of the highest growth.

Key future SHV drivers in India

Some of the following are likely to impact the SHV orientation of the Indian economy in future:

● *Greater SHV orientation of domestic government-owned funds.* Pressure is mounting on them to produce adequate returns, and to become more accountable to their own shareholders/unit trust holders. They are likely to become more active in managing their investments and will be seeking improved shareholder value performance from them in the future.

- *The growth in importance of private institutional investors.* Private domestic mutual funds, which have had slow growth in the past, are beginning to attract the attention of domestic retail investors and are expected to play a much more important role in mobilizing domestic equity funds in future. Most FII and GDR (global depositary) investments will continue to be guided by macro-economic factors, as also by the presence of SHV-oriented, globally competitive Indian companies.

- *Privatization.* Increased privatization will mean a greater exposure of government-owned companies to equity markets and lead to a change in management that will place greater emphasis on SHV. Although the process will occasionally be fitful, we think that it has now gained sufficient momentum to bring about a heightened awareness of SHV issues in the Indian equity market in the future.

- *The Indian Corporates.* They will learn to play the game better, and realize by doing so that they will increase their chances of attracting fresh capital to their undertakings.

SUMMARY

After drawing distinctions between "shareholder-friendly" and "stakeholder" economies in terms of ownership, control and stock market development, we have looked at a variety of countries and the extent to which they are utilizing SHV concepts, or have the potential to utilize them. The stakeholder approach, it is clear, is losing ground all over the world to the demands of value creation.

Notes

1. Based on Marco Becht *et al.* (1997) *Preliminary Report: The Separation of Ownership and Control: A Survey of Seven European Countries*, Vols. 1–3. Brussels: European Corporate Governance Network, for DG 3 of the European Commission.

2. Berle, A.A. and Means, G.C. (1991) *The Modern Corporation and Private Property*, New York and London, Macmillan.

3. Source: DAI (Deutsche Aktien Institut) Factbook 1998.

4. Another example is the Calvert Group.

5. "Shareholders back unions in Rio Tinto call," *Financial Times*, 4 May.

6. See, for instance, Kaplan, Robert S. and Norton, David P., "The Balanced Scorecard – Measures that Drive Performance," *Harvard Business Review*, January–February 1992.

7. *Aligning Strategic Performance Measures and Results*. The Conference Board, 1999, and authors' estimates.

8. Ibid.

9. Ibid.

10. Ibid.

11. Terry Smith (1996) *Accounting for Growth: Stripping the Camouflage from Company Accounts*, 2nd edition (London: Century Business).

12. Bagnell, P. (1999) "MVA 300 – Nortel leads in creating value: Shareholder boost," *Financial Post*, 3 July.

13. Kapitan, J. (1999) "Banks continue their upward push: Greater efficiency," *Financial Post*, 3 July.

14. Milner, B. (1999) "Canadian firms lag US in disclosing information: Survey – Money managers also believe less attention is paid to shareholder concerns and wealth creation," *Globe and Mail*, 25 October.

15. Eccles, R.G. and Weibel, P.F. (1999) *The Information Reporting Gap in the Swiss Capital Markets* Zurich: PwC.

16. *Value Based Management: 1999 Swiss Implementation Study* (Zurich: PwC).

17. Quoted in Macro Becht *et al.* (see note 1).

18. The example referred to here is the Wenger versus Siemens case.

19. Herr Strenger from the DWS is an honorable exception to this; he has been keen to bring more SHV thinking to bear on his organization's investment strategy.

20. Price Waterhouse and Hannebohm, D. (1996) *Fundamental Share Analysis and Survey of Investors*.

21. L'Helias, S. (1996) "Corporate Governance Developments in France," presentation to Euromanagement conference on Creating Shareholder Value, Amsterdam.

22. Lionel Jospin, French Prime Minister, has said "Repartition is the symbol of the chain of solidarity which links the generations. It is one of the most important terms in the nation's social pact." 21 March speech 1999 as reported in *The Economist*.

23. Yukihiro Asano (1996), *The Stock Market from Investors' Viewpoint* (Chuo Koron).

24. In one emerging market, a CFO, apparently unaware of the changes taking place in his world, was asked what his attitude to cash was – after we had spent some time stressing the importance of cash flows. He replied that cash was something he got from the bank "at the end of the year," and expressed surprise at the importance we attached to it. He was replaced soon after!

25. Plender, J. (2000) "A Big Voice for the Small Man," *Financial Times*, 4 May.

26. Stern Stewart was the main consultant to the government.

PART

4

BRINGING IT ALL TOGETHER

REPORTING ON THE FUTURE: THE BLUEPRINT

People in every walk of life are affected by financial reporting, the cornerstone on which our process of capital allocation is built. An effective allocation process ... provides an efficient and liquid market for buying and selling securities and obtaining and granting credit, [whereas] a flawed process supports unproductive practices, denies cost-effective capital to companies and undermines the securities market.

American Institute of Certified Public Accountants (AICPA)
Special Committee on Financial Reporting, 1994

Reporting on the future? The title of this chapter may seem paradoxical – after all, we normally report on the past and predict the future – but there is a point to it.

As we have said throughout this book, creating value is the central imperative in today's business environment, where globalization, the computer revolution and the free flow of capital are combining to demand as much information as possible about company performance. What's more, the performance information that investors need is not simply *historical* information; they – and the managers of the companies they invest in – need information that is oriented towards the *future*.

Of course, information is available, to some extent. The closely regulated obligations of annual reports, prospectuses, proxy statements and other formal documents ensure that there are data about company performance out there to be studied. But a gap has always existed between these facts and figures and a management's own information. Some part of that gap can be explained by the confidentiality that any commercial enterprise needs – and anyway, market analysts will often fill part of the gap with their own reports and projections. Information about a company's plans will eventually reach the public domain when its financial statements have to reflect changes in circumstances. But it's not a systematic matter: future-oriented information, reflecting financial management and investment policies, is not subject to disclosure requirements.

However, because of the rise of SHV, we believe it is in managements' interest to make their companies more transparent. A new kind of reporting is emerging that focusses on long-term cash flow and other key financial performance metrics.

This chapter, then, is about *Value Reporting* – the new kind of reporting that will be in growing demand as SHV imperatives take hold throughout the world. To help explain what it all means, we have drawn up a value report for a fictional company, Blueprint Inc.,[1] and this is printed as an appendix at the end of this chapter. But first, let us go back and remind ourselves of the market forces that are causing a shift in emphasis from point-in-time reporting to value-oriented financial reporting.

THE MARKET PRESSURES

Throughout this book we have documented how globalization, capital market liberalization and the break-up of the old "stakeholder" relationships are all increasing the competitive pressure on firms. Companies, as we have noted, are having to pay ever closer attention to what they tell the financial markets. More than ever, they need to ensure that what they do is what they said they were going to do. In short, increasingly sophisticated investors and analysts are keen to be adequately and accurately informed about what the managements of the companies they invest in are doing. Since the first edition of this book, pressure has been further magnified by the emergence of "dot com" companies valued at multiples many times greater than those achievable by so-called "old economy" companies. Old-established companies are now expected to perform apparent miracles in order to maintain their attractiveness against the new upstarts.

We think these pressures, towards better performance and greater disclosure, are pointing towards what we call value reporting. Consider the example of three companies and their response to current circumstances:

● **Boeing**, challenged by Airbus and suffering from an irate labor force is taking steps to increase its transparency to investors. In the first quarter of 1999 it announced a "managing for value" program, followed up by a "value scorecard" that included four public performance metrics to enable the investing public to check progress against published targets. This was well received by the market.

● Following the merger of **Daimler and Chrysler**, the market was uncertain how to categorize the company; US investors were upset at the loss of disclosure at Chrysler, a stock they had previously followed closely, and share price performance suffered. As a result, post-merger divisional reporting has been improved, for the Daimler as well as for the Chrysler parts of the company, and skeptical investors have been convinced that the merger is going to create value for shareholders.

- **Eastman Kodak** abandoned traditionally secretive disclosure policies in the first quarter of 1999 by announcing a profit warning and simultaneously showing how it was going to achieve better returns for the rest of the year. Although analysts' forecasts were lowered, the share price responded to the company's candor by gaining. Analysts and investors were prepared to give the management a fair chance at showing what they could achieve.

Old disclosure standards are progressively being overturned, and we think that great swathes of the so-called "old economy" may find it expedient to be more forthcoming about both their strengths and their weaknesses – particularly in the light of the challenge posed by new e-commerce companies. Oddly enough, improved disclosure by the "old" companies may well help to underline the shakiness of many dot com valuations.

The actual users of the documents and reports currently prepared for financial reporting purposes are also exerting pressure. In a survey recently conducted by PricewaterhouseCoopers of companies, analysts and investors, nearly 40 per cent of the companies polled thought their own reports were "very useful."[2] This sentiment was not shared by the main users of the reports, the investors and the analysts. Under 20 per cent of them thought the reports were very useful, and around 17 per cent thought the financial reports were "not very useful" at all. So there is some room for improvement.

This kind of sentiment is finding a strong echo among several official and accounting bodies that advise on the format and content of financial reports. For instance, the American Institute of Certified Public Accountants (AICPA) has recommended that financial reports should "provide more information with a forward-looking perspective … [and] focus on factors that create longer-term value, including non-financial measures indicating how key business processes are performing."[3] The International Accounting Standards Committee (IASC) has improved financial reporting by requiring greater detail in segment reporting and calling for minimum structure and content to interim financial statements. The need for improved disclosure is echoed by the president of the Institute of Chartered Accountants in England and Wales, Chris Swinson, who has stated that "annual reports must answer the market's call for more information … historical cost financial reports do not attempt to meet the information needs of users."

In the USA again, Lynn Turner, chief accountant to the US Securities and Exchange Commission, has said:

> The capital markets, and the investors who drive them, need high quality financial reporting more than ever before. ... *I would recommend that financial executives consider how value creation in a business, which many of us deal with daily, should translate into disclosures in public filings.* While research shows that earnings remain the most relevant information today, it also shows other measurements are becoming increasingly important.[4]

The regulators have also turned their attention to the use of the internet, which they believe is starting to change the nature of the relationship between the market participants. A recent report by the US FASB (Financial Accounting Standards Board) on business reporting and the internet concluded that a revolution was taking place. The internet was increasing the amount of information available and the speed with which it is being delivered:

> The broadening of access cannot help but to alter the relationships among participants in the marketplace. ... The changes are unpredictable, but it seems clear that the value of being in the know will necessarily decline and be replaced by the value added insight or usefulness to information.[5]

All the above, we think, point towards greater awareness and information on a company's SHV-generating properties, and this means paying closer attention to the sort of things we have been talking about in Part 1 of this book. If you provide sufficient cash to stockholders through dividends, or invest it in ways approved of by investors – in new technology, products, brands, or new management structures – markets typically show their gratitude by increasing your share price.

WHY ASK ACCOUNTANTS?

This book has been written by people who work for a firm best known for its "core competence" of accountancy and auditing; yet much of this book has been written as if that activity is only marginally involved in the transformations that we foresee. In fact, the fates of corporations, investors and professional services firms such as PricewaterhouseCoopers are intertwined.

In the new business climate, corporate management and investors are hungry for information that bears on the future of a business. Investors will exert more pressure on businesses, who will look to their service providers to help them address these demands in various ways. Identifying areas where value can be built, and supporting management's subsequent reporting on that value, is emerging as an important focus of professional services firms.

We believe that value reporting (VR) promises to have extraordinary power, and that power lies in its twofold potential: first, to integrate the principles of traditional financial reporting, investment reporting, and management reporting; and second, to help professional firms' services evolve so that they provide even further benefit to the investment community, company boards and executive management. *Helping management focus on areas in which to build value and reporting on it* is emerging as the central focus of professional services firms in the business marketplace of the new century. Meeting company needs in the coming years will require new professional services – and VR will be at the center of these.

The public accounting profession is keenly aware of the potential impact of the changing business environment on its ability to meet the needs of companies and investors. The profession's thinking on these issues is being led by the AICPA, whose Special Committee on Financial Reporting, established in 1992, we have already quoted. Set up to consider the relevance and usefulness of financial reporting and the ways it is changing to meet today's business requirements, it gave as its view that:

> Financial reports are losing their significance because they are not future oriented and do not provide value-based information. … To meet users' changing needs, business reporting must: provide more information about plans, opportunities, risks, and uncertainties, focus more on the factors that create longer-term value, including non-financial measures indicating how key business processes are performing, [and] better align information reported externally with the information reported internally to senior management to manage the business.[6]

As we have seen, there are probably more adherents of this point of view today, and we expect their number to grow.

THREE AREAS OF ACCOUNTING MERGE

VR will be made possible through the convergence of the three important areas of accounting: traditional or historical financial reporting, investment or shareholder accounting, and management accounting.

Traditional financial reporting

We can be pretty certain that external reporting of financial results will always exist in some form. Governments will always require accurate financial reporting as a basis for levying taxation. In fact, more external reporting may be demanded as investors ask for more frequent communication, and in more areas, regarding management's stewardship. Such communication will be made possible by the ubiquitous nature of communications technology.

Investment accounting

A critical driver of corporate market wealth is the market's perception of how long the cash flow a company is generating can be sustained to benefit investors. If the market concludes that the cash flow will not last, investors will leave skid marks in abandoning the stock. This perception of how long the company can reasonably expect to have good times ahead is exceptionally important; the market is judging the company's actions in such areas as new technology, new products, patents, and long-term strategic planning. Historical financial reporting is just one key element of communication.

Management accounting

Management accounting is directed towards the analyses that managers need in order to make important business decisions. This branch of accounting relies on internal and external information in areas such as revenues, cost, pricing, budgeting, and profits. For example, management accounting information would indicate margin by product line, inventory value at current standard costs and anticipated internal rate of return of a capital expenditure. An important part of management accounting is assessing the capital planning and control process in order to gauge how the company will make decisions that are strategically relevant to its future performance.

We predict that, in the business environment of the future, these three areas of accounting – traditional, investment, and management – will come closer and perhaps even combine to some extent as companies make the changes necessary to meet the new requirements of the marketplace, their business partners, and investors.

THE SEVEN CORE COMPONENTS OF VR

The value reporting approach consists of seven core activities that a professional services firm, working with company executive management, will incorporate into its work. It will:

- *Perform a preliminary evaluation of the financial drivers of the company – the levers of SHV.* Especially in the USA, and increasingly in Europe, management has already performed this type of analysis. VR incorporates this analysis and the assumptions that have gone into the evaluation.

- *Determine how management has embodied these drivers in the corporation's objectives and how these drivers are shaping business operations.* For instance, the company's objective might be, in numerical terms, a 10 percent free cash flow improvement, a 15 percent share of the market, and 30 percent of revenues from products less than five years old.

- *Understand how management has developed the strategies to achieve these objectives* – e.g. by raising prices for slow-moving items, concentrating on large customers, investing more in new products, and streamlining the R&D process.

- *Determine whether these objectives and strategies are supported by performance measurements, and assess the quality of the measurement data provided to management.* The financial drivers should be linked to a "balanced scorecard" of financial and non-financial metrics (see below) that reinforce the SHV message at all levels of the company. These metrics will need to be reviewed periodically to assure management that the information it receives is accurate.

- *Assess whether management processes foster value creation.* Such processes would include goal setting, capital planning and acquisitions, budgeting, strategic planning, product/service planning, management forums, and executive compensation. Is the value-creation message being communicated effectively to the individuals who are responsible (and accountable) for all these corporate processes?

- *Draw up the "big picture" from all of the foregoing, and select the most relevant points to communicate with the investing public about value-creating strategies, processes, goals, and results.* In some companies, such management communication has in itself enhanced the stock price – because, as the management's actions have become more transparent to investors, so investors perceive there is less risk. Naturally, management must deliver on its expectations. This would mean giving the investor information about whether the company's strategies and processes are effective. In some companies, such management communication, by itself, can enhance the stock price, as we have seen in the example of Eastman Kodak quoted above.

● *Review, on a rotating basis, how effectively the major processes of the company are functioning, and fix what needs to be fixed.* Processes here would again be things like capital planning and acquisitions, budgeting, strategic planning, product/service planning, management forums, and executive compensation.

EXTERNAL REPORTING

A significant benefit of value reporting is that it enables you as a manager to communicate your VR conclusions about company strategies, measurements, and processes to the external business and investment communities – perhaps, in the case of measurements, accompanied by an opinion from an independent accountant. Such external reporting makes sense only if several criteria are met: that your investors desire additional information; that your proprietary information can be protected; and that effective "safe harbor" rules are established to protect you from lawsuits. (Forward-looking information may lead some investors to expect more positive results than you subsequently deliver.)

Topics for external reporting that might be useful include: product development, market share for major lines of business or products, average cost of capital (and investment hurdle rates), additions to intellectual capital, and customer satisfaction survey highlights. These might be organized around a "Statement of Shareholder Value Achieved" template, an example of which is shown in Table 12.1 which is based on the publicly reported information of a US company, supplemented by some estimates.

In general, you should take a balanced attitude to external reporting – particularly the commentary associated with such reporting. You should give weight to earnings per share while also emphasizing the statement of cash flow, SHV achieved, cash flow return on investments, and the primary drivers of long-term financial success. These could include such things as product development, number of new patents being obtained, changes in market share, percentage of revenues from products less than five years old, new technology and industry-specific factors that affect shareholder wealth.

TABLE 12.1 ● **Statement of shareholder value achieved**

	2000	2001	2002
Sales and other income	7,058	6,331	5,754
Cost of product sold	4,212	3,866	3,633
Gross margin	2,846	2,465	2,121
Selling, general, administrative, and other expenses	1,213	1,137	1,073
Other operating expenses, net of other income	95	72	36
Operating earnings before interest, taxes, etc. (EBITDA)	1,538	1,256	1,012
Capital expenditures required for normal operations (Note 1)	352	335	350
Net operating profit before taxes	1,186	921	662
Cash taxes (Note 2)	401	286	314
Net operating profit after taxes (NOPAT)	**785**	**635**	**348**
Capital charge for invested capital			
Net receivables and operating cash	1,351	1,291	1,109
Inventories @ FIFO	941	886	893
Current working assets	2,292	2,177	2,002
Accounts payable and accrued expenses	(1,104)	(1,034)	(921)
Net operating working capital	1,188	1,143	1,081
Net property, plant and equipment	2,835	2,742	2,787
Other operating assets, net of other liabilities	27	54	82
Net operating assets	4,050	3,939	3,950
Weighted average cost of capital (WACC) (Note 3)	11.3%	11.5%	11.0%
Capital charge (on beginning asset values)	**445**	**454**	**—**
Shareholder value achieved			
Net operating profit after taxes (NOPAT)	785	635	—
Capital charge (on beginning asset values)	445	454	—
Economic profit/shareholder value achieved	**340**	**181**	**—**

TABLE 12.1 ● **Notes**

	2000	2001	2002
Note 1: Depreciation and amortization from the statement of cash flows has been used as an approximation.			
Note 2: Cash taxes on EBIT (adjusted for non operating items)			
Effective income tax rate	*38%*	*38%*	*43%*
Interest expense	*85*	*86*	*103*
Non operating <income> expenses	*(162)*	*(20)*	*15*
Tax effect of interest and non-operating expenses	(29)	25	51
Provision for income taxes	480	325	236
Decrease <increase> in deferred taxes	(50)	(64)	27
Cash taxes	**401**	**286**	**314**
Note 3: Weighted average cost of capital (WACC)	1996	1995	1994
Cost of equity			
Expected return on US equities market	11.3%	11.7%	11.3%
Risk free cost of capital (US ten year treasury bond)	6.6%	6.9%	7.3%
Market risk premium for US equities	4.7%	4.8%	4.0%
Beta for company			
(Measure of risk adjusted for financial leverage)	1.13	1.11	1.08
Cost of equity			
(Return for business and financial risk of shareholders)	**11.9%**	**12.2%**	**11.6%**
Cost of debt			
Marginal cost of debt	7.9%	7.8%	7.8%
Tax adjustment	–3.0%	–3.0%	–3.4%
After tax cost of debt	**4.9%**	**4.8%**	**4.4%**
Total market value			
Total shares	291	291	145
Share price	45.750	37.125	75.875
Total market value	13,313	10,803	11,002
Total debt outstanding	1,221	1,144	1,129
Total value of Invested capital	14,534	11,947	12,131
Weighted average cost of capital			
Equity percentage of total capital	91.6%	90.4%	90.7%
Debt percentage of total capital	8.4%	9.6%	9.3%
Equity contribution to WACC	10.9%	11.0%	10.6%
Debt contribution to WACC	0.4%	0.5%	0.4%
Market cost of capital	**11.3%**	**11.5%**	**11.0%**

Source: Illustrative, based on publicly reported information of a US company and estimates

APPLYING VR: A HYPOTHETICAL CASE

How could your company make use of and benefit from value reporting? To begin answering this question, let us take a hypothetical company undergoing a VR analysis in conjunction with its independent accounting firm. This can be seen as a fourfold process that differs from, although it can draw on some of the knowledge gained in, the traditional annual financial audit, which will still be carried out.

Identifying the value levers

Since most companies' top goals include enhancing SHV, this is the first area that the VR process addresses. To identify the levers of SHV in an organization, the VR approach *develops a thorough understanding of the company's processes*, and thereby *identifies key SHV areas,* including those that may not be included in annual reports today. Some of these matters may have an associated degree of attestation.

Areas that could affect the company's future, and therefore interest investors, may include: tight definitions of product development – the total amount the company is really spending; the percentage of revenues coming from "younger" products; the number of patents being obtained; and the company's market share. In addition, VR activity would identify industry-specific SHV factors that may help investors in making judgements about the company's future.

VR also *demonstrates how the company resolves its most important strategic issues.* Generally, these issues might include acquisitions, divestitures, investment in new products and establishing new plants. These are the kinds of matters which could be the basis for informed recommendations concerning:

- how to improve the business's internal processes relating to such areas as revenues, costs, working capital, and capital expenditure planning;
- the impact of possible decisions and actions on SHV;
- event-related matters such as how the company should set about merging the cultures and systems of a new acquisition.

During the first year of the VR process (which would be conducted on top of regular financial auditing work), the VR project team's initial operational steps would include *developing a thorough understanding of the factors that enhance SHV and influence strategic decisions* in this particular organization. Firstly, the project team, in conjunction with management, would assess the company's key financial indicators in relation to those of its competitors, to obtain an external benchmark of how this company is performing compared to others. This effort might include learning about such areas as revenue growth, margin growth, cash tax rates, how the company absorbs its working capital for its incremental sales, capital expenditures, and so on. Additionally, since most large corporations have many divisions and an array of product lines and markets, the team may want to expand the benchmark efforts to encompass all of the company's individual business segments.

The project team would then proceed to *pinpoint the locations of the company's areas of financial strength and weakness – the value levers of the organization.* The team would convey this information to executive management, and suggest that the accounting firm should continue using the VR concept in this attestation function for the next several years.

At this point, the team – and the company – would be well placed to move from a primary focus on diagnostics to value creation through performance enhancement. The aim would be to understand which factors within the company improve the drivers of financial success; for example, what improves revenue generation, what improves margin, what improves working capital utilization, how are capital expenditures authorized, and so on.

Creating a metrics scorecard

Equally important, the project team would want to learn whether this company had *performance-measurement metrics* in place that could help determine whether its value objectives and other strategic goals were being achieved. If work is needed in this area, the team would help the company *link its financial drivers of SHV with a "balanced scorecard" of performance-measurement metrics* as it proceeded with the VR work. The metrics would not be abstract algorithms but would be straightforward and meaningful to employees at all levels. They would tell them what counts.

In creating this metrics scorecard, the project team would work with management to select a balanced set of performance measures designed to achieve goals at the corporate level – goals that it would then "drill down" into its business units. Some of these measurements would be financial, others would be related to customer service and other factors; but all would be expressed in quantitative terms and have a common focus on long-term sustainable value. They would include such matters as: average time to market for new products, new product development expense as a percentage of sales, product return on investment, new product sales dollars as a percentage of total sales dollars, product quality and margin, and customer satisfaction. (See Fig. 12.1.)

Testing reliability and effectiveness

Towards the end of the first year, or possibly in the second year with this hypothetical company, the VR team would ask: How effective are the organization's existing processes and its systems for reporting performance measure-

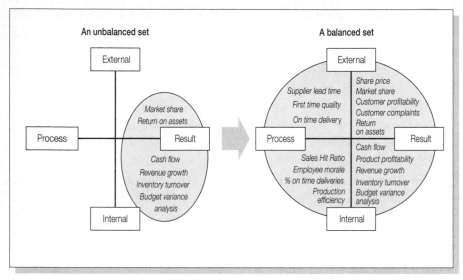

FIG 12.1 ● Example of balanced scorecard

ments? Is the system bringing about positive changes in the drivers of SHV? At this stage, the project team would probably select one or two of the company's key processes – for example, the capital spending process, or the R&D effort – to test the reliability of the information derived from the metrics. The VR team would plan, in future years, to test processes for effectiveness in such areas as budgeting and planning, purchasing, and customer acquisition.

In some situations, the company may decide that it could benefit from VR through creation of a continuing role for the accounting firm as external reviewer and adviser. This role would have two parts: on a recurring basis, each year, the firm would ensure that the metrics were providing the correct information; and on a rotating basis, the firm would "audit" or test the company's key value-driving processes to ensure that they were functioning effectively. And of course, the firm would comment on the reliability of such information and processes for executive management.

Senior executives may want to enlist their professional advisers' help in looking down through the layers of middle management to understand better what is really happening in the company. Top executives value objective, dependable information about how well the company's processes and metrics are working, brought to them by an external party who has free access to all parts of the organization.

In later years, a value reporting team might turn to examining other processes within the company, seeking areas in which to improve efficiency and reduce costs. These might include the processes for strategic planning, customer relationships, product delivery, quality assurance, environmental affairs and risk management. In each of these areas, the team would issue a report with commentary for management. So many people will be involved that reviewing these processes will not be easy; field guides, process descriptions, and training will be needed. Nevertheless, such an activity, even though it involves areas not traditionally addressed by accounting firms, is not substantially different from understanding whether a company's accounts receivable process is working effectively.

In essence, the long-established skills and worldwide trust enjoyed by leading public accounting firms would act as a security for any company that decided to apply VR. After all, what they do now is conduct independent testing of data and report on the quality of processes that produce the data. With VR, a firm will have to test different bases and examine different processes to see whether they are effective – but the principles are the same.

Communicating to investors

At the appropriate time – probably not before the second year – executive management may want to share publicly certain information (such as market share or new products/services) that could help investors gauge what the company is doing to ensure shareholder wealth. Obviously, it is critical that such information should be reliable; this is where attestation becomes important.

In line with the investing public's expectations of reporting, a shift away from commentary regarding earnings per share and towards a Statement of Shareholder Value Achieved, as in Table 12.1, may be in order. Attestation by the independent accounting firm as to the reliability of such information becomes important here.

During the second or third year, management may consider modifying the information given in the annual report, by starting to emphasize cash and SHV. This approach could include a substantial amount of commentary; for example, the management and discussion analysis (MD&A) could include analyses of the outcomes of new performance measurements, thus enabling investors to judge how today's actions will enhance future value.

Subsequently, based on the accounting firm's assurance that the key metrics were reporting accurate information, management and the board may consider expanding the company's communication of SHV information to investors. By now, management will be more comfortable with this information, whose reliability will have the additional assurance provided by the attestation work of external accountants.

All of which is something close to an ideal in investor communication; providing information of this type sets your flag on impressively high ground. As a company you will send the message that you are changing, that you have put new metrics in place, and that you are doing much to monitor their progress. This type of communication will, in itself, start changing the investor's view of your company.

THE FUTURE OF VALUE

Value reporting holds exceptional significance for corporations, the investment community, and public accounting firms and other professional services providers worldwide. We anticipate that investors will continue to pressure companies for more disclosure of performance measurements, possibly including an annual statement of SHV achieved or even a more detailed annual value report. This is the demand that our hypothetical "Blueprint Inc." model (see Appendix 1) has been drawn up to meet. It may seem to some readers to be somewhat extreme in terms of types of disclosures made; but the reporting environment of (say) the year 2005 could be strikingly different.

Value reporting, then, is the consequence of the SHV imperative that has been with us in this book from the beginning – and is an integral part of "value realization" the last step in the value transformation process that we met in Part 2.

As we enter a new millennium, the thirst for value will not abate. The causes of this thirst – globalization, the information revolution and the mobility of capital – are not easily satisfied and are increasing in momentum. Scope and scale, the competitive drivers of the last century, are being augmented by speed and knowledge management.

As we have described it in this book, the creation of value is a synthesizing process of analysis, action and communication. It requires the reconciliation of the strategic and economic with accounting approaches to analysis; it necessitates the coordination of changes in culture and mindset with new measurement systems; and it now demands the integration of separate management, investor and financial reporting practices.

To rise to the challenge of value creation, to understand it and improve on it, is no easy task. But all around the globe, it is a challenge that investors, managements and their advisers are focussing on. We trust we have helped you focus on it too.

If you would like further information about the shareholder value services that Pricewaterhouse-Coopers can provide through its ValueBuilder™ process and in other ways, contact your local PwC office or telephone Andrew Black or Philip Wright at 020 7804 3000 in the UK (+44 20 7804 3000 elsewhere). See also the website at www.pwcglobal.com

Notes

1. The name "Blueprint" is, in the context of this book, fictional and does not (nor is intended to) refer to any real entity, product or service.

2. Quoted in Eccles, R. (1998) *Value Creation, Preservation and Realization* (London: PwC).

3. *Preliminary Report of the Special Committee on Financial Reporting*, New York: American Institute of Certified Public Accountants, July 1992.

4 "21st Century Financial Reporting," speech at the 27th National AICPA conference.

5. *Electronic Distribution of Business Reporting Information*, US Financial Accounting Standards Board Business Reporting Research Project, 31 January 2000.

6. *Preliminary Report of the Special Committee on Financial Reporting*, New York: American Institute of Certified Public Accountants, July 1992.

BLUEPRINT INC.[1]

T he following report is an illustration of the possible structure and content of corporate reporting in the future. The extent to which this type of information will be disclosed publicly may be difficult to assess today. What is clear, however, is that this form of analysis should be at the heart of any company's internal reporting and measurement systems because it links value analysis to measurable performance indicators.

Company executives may be wary of demands for more disclosure. But as institutional investors master SHV analysis, their ability to scrutinize and probe publicly quoted companies will improve. Indeed, executives may see a considerable advantage to be had by improving the flow of relevant information to the market.

BLUEPRINT INC.

Mission statement

The key to our corporate success is cash generation. Our ambition is to build value by exploiting our core competencies to achieve this goal. We must identify those pulses that contribute to the long-term enhancement of cash flow – customer satisfaction, employee satisfaction, growth and innovation. These and all value-achievement matters must be embedded in our business processes and our actions.

Letter from the Chief Executive Officer

I am pleased to report another successful year in which the Company's value has been further enhanced. Our progress in creating value has contributed significantly to the Company's successful performance in the areas of productivity, competitiveness, revenue growth and profitability.

Set out below are the key features of our value reporting model. Developed last year, it provides the structure of our value report for the year ended 31 December 1996.

The Company's main mission is to maximize long-term value. We will achieve this by consistently delivering superior performance relative to our competitors year after year. We measure value in terms of both financial and non-financial indicators, reflected through their effect on past and future cash flows.

The financial measures we use are based on the drivers of past and future cash flows and are not the traditional earnings-based indicators. The non-financial measures help to assess the value of several critical areas, which are emphasized in our mission statement: our customers, employees, growth and innovation, and internal processes. Only by improving these indicators continuously can we improve financial performance and, hence, value.

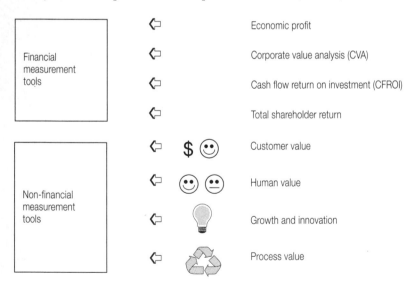

Financial measurement tools		Economic profit
		Corporate value analysis (CVA)
		Cash flow return on investment (CFROI)
		Total shareholder return
Non-financial measurement tools		Customer value
		Human value
		Growth and innovation
		Process value

All financial measurement categories consider the extent to which value has been increased or decreased in the financial period. The non-financial indicators are the activities which underpin historic financial performance and which, if managed effectively, provide the basis for sustainable growth in value.

Blueprint Inc. value drivers

Value drivers are the framework we use to analyze the free cash flow in the business and to understand which levers will have the most effect on corporate value. The cube below illustrates the fact that all drivers, whether financial or non-financial, are interrelated.

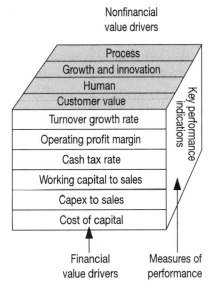

The table below demonstrates which non-financial value drivers have an impact on the financial value drivers.

	Customer	People	Growth and innovation	Processes
Turnover growth rate	✓	✓	✓	
Operating profit margin		✓	✓	✓
Cash tax rate		✓		
Working capital to sales	✓	✓		✓
Capex to sales		✓		✓
Cost of capital		✓		

In operating the company, we need to be able to focus on the activities which provide sustainable growth in value. We have accordingly developed a series of performance indicators which we believe ensure that the management team and the rest of the organization commit their time and resources to the key value-adding activities.

On the next few pages, we consider some of these primary performance indicators. We have not significantly changed the indicators in the last 12 months, although improvements have been made in the way performance is measured, particularly in the area of "people value," which we believe will be the most important factor in the Company's long-term success. This conclusion is clear if one analyzes the relative impact of each value generator on the financial drivers.

Blueprint Inc. financial value drivers

| | £million | | | | | |
| | Actual | | | | | Projected |
	1994	1995	1996	1997	1998 ...	2006
Sales and other income	**5,754**	**6,331**	**7,058**	**7,868**	**8,770**	**... 20,914**
Free cash flow						
Operating earnings before interest, taxes, depreciation and amortization (EBITDA)	**1,012**	**1,256**	**1,538**	**1,636**	**1,824**	**... 4,350**
Depreciation and amortization	350	335	352	365	371	... 424
Operating earnings before interest and taxes (EBIT)	**662**	**921**	**1,186**	**1,271**	**1,453**	**... 3,926**
Cash taxes on EBIT (note 1)	314	286	401	496	567	... 1,531
Net Operating Profit After Tax (NOPAT)	**348**	**635**	**785**	**775**	**886**	**... 2,395**
Add back depreciation and amortization	350	335	352	365	371	... 424
Gross cash flow	**698**	**970**	**1,137**	**1,140**	**1,257**	**... 2,819**
Less: reinvestment of cash flow						
Increase in working capital		34	18	(92)	129	... 307
Capital expenditures		356	454	388	395	... 451
		390	472	296	524	... 758
Free cash flow before dividends and scheduled debt repayment (FCF)		580	665	844	733	... 2,061

				£million			
		Actual					Projected
	1994	1995	1996	1997	1998	...	2006
Net assets							
Property, plant and equipment							
Original cost – balance at January 1	6,158	6,042	6,163	6,464	6,572	...	7,503
Capital expenditures	293	356	454	388	395	...	451
Gross retirements	409	235	153	280	285	...	326
Original cost – balance at December 31	6,042	6,163	6,464	6,572	6,682	...	7,628
Accumulated depreciation – balance at January 1	3,187	3,255	3,421	3,629	3,714	...	4,446
Depreciation and amortization	350	335	352	365	371	...	424
Accumulated depreciation on retirements	282	169	144	280	285	...	326
Accumulated depreciation – balance at December 31	3,255	3,421	3,629	3,714	3,800	...	4,544
Net property, plant and equipment	**2,787**	**2,742**	**2,835**	**2,858**	**2,882**	...	**3,084**
Operating cash and equivalents	112	62	106	116	129	...	308
Receivables	997	1,229	1,245	1,388	1,547	...	3,690
Inventories at LIFO	683	687	738	822	917	...	2,186
Adjustment for FIFO	210	199	203	0	0	...	0
	2,002	2,177	2,292	2,326	2,593	...	6,184
Accounts payable and accrued expenses	921	1,034	1,104	1,230	1,371	...	3,270
Other current assets net of other current liabilities	82	54	27	27	30	...	72
Net operating working capital	**1,163**	**1,197**	**1,215**	**1,123**	**1,252**	...	**2,986**
Invested capital	**3,950**	**3,939**	**4,050**	**3,981**	**4,134**	...	**6,070**

	1994	1995	1996
Note 1 – Cash taxes on EBIT			
Effective income tax rate	43%	38%	38%
Interest expense	103	86	85
Non-operating (income) expenses	15	(20)	(162)
Tax effect of interest and non-operating expenses	51	25	(29)
Provision for income taxes	236	325	480
Decrease (increase) in deferred taxes	27	(64)	(50)
Cash taxes	**314**	**286**	**401**
Note 2 – Weighted average cost of capital (WACC)			
Market value			
Total shares	145	291	291
Share price	75.875	37.125	45.750
Total market value	11,002	10,803	13,313
Total debt outstanding	1,129	1,144	1,221
Total market value of invested capital	12,131	11,947	14,534
Cost of debt			
Marginal borrowing rate	7.8%	7.8%	7.9%
Tax adjustment	3.4%	3.0%	3.0%
After-tax cost of debt	4.4%	4.8%	4.9%
Cost of equity			
Expected return on US equities market	11.3%	11.7%	11.3%
Risk-free cost of capital	7.3%	6.9%	6.6%
Market risk premium for US equities	4.0%	4.8%	4.7%
Beta	1.08	1.11	1.13
	11.6%	**12.2%**	**11.9%**
WACC			
Equity percentage of total capital	90.7%	90.4%	91.6%
Debt percentage of total capital	9.3%	9.6%	8.4%
Equity contribution to WACC	10.6%	11.0%	10.9%
Debt contribution to WACC	0.4%	0.5%	0.4%
	11.0%	**11.5%**	**11.3%**

Financial value drivers

We use a number of cash flow-based financial measures. All of these are linked and the source of data from which they are calculated is shown above.

1 Economic profit

The operating profit created during the year in excess of the cost of invested capital.

	£ million		
	1994	1995	1996
Net operating profit after tax (NOPAT)	348	635	785
Less: Capital charge (WACC x opening invested capital)	(428)	(454)	(445)
Economic (loss)/profit	(80)	181	340

As indicated, in 1994 the cost of capital was not covered by NOPAT, which resulted in a loss of value. The following two years, however, saw a period of positive growth; value reached an all-time high of $340 in the current year. The economic value calculation above looks only at each year in isolation. The projected economic profit can be discounted at the cost of capital to give a value for the Group.

	$ million		
	1994	1995	1996
Present value of economic profit at cost of capital	8,232	8,949	10,737
Add: Invested capital	3,950	3,939	4,050
Less: Value of debt	(1,129)	(1,144)	(1,221)
Internal value	11,053	11,744	13,566
Market capitalization	11,002	10,803	13,313
Over/under valuation	(51)	(941)	(253)

The value of the Company in 1994 was very close to its market value despite loss of value in that year, showing that the value and market value reflect the Company's prospects.

2 Free cash flow (FCF)

The free cash flows discounted to a net present value at the company's cost of capital, less company debt.

	$ million		
	1994	1995	1996
Present value of free cash flows discounted at cost of capital	12,182	12,888	14,787
Less: Value of debt	(1,129)	(1,144)	(1,221)
Internal value	11,053	11,744	13,566
Market capitalization	11,002	10,803	13,313
Under-valuation	(51)	(941)	(253)

In 1995, because our implicit value was significantly in excess of our Company's market capitalization, management embarked upon an extensive series of roadshows to more fully explain our strategy and future plans. We believe that this has been reflected in the reduced under-valuation.

3 Cash flow return on investment (CFROI)

The discount rate at which the net present value of the inflation-adjusted cash flows are available to capital holders equals the value of invested capital. The value of capital invested is adjusted for depreciating assets and the residual value of non-depreciating assets such as land and working capital.

	1994	1995	1996
CFROI	6.5%	9.8%	11.0%
Assumed investors' required real rate of return	7.0%	7.0%	7.0%
(Discount)/Premium	(0.5%)	2.8%	4.0%

In 1996, the Company again achieved a cash flow return on investment in excess of the assumed real rate of return required by investors. Based on our internal projections, we believe this position is sustainable provided we continue to invest carefully in technical innovation and human capital.

4 Total shareholder return

The total return available to the equity shareholder. This represents any dividends paid and movement in the share price.

	1994	1995	1996
Share price	75.88	37.13	45.75
Share price movement (%, adjusted for stock split)	15.18	(2.14)	23.22
Dividend per share	1.04	1.12	1.18
Total shareholder return	17.72%*	0.075%	26.88%

In 1995, there was a stock split resulting in an adjustment to the share price. Coupled with market uncertainty, the share price fell 2.14 percent. In 1996, the share price recovered to $45.75, showing an improvement of 23.22 percent on the year, which together with the full year dividend gave an overall shareholder return of 26.88 percent.

* The figures in the tables above are for illustrative purposes only.

Market share

We have continued to maintain our global market share while many of our competitors have lost theirs to new entrants from the Pacific Rim. We believe our position as market leaders has been secured through our customer care program and our focus on product innovation and quality.

Share of customer

We have been building strong relationships with our customers over many years, and once again have maintained our average percentage share of their spending on consumables. Our acquisition of Jupiter, Inc. will enable us to expand our current product list, and we believe it should enable us to increase our share of customer spending in the future.

Customer satisfaction

Our latest annual customer satisfaction survey undertaken by Pricewaterhouse-Coopers showed room for improvement in certain areas but, overall, a promising result. We have already commissioned a review of our pre-sales service and our ability to deliver on time. Furthermore, the results of our two-year project into the redesign of our core "K" product will address the "value for money" concern expressed by our customers.

Product defects

Product defects continued to fall, and we are now close to achieving our "six sigma" target set two years ago. We continue to invest in new technology and procedures, and have been particularly pleased with the input provided by our workforce around the world through our "Kreative" ideas initiative introduced in 1996. Further, we have introduced a "no quibble product guarantee" in which any defective product is replaced within 12 hours with no questions asked.

Blueprint Inc. people value

Employee survey index

Having been disappointed with the poor results of the 1995 employee survey, we invested heavily in 1996 to address a number of the key weaknesses. In particular, our increase in investment in training has been reflected in an above-average score on skills building, and our move to greater teleworking, our "time out" and "children at work" initiatives have significantly improved the Company's overall lifestyle rating.

Intellect index

We continue to measure and monitor the intellectual capacity of the Company through our "Global Intellect Index," which is based on qualifications held and relevant experience of all our employees. We are pleased to report that the investment in recruitment made in 1994 is already having a marked effect on the level of innovation and creativity

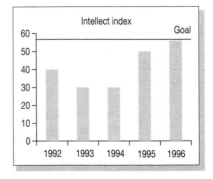

at the junior management level.
Further work is required in this area
if we are to achieve the levels of
performance currently recorded by
competitors in Singapore and South Korea.

Resources and cultural balance

We have continued to invest in our
program to realign culturally and
numerically our human resources with
the markets we serve. This has
resulted in $30 million being spent on
recruitment in the Pacific Rim and $20
million on cultural training for our
senior executives in North America
and Europe.

	% of world population	Company resources
North America	5	30
Europe	11	20
South America	10	8
China	54	25
Russia	5	5
Africa	14	6
Australasia	1	6
	100%	100%

Training

We continue to invest heavily in training and have, in the current year,
achieved a per-capita expenditure on
training equivalent to 49 percent of
wage cost. This puts the Company in
the top quartile of global companies,
and will be surpassed next year as a
result of the introduction of the spon-
sored MBA program for middle managers, to be delivered via the internet.
Funding for this development is made
possible by our ability to close two
global training centers no longer
needed in the new telecommunications
environment.

Blueprint Inc. growth and innovation

Research and development

Our long-term strategy has been to
invest heavily in Research and Development and in the intellectual capacity of the business. These investments
are now providing valuable payback

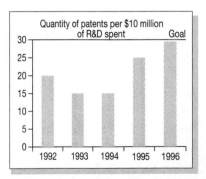

in the form of market leadership. The Company is in the top ten percentile of all companies in number of patents obtained in 1996 for every $10 million spent on R&D. One disappointing event in the year was the negative outcome of our litigation against Pluto, Inc. over the "Q" patent, which we believed we had secured.

New product pipeline

Our new product pipeline remains very healthy although we have been disappointed to have brought only ten products to market in the last 12 months. We are currently reviewing the speed with which we test quality and market demand in order to reduce significantly our future development time. Sales of our new K2 product suffered in the year due to a major competitor's achieving a market launch one month earlier.

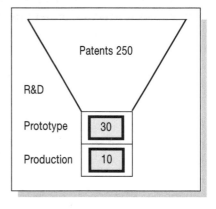

Structured thinking

We set a target of 18 percent for structured thinking in the Company in 1994. After two years we have achieved 17 percent through our scenario planning, product innovation, employee development, and process reengineering programmes. This level of performance is still considered unsatisfactory, and further initiatives are being introduced to encourage structured thinking time and to protect staff from low value-creating activities.

Brands

The Company's brands continue to be strong despite tough competition from our main rivals. We have in particular seen a strengthening in our brand positioning in the developing economies in which we have increased our marketing and promotional activity in the last 12 months, and have started to build the pre- and post-sales infrastructure present in the more developed OECD markets.

Each square represents the relative strength to competitors of our brands throughout the world

N. America	Europe	Asia
□ □ □	□ □ □ □ □ □	□ □ □ □ □
□ □ □	□ □ □ □ □ □	□ □ □ □ □

S. America	Africa	Russia	Australia
□ □	□ □ □ □	□ □	□ □ □ □
□ □	□ □ □ □	□ □	□ □ □ □

Blueprint Inc. process value

Process cost per transaction

Because process cost has a direct impact on profitability, we aim to reduce this cost per transaction to $1 by introducing more efficient processing methods and eliminating all tasks which do not add value (particularly tasks which occur for internal reasons only).

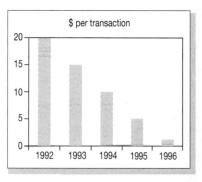

Efficiency rating

We have again participated in the "PWC World Process Benchmarking Study," which has shown that the Company remains in the top quartile of MNCs on process efficiency. While this reflects the investment made in new systems and the interactive database, we believe significant opportunity still remains to enhance our efficiency rating.

Office space

We have successfully reduced the most under-utilized asset in the business – our office space – and have enhanced employee satisfaction by encouraging more staff to telecommute. This has resulted in a reduction of 10,000 sq. metres in our office space requirements and an increase in capex of $20 million for the provision of mobile work stations and technology support services.

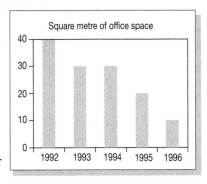

Outsourcing cost

We have continued the strategic push to outsource all non-value-adding activities to major recognized outsourcing providers. As noted earlier, we have out-sourced all finance-related functions in the year, saving us $180 million over the next ten years. This follows the outsourcing of information technology, primary manufacturing, and distribution in pre-vious years.

	Annualized cost savings
Financial transactions	$$$$
Primary manufacturing	$$$
Information technology	$$
Distribution	$

Note

1 For the purposes of this book, the name "Blueprint Inc." is fictional and does not (and is not intended to) relate to any real entity, product or service.

APPENDIX 2

BETAS

....

ESTIMATING BETA-LEVERAGE EFFECTS

We typically observe levered betas, since companies mostly have some debt; but this can be thought of as a function of a hidden "undiscovered" beta.

$$\beta \text{ levered} = \{1 + (1 - T_m) D/E\} \beta \text{ unlevered},$$

where T_m = the marginal corporate tax rate,
   D = market value of debt,
   E = market value of equity

$$\beta \text{ unlevered} = \beta \text{ levered}/\{1 + (1 - T_m) D/E\}$$

If we assume that β levered = 1.2, D = 1300, E = 1000 and T_m is 0.3, then in equation 2 we would get

$$\beta \text{ unlevered} = 1.2/1 + (1 - 0.3) \times 1.2 = 0.652$$

Assume a new debt/equity ratio = 1.4, put back into equation 1

$$\beta \text{ levered} = \{1 + (1 - 0.3) \times 1.4\} \times 0.652$$

$$\beta \text{ levered} = 1.291$$

ESTIMATING THE BETA-LEVERAGE EFFECTS
AND THE IMPACT ON THE COST OF CAPITAL

An upwards move in the gearing or leverage, from 1.3 to 1.4, moved the levered beta from 1.2 to 1.291, which is a reasonably large shift.

Impact on the cost of capital:

K_e old 9.8%; K_d old 4.2%

(where K_e is cost of equity and K_d is cost of debt)

Old equity = 43.5% of total; old debt 56.5% of total

So K_e old is 4.26%, K_d old 2.37%, which makes a WACC of 6.63%

K_e new 9.91%; K_d new 4.2%

New equity = 41.7% of total, new debt 58.3% of total

So K_e new is 4.13%, K_d new 2.449, which makes a WACC of 6.57%.

Summary: the higher the leverage (or gearing), the higher the cost of equity – the cost of equity is raised by the higher beta. On the other hand, you now have more low-cost debt, which reduces the WACC. The net impact of higher leverages and re-levering the betas, is to lower the WACC, but by less than if the betas had not been changed.

Impact of tax changes

- After levering and unlevering the betas, a rise in the debt portion reduces the WACC, but by slightly less than you might have expected if you had not changed the betas.

- If the debt is redistributed to higher tax areas, then their impact will be to lower the betas and hence lower the cost of capital.

- Counter-intuitive result: reducing the tax burden will raise the cost of capital and lower shareholder value.

- Debt redistributed to a lower tax regime – releveraging beta will have a greater impact on WACC.

BIBLIOGRAPHY

Aligning Strategic Performance Measures and Results (Conference Board Europe, 1999)

American Institute of Certified Public Accountants, *Preliminary Report of the Special Committee on Financial Reporting* (New York: AICPA, July 1992)

Asano, Yukihiro, "The Stock Market from Investors' Viewpoint" (*Toushika kara mita kabusiki shijo*), *Chuo Koron*, April 1996

Asquith, P., Bruner, R.F., and Mullins, D., Jr, "The Gains for Bidding Firms from Merger," *Journal of Financial Economics*, Vol. 11 (1983), pp.121–39

Bealey, R., and Myers, S., *Principles of Corporate Finance*, 2nd edition (London and New York: McGraw-Hill, 1984)

Becht, M., *et al.*, *Preliminary Report: The Separation of Ownership and Control, A Survey of Seven European Countries*, Vols. 1–3 (Brussels: European Corporate Governance Network, 1997)

Berle, A.A., and Means, G.C., *The Modern Corporation and Private Property* (New York and London: Macmillan, 1932, republished 1991)

Black, F., Jensen, M., and Scholes, M., "The Capital Asset Pricing Model: some empirical tests," in *Studies in the Theory of Capital Markets* (Praeger, 1992)

Boutis, Nick, Dragonetti, Nicola, Jacobsen, Kristina, and Roos, Goran, "The Knowledge Tool-Box: A Review of the Tools Available to Measure and Manage Intangible Resources," *European Management Journal*, Vol. 17, No. 4 (1999), pp. 391–402

Bradley, M., Desai, A., and Kim, E.H., "Synergistic Gains from Corporate Acquisitions and their Division between Stockholders of Target and Acquiring Firms," *Journal of Financial Economics*, Vol.21 (1988), pp.3–40

"Cadbury Committee report:" *Financial Aspects of Corporate Governance* (London, 1992)

Carman, Peter, "The Equity Risk Premium and Tactical Asset Allocation," in: Stephan Lofthouse, *Readings in Investments*, Wiley 1995

Cooper, I., *Arithmetic versus Geometric Mean Risk Framed: Setting Discount Rates for Capital Budgeting* (IFA working paper 174–195, September 1995)

CFO 2000: The Global CFO as Strategic Business Partner (Conference Board Europe, 1997)

Copeland, Tom, Koller, Tim, and Murrin, Jack (McKinsey & Company, Inc.), *Valuation*, 2nd edition (New York: John Wiley, 1996)

Datta, Narayanan, and Pinches, "Factors Influencing Wealth Creation from Mergers," *Strategic Management Journal*, Vol.13 (1992), pp.67–84

Eccles, R., *Value Creation, Preservation and Realization* (London: PwC, 1998)

Eccles, Robert G., Lanes, Kirsten L., and Wilson, Thomas C., "Are You Paying Too Much for That Acquisition?" *Harvard Business Review*, July–August 1999

Fama, Eugene, and French, Kenneth R., "Permanent and Temporary Components of Stock Prices," *Journal of Political Economy*, April 1988, pp. 246–73

Fama, E., and French, K., "Dividend Yields and Expected Stock Returns," *Journal of Financial Economics*, October 1988, pp.3–25

Fama, E., and French, K., "Cross-Section of Expected Stock Returns," *Journal of Finance*, No.42 (June 1992), pp.427–65

Friend, Irwin, and Blume, Marshall E., "A New Look at the Capital Asset Pricing Model," *Journal of Finance* (1973), pp.19–33

Gates, Stephen, *Aligning Performance Measures and Incentives in the European Community Results* (Brussels and NY: Conference Board research report 1252–99–RR, 1999)

Gates, Stephen, *Aligning Strategic Performance Measures and Results* (Brussels and NY: Conference Board research report 1261–99–RR, 1999)

Gregory, Bruce, *Defending SHV in an Era of Deflation* (London: PwC pamphlet, 1999)

Hannebohm, D., *Fundamental Share Analysis and Survey of Investors* (Price Waterhouse, 1996)

Hempel Committee on Corporate Governance, final report (London, January 1998)

Howell, S.D., and Jägle, A.J., "Evidence of How Managers Intuitively Manage Growth Options," *Journal of Business Finance and Accounting*, Spring 1997

Ibbotson Associates, *Stocks, Bonds, Bills and Inflation Yearbook* (Chicago, 2000)

Institute of Chartered Accountants in England and Wales, *Inside Out: Reporting on Shareholder Value* (London: ICAEW, October 1999)

Jarrel, G.A., Brickley, J.A., and Netter, J.M., "The Market for Corporate Control: The Empirical Evidence Since 1980," *Journal of Economic Perspectives*, Vol.2 (1988), pp.21–48

Kaplan, Robert S., and Norton, David P., "The Balanced Scorecard – Measures that Drive Performance," *Harvard Business Review*, January–February 1992

Lev, B.L., and Sougiannis, T., "The Capitalization, Amortization and Value of R&D," *Journal of Accounting and Economics*, 21 (1996), pp.107–38

Lo, and Macinlay, "Stock Market Prices Do Not Follow Random Walks: Evidence from a Simple Specification Test," *Review of Financial Studies*, Spring 1988

Loderer, C., and Martin, K., "Corporate Acquisitions by NYSE and AMEX firms: The experience of a Comprehensive Sample," *Financial Management* (Winter 1990), pp.17–33

Luehrman, Timothy A., "Investment Opportunities as Real Options: Getting Started on the Numbers," *Harvard Business Review*, July–August 1998

Luehrman, Timothy A., "Using APV: A Better Tool for Valuing Operations," *Harvard Business Review*, May–June 1997

Luehrman, Timothy A., "What's It Worth? A General Manager's Guide to Valuation," *Harvard Business Review*, May–June 1997

Madden, C., *Managing Bank Capital* (John Wiley, 1996)

Miller, W.D., *Commercial Bank Valuation* (New York: John Wiley, 1995)

Mills, Roger C., *The Dynamics of Shareholder Value* (Gloucester, England: Mars Business Associates)

Myers, Stewart C., "Corporate Finance Behaviour," *Journal of Finance*, July 1984 Vol.xxxix No.3, pp.575–91

Myers, S., and Kajluf, N.S., "Corporate Financing and Investment Decisions When Firms Have Information that Investors Do Not Have,", *Journal of Financial Economics*, Vol.13, pp.187–221

Myners, Paul, *Developing a Winning Partnership: How companies and institutional investors are working together* (Report of a joint city/industry working party established under the chairmanship of Paul Myners of Gartmore plc, second edition 1996)

Porter, Michael, *Competitive Strategy: Techniques for Analysing Industries and Competitors* (New York: Free Press, 1980)

Plender, John, *A Stake in the Future* (London: Nicholas Brealey, 1997)

Prahalad, C.K., and Hamel, Gary, "The Core Competence of the Corporation," *Harvard Business Review*, May–June 1990

Price Waterhouse Change Integration Team, *The Paradox Principles: How High-Performance Companies Manage Chaos, Complexity and Contradiction to Achieve Superior Results* (Chicago: Irwin Professional Publishing, 1996)

PricewaterhouseCoopers, *International Accounting Standards: Similarities and Differences* (1998)

Purie, A., and Malhotra, V., *Cost of Capital: Survey of Issues and Trends in India* (New Delhi: PwC Publications, 1999)

Puschaver, Lee, and Eccles, Robert G., "In Pursuit of the Upside: The New Opportunity in Risk Management," *PW Review*, December 1996, p.7ff

Rappaport, Alfred, *Creating Shareholder Value* (New York: Free Press, 1986)

Reimann, Bernard C., *Managing for Value* (Oxford and London: Blackwell, in association with the Planning Forum, 1989)

Schell, Charles, *Earnings and Cash Flow as Predictors of Value Creation*, Manchester Business School Working Paper, 1998

Sirower, Mark L., *The Synergy Trap* (New York: The Free Press, 1997)

Smith, Terry, *Accounting for Growth: Stripping the Camouflage from Company Accounts*, 2nd edition (London: Century Business, 1996)

Stewart, G. Bennett, *The Quest for Value* (New York: Harper Business, 1991)

Stigler, George, *The Regularity of Regulation* (London: David Hume Institute, 1986)

Thomas, Rawley, and Lipson, Marvin, *Linking Corporate Return Measures to Stock Prices* (St Charles, Illinois: Holt Planning Associates 1985)

Travlos, N.G., "Corporate Takeover Bids, Methods of Payment, and Bidding Firm's Stock Returns," *Journal of Finance*, Vol.42, pp.943–6

Weissenrieder, Frederik, and Ottosen, Eric, "Cash Value Added, A New Method for Measuring Financial Performance," Gothenburg University Working Paper 1996, No. 1

Websites

The American Institute of Certified Public Accountants: www.aicpa.org

Berkshire Hathaway annual reports: www.berkshirehathaway.com

CalPERS (California Public Employees Retirement System): www.calpers.ca.gov

The Corporate Governance Network: www.corpgov.net

European Corporate Governance Network: www.ecgn.ulb.ac.be/ecgn/

ICAEW (Institute of Chartered Accountants in England and Wales): www.icaew.co.uk

PIRC (Pensions Investment Research Consultants): www.pirc.co.uk

PricewaterhouseCoopers: www.pwcglobal.com

INDEX

Tables and figures are shown in *italics*

GATT (General Agreement on Tariffs and
    Trade) 6
General Electric 25, 98, 99, 102
generic
    competition 208
    models 225
Germany 7–8, 277–86, 280–1
    after-tax profits 160
    companies 7, 244
    company managements 284–6
    equities 38
    forecasts of share price movements
        (1994) 51
    international capital markets 125, 248–9
    managers and analysts 49
    Neue Markt 8, 280, 281
    new accounting 283–4
    privatizations 246
    social provision 13
    strategic investments in industry 17–18
global
    benchmarking alliances 114
    economic development 20
    M&A activity (1984–98) 133
    markets, financial assets 6
Global Reporting Initiative 253
Goizueta, Roberto C. 14–15, 23
Golden, Charles 256
goodwill 186, 188
Granada Forte 145, 151
Grand Metropolitan 260
Greenbury committee report 258–9
gross investment 50
growth 60–1
    affect on shareholder value 60, 61
    and corporate planning 63–5, 63–4
    in operating assets 194
    and value agendas 110
GSM hand sets 152
GTE 152
Guiness 260

Ha Sung, Jang 308
Hamel, Gary 21
Hampel committee 258–9
Havas 291

health and social security 5
Helsinki, Stock Exchange 274, 293
Hermes Pension Fund Management (UK)
    255, 261
high technology 189, 206, 211–21
    companies 91
    micro drivers 213–14
    options 214–16, 215
    real options drivers 217–21, 218–22
    two components of high-tech value
        212–13, 213
    valuing innovation 216–17
high-inflation countries 31
historical
    accounting earnings and stock market
        performance, correlation between
        10
    financial reporting 323
history of value 19–26
Holt Value company 78
Holzman, Philip 283
Honeywell 255–6
Hong Kong, market capitalization 248–9
hostile takeovers, European markets 7
Hoya 300
Hungary
    and other Eastern European Countries
        301–3
    privatization act (1997) 302
hurdle rates 28–9, 45
Hyderabad 311

IAS see International Accounting Standards
        Committee (IASC)
ICI 25, 271
ILO conventions 255
IN (intelligent network) 228
inappropriate expansion strategy 168
income generation 143, 146–7
income/average funds under management
        (FUM) 102
    growth 203
India 303, 310–12, 311
    foreign institutional investors (FIIs) 310
individual business units 104
industry structure 232